Contents W9-APR-915

Eastern Region—Access from Forest Roads 25, 26, and 99 135

Northern Region—Access From US 12 and Forest Roads 25, 26 189

Summit Climb 234

Hiking
Mount St. Helens

Fred Barstad

FALCON®

HELENA, MONTANA

A **FALCON** GUIDE®

Falcon® Publishing is continually expanding its list of recreational guidebooks. All books include detailed descriptions, accurate maps, and all the information necessary for enjoyable trips. You can order extra copies of this book and get information and prices for other Falcon® books by writing Falcon, P.O. Box 1718, Helena, MT 59624 or calling toll free 1-800-582-2665. Also, please ask for a free copy of our current catalog. Visit our website at www.FalconOutdoors.com or contact us via e-mail at www.falcon.com.

©1999 Falcon® Publishing, Inc., Helena, Montana
Printed in the United States of America.

1 2 3 4 5 6 7 8 9 0 MG 04 03 02 01 00 99

Falcon and FalconGuide are registered trademarks of Falcon® Publishing, Inc.

All photos by author unless otherwise noted.

Library of Congress Cataloging-in-Publication Data
Barstad, Fred
  Hiking Mount St. Helens / by Fred Barstad.
    p. cm. -- (A Falcon guide)
    Includes bibliographical references and index.
    ISBN 1-56044-696-X
    1. Hiking--Washington (State)--Saint Helens, Mount--Guidebooks. 2. Trails--Washington (State)--Saint Helens, Mount--Guidebooks. 3. Saint Helens, Mount (Wash.)--Guidebooks. I. Title. II. Title: Hiking Mount Saint Helens. III. Series.
GV199.42.W22S353 1999
917.97'84--dc21   98-50261
                                                              CIP

CAUTION

Outdoor recreational activities are by their very nature potentially hazardous. All participants in such activities must assume the responsibility for their own actions and safety. The information contained in this guidebook cannot replace sound judgment and good decision-making skills, which help reduce risk exposure, nor does the scope of this book allow for disclosure of all the potential hazards and risks involved in such activities.

Learn as much as possible about the outdoor recreational activities in which you participate, prepare for the unexpected, and be cautious. The reward will be a safer and more enjoyable experience.

♻ Text pages printed on recycled paper.

Acknowledgments

Many people helped gather information and put this book together. Thanks go to Walt Doan, Chief Cartographer of the Gifford Pinchot National Forest, for reviewing the text and Jim Nieland, Recreation Planner for Mount St. Helens National Volcanic Monument, for information. Thanks also to Brian Spite, Climbing Ranger, and Robert Larson at Coldwater Ridge Visitor Center for information. Thanks to Helen and Alex Hoppe for shuttles and companionship. Thanks to Dave Martin for camping with me and helping with car shuttles. Thanks to Karla Evans for hiking and camping with me. Thanks to Eric Valentine and Scout Troop 514 for backpacking with me and contributing photos. Thanks to Jim Glick, pilot at Precision Helicopters, for an over-flight. Many thanks to Mike Barstad for backpacking with me, contributing photos, providing an over-flight and a place to stay. Thanks to Gary Fletcher for proofreading. Most of all thanks to my wife Suzi Barstad for hiking and camping with me, helping with car shuttles and proofreading the text.

Legend

Interstate	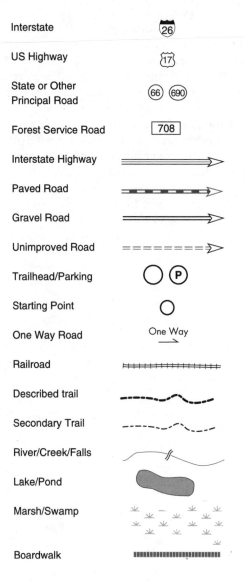	Campground	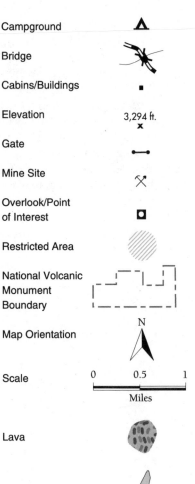
US Highway		Bridge	
State or Other Principal Road		Cabins/Buildings	
Forest Service Road		Elevation	3,294 ft.
Interstate Highway		Gate	
Paved Road		Mine Site	
Gravel Road		Overlook/Point of Interest	
Unimproved Road		Restricted Area	
Trailhead/Parking		National Volcanic Monument Boundary	
Starting Point			
One Way Road		Map Orientation	N
Railroad		Scale	0 0.5 1 Miles
Described trail			
Secondary Trail			
River/Creek/Falls		Lava	
Lake/Pond		Lahar	
Marsh/Swamp			
Boardwalk			

Overview Map

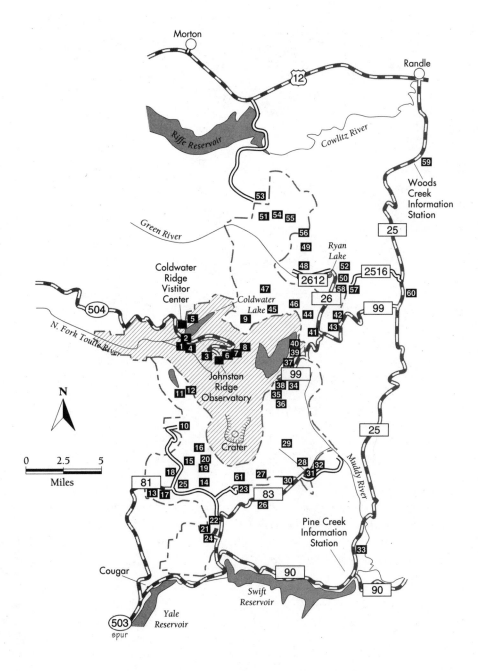

USGS Topo Map Index

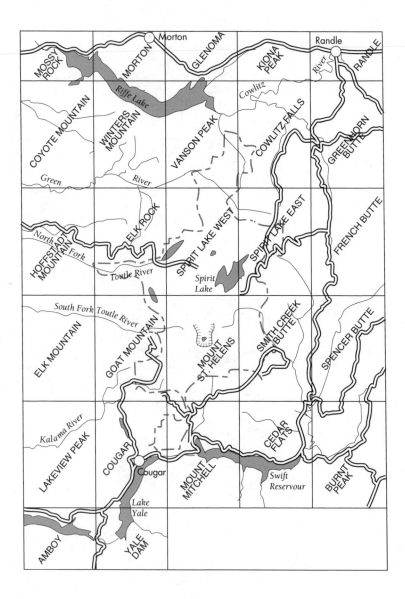

Introduction

A BRIEF GEOLOGIC HISTORY OF MOUNT ST. HELENS

We should have known that Mount St. Helens was not the benevolent remains of a dead volcano that it appeared to be. The signs were all there. St. Helens's smooth sides, little scarred by erosion, made it one of the most beautiful mountains in the Cascades. Its modest glaciers had not dug deeply into its flanks like they had on other Cascade volcanoes. Pumice covered many of its slopes, and the timberline was much lower than that of its close neighbors. Layers of fine white soil were found close to the surface in many areas near the mountain.

Native Americans and early day European settlers told stories of fire, smoke, and hot rocks being ejected from the heights. They spoke in awe of Spirit Lake where the rocks (pumice) floated and the wood (wet hemlock) sank.

The low timberline existed because trees take several centuries to work their way back up a volcano's slopes after an eruption has removed them. The smooth, pumice-covered slopes that had not had the time to become deeply eroded indicated that not many centuries had passed since the volcano last erupted. The pumice rocks that floated in Spirit Lake also pointed to recent volcanic activity, confirming the old timers' reports of smoke and fire. It was not until the middle of the twentieth century, however, that scientists began to realize that Mount St. Helens was not an extinct volcano, but a very much alive mountain that was just resting between eruptive cycles. But even with new information, most people thought that the mountain would retain its beautiful and benign character forever. Fun-seekers flocked to the shores of Spirit Lake and climbers ascended the ice-covered north slopes.

Everything began to change in March of 1980. Swarms of small earthquakes rumbled beneath the snow-covered mountain, and a small crater formed after a blast through the ice near its summit. This crater grew larger with successive minor eruptions. Monitoring sites were set up by the United States Geological Survey to keep track of the volcano's antics. A 10-mile-wide circle around the mountain was made off-limits to all people without special permission. This circle, called the Red Zone, was thought to be big enough to keep people mostly out of danger. Still, many people did not take the danger seriously. I must admit that I was one of these people; I was in the Red Zone in April of 1980.

On May 18, 1980, at 8:32 A.M., a much larger earthquake shook the mountain. Within seconds the largest landslide in recorded history slid from its north face. This slide, called the Debris Avalanche, swept into Spirit Lake and over Johnston Ridge, leaving pieces of the once-symmetrical mountain miles from their previous locations.

As the Debris Avalanche slid from the side of the mountain, the tremendous pressure that had been building beneath was released. This release of pressure caused a lateral blast to charge north at more than 500 miles per hour. Made up of hot gasses, boulders, and ash, this blast traveled as far as 16 miles north of the mountain. It flattened nearly all the vegetation in a 180-degree arc for approximately 12 miles from the crater. The eruption continued for nine hours.

Later that day, mudflows, called lahars, rushed down many of the streams radiating from the peak. The largest and most destructive lahar followed the Toutle River Valley all the way to the Cowlitz and Columbia Rivers. The sediment choked the shipping channel in the Columbia River, reducing its depth from nearly 40 feet to only 12 feet. Two new lakes and many ponds were formed when the Debris Avalanche dammed streams and made depressions that held water between the hummocks.

As you might guess, the 10-mile-wide Red Zone was not nearly big enough on the north side of the mountain. Fifty-seven people were killed in the eruption. In a few cases their bodies and even their cars were never found. Nearly all of these people died from asphyxiation from the ash and hot gases. Most of these people were outside the perimeter of the Red Zone.

Mount St. Helens erupted with decreasing frequency and intensity between 1980 and 1986. Since then its activity has been confined to small earthquakes and minor steam emissions from the lava dome in its crater. Mudflows have originated from the mountain during this time. These mudflows are not necessarily caused by volcanic heat, but by normal precipitation saturating the loose volcanic soils.

CHANGE AND RECOVERY

It may seem as if the volcano destroyed everything in its path. However this is not really what has happened. Nature does not waste anything, it only recycles. While the eruption did destroy much of the life close to it, it also covered the ground with nutrient-rich volcanic ash. The downed or buried logs will rot and add organic matter to the new soil, preparing it for new plant growth. The time it takes nature to recycle may be beyond our comprehension but it will still occur.

Animals are quickly returning to the Blast Zone. Some of them, like the elk, have actually benefited from the loss of the dense forest. The open ground allows more grasses and brush to grow—their favorite foods. The chances of seeing elk from Washington Highway 504 are excellent, especially in the spring while they are still on their winter range. The Lakes Trail and the Hummocks Trail have the best elk viewing potential. By mid-June most of the elk have moved to higher ground.

Fish survived in many of the lakes that were still snow covered when the eruption occured. They had a difficult time surviving in the heavily silted water at first, but now they are doing very well in several lakes. All of the fish in Spirit Lake were killed by the eruption, but now wild fish have been found there, thought perhaps to have come down from St. Helens Lake. St.

Helens Lake, at a higher elevation than Spirit Lake, was covered with snow at the time of the eruption. A stream connects the lakes, but there are waterfalls in the stream. If fish did come down the stream it must have been an exciting ride. Many burrowing animals also survived the blast as they stayed beneath the snow cover; those that did survive quickly went to work repopulating the area.

ACCESS

The hike descriptions in this book are arranged by the access routes that you take to reach them. Reach the west side hikes from Washington Highway 504. Access the trailheads on the south side of the monument from forest roads off WA 503 spur. Reach the east side hikes from Forest Roads 25, 99, and 26. Accessing the north side trailheads is a little more complicated. Use the timber company roads off US Highway 12 for some and FR 25 and 26 south of Randle for others. Each hike has its own driving directions.

The Finding the trailhead section for each hike assumes that the hiker is coming from Interstate 5, either from the south (Portland) or the north (Seattle). The west side trails can be reached from I-5. However, the south, east, and north trails are also accessible from I-84, which runs east of I-5. From I-84, leave the freeway at Hood River. Cross the bridge over the Columbia River and turn west on WA 14. Follow WA 14 west for 15 miles, then turn north and drive 1 mile to Carson. Head north from Carson for 13 miles then turn right on Wind River Road. This junction is just past the Carson Fish Hatchery. Follow Wind River Road for 13.5 miles to the junction with Curly Creek Road (FR 51). Turn left (northwest) on Curly Creek Road and drive 6.9 miles to the junction with FR 90. The last 1.1 miles of Curly Creek Road is gravel. Turn left on paved FR 90 and follow it west for 5.3 miles to the junction with FR 25. If you are headed for the south side trails, turn left at the junction and stay on FR 90. To reach the east and north side trails, turn right on FR 25. The junction of FR 90 and FR 25 is mentioned in each hike's "Finding the trailhead" section. This junction is 24.3 miles south of the junction of FR 25 and FR 99, or 18.6 miles east of Cougar. To reach the west side trails it is necessary to come in from I-5 and access WA 504.

You can also reach the south, east, and north side trails from Exit 110 on I-90 at Ellensburg, Washington. From Exit 110 take I-82 south for 31 miles to Exit 31 at Yakima. Then turn west on US 12 and follow it 89 miles to Randle. Pick up the driving directions from Randle in the Finding the trailhead section of the hike descriptions.

How To Use This Guide

HOW THE INFORMATION FOR THIS GUIDE WAS GATHERED

I hiked nearly all of these trails in the summer of 1998, many of them in both directions. The mileage was very difficult to gauge exactly. I took mileage from Forest Service signs and maps into account whenever possible. I also kept records of the time it took to complete each hike. By knowing approximately what speed I hiked over various types of trail I calculated the mileage by combining these means and in some cases by pacing off the distance.

DIFFICULTY RATINGS

The trails in this book are rated easy, moderate, or strenuous with the length of the trail and the time involved in hiking it not taken into account. Only steepness of the grade, roughness of the trail, extent of erosion or rockiness, and elevation changes are considered.

The trails that are rated "easy" generally have gentle grades and be mostly smooth; however, there may be short sections of rocky or eroded areas. Anyone in reasonable condition can hike easy trails given enough time.

Trails rated as "moderate" climb or descend more steeply than easy trails. They may climb 500 or 600 feet per mile and have fairly long sections that are rough or eroded. A person in good physical condition can hike these trails with no problem. However, people in poor condition and small children may find them grueling.

Trails rated as "strenuous" are best left to expert backpackers and mountaineers. These trails may climb or descend 1,000 feet or more per mile and be very rough. In some cases these trails require good route-finding and map-reading skills to follow safely.

TRAIL MILEAGE

Distances for loop hikes and shuttle hikes are given in the amount of the one-way distance as it will be the entire distance you will hike. Out and back hikes are stated round trip, so you will hike the stated distance to make the complete trip. The additional hiking options listed after the Type of hike are not taken into consideration for the mileage in Total distance. A few hikes described in this book are internal trails that start and/or finish at a trail junction rather than at a trailhead. In these cases you will have to add the distance of the hike to the distance between the junction and your trailhead or starting point to get the total distance you must cover.

MAPS

If you want one map for the whole Mount St. Helens area, the USDA Forest Service map for Mount St. Helens National Volcanic Monument, with the waterfall on the cover, is the map to get. This topo map (AKA the Brown Map) is referred to in this book as MSHNVM and covers the entire area. Most but not all of the trails are shown on this map. The scale of 1:63,360 is a bit small and the tiny printing can be difficult to read for some people, but this map is adequate for most hikes in the monument.

Many of the trails in the monument are fairly new and some of the United States Geological Survey quad maps have not yet been updated to show them. In each hike description the names of the quad maps that cover the area are included as well as an indication as to whether they have the trails on them or not.

To find the out-of-the-way trailheads on the northwest side of the monument, the Weyerhaeuser Mount St. Helens Tree Farm map is very helpful. This map can be purchased at Jack's Restaurant located 5 miles west of Cougar on Washington 503, or directly from the Weyerhaeuser Company. See Appendix A.

Nearly all maps are labeled with trail numbers. Most hikers use names rather than numbers when referring to a certain trail. This can cause confusion as to which trail we are talking about or looking at on a map. To help clear up this confusion the Trail User Table lists the hike number, the hike name and the trail number or numbers for each hike.

ELEVATION PROFILES

Elevation profile graphs are provided for each hike. These profiles show the major elevation changes of the hike, but because of the size limitations they may not show small elevation changes.

Backcountry Safety and Hazards

There are a few simple things you can do that will improve your chances of staying safe and healthy while you are on your hikes.

One of the most important things to do is to be careful of your drinking water supply. There are only a few places in the monument where you can get water from a tap. All surface water should be filtered, chemically treated, or boiled before drinking it or washing utensils or brushing your teeth with it. The water may look clean and pure, and it may actually be, but you can never be sure. In many cases there is no water along the trail so you need to take along all that you will need. If you use a filter be sure it has a fairly new cartridge or one that has been recently cleaned before you leave on your hike. The lightly silted water in many streams at Mount St. Helens clogs filters quickly.

Perhaps the second-best piece of safety advice is to tell somebody where you're going and when you plan to return. Pilots must file flight plans before every trip, and anybody venturing into a blank spot on the map should do the same. File your "flight plan" with a friend or relative before taking off.

Check the weather report before heading into the mountains. Stormy weather with wind, rain, and even snow is possible at any time of year. Cool temperatures with fog in the mornings are common through much of the summer making hypothermia one of the most frequent problems in this damp climate. Be sure to have rain and wind gear along and a change of dry clothes for when you stop moving. When the opposite weather conditions prevail, warm sunny weather on the exposed slopes or on the pumice plain can cause quick dehydration. At these times light-colored, loose fitting clothes and lots of sunscreen are what you need. Keep well fed and drink plenty of liquids.

If you are planning a long or difficult hike be sure to get into shape ahead of time. Because of the relatively low elevation of most of the hikes (with the exception of the Summit Climb), altitude-related problems are generally minimal for most hikers. Still, being fit not only makes wilderness travel more fun, it makes it safer.

Volcanic hazards are always present on this active volcano. There is the chance of an unexpected eruption at any time. The chance, however, is small that the scientists monitoring the mountain will not be able to predict an eruption in advance. Almost any information about volcanic activity or potential volcanic activity at Mount St. Helens is broadcast over the local TV stations. If there is any question about possible volcanic activity check with the Forest Service at monument headquarters or at one of the visitor centers before your begin your hike.

To whet your appetite for more knowledge of wilderness safety and preparedness, here are a few more tips.

- Check the weather forecast. Be careful not to get caught at high altitude by a bad storm or along a stream in a flash flood. Watch cloud formations closely, to avoid getting stranded on a ridgeline during a lightning storm. Avoid traveling during prolonged periods of cold weather.

- Avoid traveling alone in the wilderness.

- Keep your party together.

- Study basic survival and first aid before leaving home.

- Don't eat wild plants unless you have positively identified them.

- Before you leave for the trailhead, find out as much as you can about the route, especially the potential hazards.

- Don't exhaust yourself or other members of your party by traveling too far or too fast. Let the slowest person set the pace.

- Don't wait until you're confused to look at your maps. Follow them as you go along, from the moment you start moving up the trail, so you have a continual fix on your location.

- If you get lost, don't panic. Sit down and relax for a few minutes while you carefully check your topo map and take a reading with your compass. Confidently plan your next move. It's often smart to retrace your steps until you find familiar ground, even if you think it might lengthen your trip. Lots of people get temporarily lost in the wilderness and survive—usually by calmly and rationally dealing with the situation.

- Stay clear of all wild animals.

- Take a first-aid kit that includes, at a minimum, the following items: sewing needle, snake-bite kit, aspirin, antibacterial ointment, two antiseptic swabs, two butterfly bandages, adhesive tape, four adhesive strips, four gauze pads, two triangular bandages, codeine tablets, two inflatable splints, Moleskin or Second Skin for blisters, one roll 3-inch gauze, CPR shield, rubber gloves, and lightweight first-aid instructions.

- Take a survival kit that includes, at a minimum, the following items: compass, whistle, matches in a waterproof container, cigarette lighter, candle, signal mirror, flashlight, fire starter, aluminum foil, water purification tablets, space blanket, and flare.

Last but not least, don't forget that the best defense against unexpected hazards is knowledge. The Boy Scouts of America have been guided for decades by what is perhaps the single best piece of safety advice—Be Prepared! For starters, this means carrying survival and first-aid materials, proper clothing, compass, and topographic map—and knowing how to use them. Read up on the latest in wilderness safety information in the recently published *Wild Country Companion* by Will Harmon (Falcon Publishing) Check the back of this guidebook for ordering information.

YOU MIGHT NEVER KNOW WHAT HIT YOU

Thunderstorms are relatively rare on Mount St. Helens, but they can happen. If you get caught by a lightning storm, take special precautions. Remember:

- Lightning can travel far ahead of the storm, so be sure to take cover before the storm hits.

- Do not try to make it back to your vehicle. It isn't worth the risk. Instead, seek shelter even if the trailhead is nearby. Lightning storms rarely last long, and from a safe vantage point, you might enjoy the sights and sounds.

- Be especially careful not to get caught on a mountaintop or exposed ridge; under large, solitary trees; in the open; or near standing water.

- Seek shelter in a low-lying area, ideally in a dense stand of small, uniformly sized trees.

- Stay away from anything that might attract lightning such as metal tent poles, graphite fishing rods, or pack frames.

- Get in a crouch position and place both feet firmly on the ground.

- If you have a pack (without a metal frame) or a sleeping pad with you, put your feet on it for extra insulation against shock.

- Do not walk or huddle together. Instead, stay 50 feet apart, so if somebody gets hit by lightning, others in your party can give first aid.

- If you're in a tent, stay there, in your sleeping bag with your feet on your sleeping pad.

THE SILENT KILLER

Be aware of the danger of hypothermia—a condition in which the body's internal temperature drops below normal. It can lead to mental and physical collapse and death.

Hypothermia is caused by exposure to cold and is aggravated by wetness, wind, and exhaustion. The moment you begin to lose heat faster than your body produces it, you are suffering from exposure. Your body starts involuntary exercise, such as shivering, to stay warm and makes involuntary adjustments to preserve normal temperature in vital organs, restricting bloodflow in the extremities. Both responses drain your energy reserves. The only way to stop the drain is to reduce the degree of exposure.

With full-blown hypothermia, as energy reserves are exhausted cold reaches the brain, depriving you of good judgment and reasoning power. You won't be aware that this is happening. You lose control of your hands. Your internal temperature slides downward. Without treatment, this slide leads to stupor, collapse, and death.

To defend against hypothermia, stay dry. When clothes get wet, they lose about 90 percent of their insulating value. Wool loses relatively less heat; cotton, down, and some synthetics lose more. Choose rain clothes that cover the head, neck, body, and legs and provide good protection against wind-driven rain. Most hypothermia cases develop in air temperatures between 30 and 50 degrees F, but hypothermia can develop in warmer temperatures.

If your party is exposed to wind, cold, and wet, think hypothermia. Watch yourself and others for these symptoms: uncontrollable fits of shivering; vague, slow, slurred speech; memory lapses; incoherence; immobile, fumbling hands; frequent stumbling or a lurching gait; drowsiness (to sleep is to die); apparent exhaustion; and inability to get up after a rest. When a member of your party has hypothermia, he or she may deny any problem. Believe the symptoms, not the victim. Even mild symptoms demand treatment, as follows:

• Get the victim out of the wind and rain.

• Strip off all wet clothes.

• If the victim is only mildly impaired, give him or her warm drinks. Then get the victim in warm clothes and a warm sleeping bag. Place well-wrapped water bottles filled with heated water close to the victim.

• If the victim is badly impaired, attempt to keep him or her awake. Put the victim in a sleeping bag with another person—both naked. If you have a double bag, put two warm people in with the victim.

BE BEAR AWARE

While still infrequent, bear sightings on Mount St. Helens have been increasing in recent years. The Mount St. Helens National Volcanic Monument Headquarters advises hikers to take all the usual precautions. In other words—be prepared. And being prepared doesn't only mean having the right equipment. It also means having the right information and right attitude. Knowledge is your best defense.

Hiking in bear country

Nobody likes surprises, and bears dislike them, too. The majority of human/bear conflicts occur when a hiker surprises a bear. Therefore, it's vital to do everything possible to avoid these surprise meetings. Perhaps the best way is to follow this five-part system of simple rules to make the chance of encountering a bear on the trail sink to the slimmest possible margin.

• Be alert.

• Do not hike alone.

• Stay on the trail.

• Do not hike in the late evening or early morning.

• Make lots of noise.

If you see a bear on the trail: Freeze and begin to slowly back away. Let the bear know you are there by clapping or talking to it in a loud voice. The bear will usually take action to avoid you. Never run from a bear, since they might consider you prey.

Cute, cuddly, and lethal: If you see a bear cub, do not go an inch closer to it. Back up and go around, or take another route, if possible. The cub might seem abandoned, but it most likely is not. Mother bear is probably very close, and female bears fiercely defend their young.

Camping in bear country

Using the correct bear country camping techniques can save you and the bears much grief. Once a bear has tasted human food, it often becomes habituated to this food source and many end up being destroyed. Remember, "A fed bear is a dead bear."

Staying overnight in bear country is not dangerous, but it adds a slight additional risk to your trip. The main difference is the presence of more food, cooking, and garbage. Plus, you are in bear country at night when bears are usually most active. But following a few basic rules greatly minimizes the risk to yourself and the bears.

Storing food and garbage: If your campsite doesn't have a permanent wire, pole, or locker in which to store food, be sure to hang your food well before dark. It's not only difficult to store food after darkness falls, but it's easier to miss a juicy morsel on the ground.

You will need the following items to properly store and hang your food:

• A good supply of zip-locked bags.

• A waterproof "dry" bag or stuff sack for storing food.

• 75 feet of strong nylon cord.

Hanging food and gargage over a tree branch.

Find a good tree branch at least 10 feet high and 4 feet from the trunk. Above treeline, hang food off cliffs and boulders. Be sure to store food in airtight, waterproof bags to contain food odors. For double protection, put food and garbage in zip-locked bags and seal everything in a larger, plastic bag.

You can get hurt hanging your food at night, so be careful. The classic method is tying a rock or piece of wood to the end of a rope, tossing it over a branch and then attaching the rope to your food storage bag and hoisting it up 10 feet or more (see illustrations). Of course, watch that the rock or wood doesn't come down on your head (it happens!). Also, don't let anybody stand under the bag until you're sure it's securely in place.

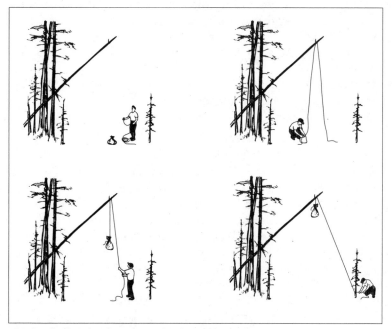

Hanging food and garbage over a leaning tree.

What to hang: To be as safe as possible, store everything that has any food odor. This includes cooking gear, eating utensils, bags used to keep food in your pack, all garbage (stored in zip-locked bags), and even clothes with food odor on them.

Your tent: an odor-free zone: You cannot be too careful in keeping food odors out of your tent. Just in case a bear has become accustomed to coming into that campsite looking for food, it is *critical* to keep all food odors out of the tent. This includes your pack, which is hard to keep odor free, as well as toothpaste, chapstick, lotions, and other odoriferous, non-food items.

How to cook: The overriding philosophy of cooking in bear country is to create as little odor as possible. Keep it simple. Use as few pans and dishes as possible. Unless you encounter a weather emergency, *never* cook in your tent.

Be careful not to spill on your clothes while cooking and eating. If you do, wash them as soon as possible and change into clean ones. Avoid leftovers by not cooking too much food and cleaning your plate to eliminate food scraps. Never bury food or dump leftovers into any water source. Take your scrap-free dish water at least 100 yards downwind and downhill from camp and pour it on the ground or in a small hole. Do dishes immediately after eating to minimize food odors.

Choosing a tent site: Cook and sleep at least 100 yards apart. If possible, pitch your tent *upwind* from the cooking area. Store or hang your food in the cooking area, or better yet, another 100 yards downwind from both the cooking and sleeping areas.

If you see a bear in camp or on the trail, report it to a ranger after your trip. If rangers get enough reports to spot a pattern, they manage the area to prevent potentially hazardous situations.

Most of the information in this section comes from *Bear Aware*, a handy, inexpensive guidebook by Falcon Publishing. The book contains even more, detailed information you need to reduce the risk of having a close encounter of the bear kind. You can get this book at your local bookseller, or by calling Falcon Publishing.

PASSING STOCK AND BIKES ON THE TRAIL

Meeting stock traffic is fairly common on the southwest side of Mount St. Helens National Volcanic Monument, as well as along and north of the Green River Trail. It's a good idea to know how to pass stock with the least possible disturbance or danger. If you meet parties with stock try to get as far off the trail as possible. Horseriders prefer that you stand on the downhill side of the trail, but there is some question if this is the safest place for a hiker. If possible I like to get well off the trail on the uphill side. It is often a good idea to talk quietly to the horses and their riders, as this seems to calm many horses. If you have the family dog with you be sure to keep it restrained and quiet. Dogs are the cause of many horse wrecks.

You might also encounter bike riders along many of the trails. See the Trail User chart to see which trails you might expect them on. It is the bicyclist's obligation to watch out for hikers and horses, but it is a good idea to watch for them too. Bikes are fast and quiet so pay close attention when you are on trails that are open to their use.

With a little common sense and consideration all types of trail users can have a safe and pleasant experience.

Leave No Trace

Going into a wild area is like visiting a famous museum. You obviously do not want to leave your mark on an art treasure in the museum. If everybody going through the museum left one little mark, the piece of art would be quickly destroyed—and of what value is a big building full of trashed art? The same goes for pristine wildlands. If we all left just one little mark on the landscape, the backcountry would soon be spoiled.

A wilderness can accommodate human use as long as everybody behaves. But a few thoughtless or uninformed visitors can ruin it for everybody who follows. All backcountry users have a responsibility to know and follow the rules of leave-no-trace camping.

THREE FALCON PRINCIPLES OF LEAVE NO TRACE

- Leave with everything you brought in.
- Leave no sign of your visit.
- Leave the landscape as you found it.

Nowadays most wilderness users want to walk softly, but some are not aware of their own poor manners. Often their actions are dictated by the outdated habits of a past generation of campers who cut green boughs for evening shelters, built campfires with fire rings, and dug trenches around tents. In the 1950s, these "camping rules" may have been acceptable. But they leave long-lasting scars, and today such behavior is absolutely unacceptable. Wild places are becoming rare, and the number of users is mushrooming. More and more camping areas show unsightly signs of heavy use.

Consequently, a new code of ethics is growing out of the necessity of coping with the unending waves of people who want a perfect backcountry experience. Today, we all must leave no clues that we were there. Enjoy the wild, but leave no trace of your visit.

Most of us know better than to litter either in or out of the backcountry. Be sure you leave nothing, regardless of how small, along the trail or at your campsite. This includes orange peels, flip tops, cigarette butts, and gum wrappers; pack out everything. Also, pick up any trash that others leave behind.

Follow the main trail. Avoid cutting switchbacks and walking on vegetation beside the trail. Shortcuts cause much erosion and destroy plant life. It is always best to stay on the trail and not take shortcuts. It also usually takes less energy to follow the trail. Where the trail is braided try to stay on the main route. Do not dismantle rock cairns, as they may be the only thing marking the route in some areas.

13

Don't pick up "souvenirs," such as rocks, antlers, or wildflowers. The next person wants to see them, too, and collecting such souvenirs violates many regulations.

Avoid making loud noises on the trail (unless you are in bear country) or in camp. Be courteous—remember, sound travels easily in the backcountry, especially across water.

Carry a lightweight trowel to bury human waste 6 to 8 inches deep at least 300 feet from any water source. Pack out used toilet paper. Keep human waste at least 300 feet from any water source.

Go without a campfire. Carry a stove for cooking and a flashlight, candle lantern, or headlamp for light. For emergencies, learn how to build a no-trace fire. If you must build a fire, be sure you extinguish it completely. Campfires are prohibited within the Blast Zone.

Conscientious and intelligent campsite selection is critical to maintaining the health of the environment. Camp in designated sites when they are available. Otherwise, camp and cook on durable surfaces such as bedrock, sand, gravel bars, or bare ground.

Make camp in the timber and avoid camping in meadows. Be careful not to trample vegetation. Camp well away from lakes and at least 100 feet from streams. Camping is prohibited in the restricted area and only permitted at designated sites within the Mount Margaret Backcountry. Check Forest Service regulations about campsite selection.

Finally, and perhaps most importantly, strictly follow the pack-in/pack-out rule. If you carry something into the backcountry, consume it or carry it out. We all need to do our part to keep our wild areas beautiful and clean forever.

Leave no trace—and put your ear to the ground and listen carefully. Thousands of people coming behind you are thanking you for your courtesy and good sense.

Details on these guidelines and recommendations of leave-no-trace principles for specific outdoor activities can be found in the guidebook *Leave No Trace* by Will Harmon (Falcon Publishing). Visit your local bookstore, or call Falcon Publishing directly.

Backcountry Regulations and Permits

Mount St. Helens National Volcanic Monument is administered by the USDA Gifford Pinchot National Forest. This is different than most national monuments in the country, which are administered by the U.S. Department of the Interior–National Park Service. This difference in administration makes regulations here different than they are in most other national parks and monuments. Mount St. Helens is a new national monument, so regulations are still being implemented to protect the unique environment and allow for the accommodation of many user groups.

Mountain bike use is allowed on many trails within the monument. Horses and other stock are prohibited in much of the Blast Zone in order to prevent the introduction of non-indigenous plants. However, there are still many trails that are open to horses, and special accommodations are made for them in places. Off-trail travel and camping are prohibited within the restricted area. See the overview map for the boundaries of the restricted area.

All in all these regulations seem to be working very well. As I hiked the trails to gather information for this book I had no unpleasant encounters with other trail users. Everyone, and especially the backcountry rangers, was friendly, courteous, and helpful.

Permits

Mount St. Helens visitors permits can be obtained at any of the visitor centers or information stations in or near the monument. They are also available at Cascade Peaks Restaurant on Forest Road 99. The cost of permits (as of 1998) is $8 for up to 3 days or $16 for an annual permit. Children are free and there is a discount for seniors.

A climbing permit is required for each person climbing higher than 4,800 feet elevation on the south side of Mount St. Helens. (The rest of the mountain is within the restricted zone so no off-trail travel is permitted.) There is a limit on the number of permits available between May 15 and October 15. Permits for dates between May 15 and October 15 can be reserved through Monument Headquarters. Call the climbing hotline (see Appendix A). Then send your application to:

Climbing Coordinator
Mount St. Helens NVM
42218 NE Yale Bridge Road
Amboy, WA 98601

Do not send money with your application. If the requested date is available you will receive a confirmation in the mail. If the date you requested is not available, you will be sent a list of alternate dates. Climbers with permit reservations must purchase their permits before 5:30 P.M. the day before the climb at Jack's Restaurant (5 miles west of Cougar on Washington 503). The cost of the permits is $15 per person.

A number of unreserved permits are available at Jack's Restaurant. These permits are made available through a lottery. Sign up for the lottery at 5:30 P.M. the day before you want to climb. The permits will be awarded at 6:00 P.M. that same day.

The rest of the year, between October 15 and May 15, you can pick up your permit at Jack's without getting a reservation or going through the lottery.

Backcountry permits are required for the Mount Margaret Backcountry. These permits may be obtained through Monument Headquarters. The fees and quota have not yet been set for these permits (as of 1998). Contact Monument Headquarters for information. See Appendix A.

Trail User Table

Hike	Trail Number	Hiker	Bike	Stock	Wheelchair
1 Hummocks Loop	229	•			
2 Birth of a Lake	246	•			•
3 Boundary Trail	1	•	•		
4 Coldwater Loop	230A, 230, 211	•	•		
5 Elk Bench	211D	•	•		
6 Boundary Coldwater Loop	1, 230, 211	•			
7 Eruption Loop	201	•			•
8 Harry's Ridge	1E (was 208)	•	•		
9 Coldwater Peak	1G	•			
10 Sheep Canyon–Crescent Ridge Loop	240, 216, 238	•	•		
11 Castle Ridge	216G	•	•		
12 Castle Lake	221	•	•		
13 Toutle Trail	238	•	•	•	
14 Toutle Trail	238	•	•	•	
15 Toutle Trail	238	•	•		
16 Blue Horse Trail	237	•	•	•	
17 Kalama Ski Trail	231	•		•	
18 Goat Marsh	237A	•	•		
19 Butte Camp	238A	•	•		
20 Loowit Trail	216	•	•		
21 Lower Ape Cave	239B	•			
22 Upper Ape Cave	239A, 239	•			
23 Ptarmigan Trail	216A	•	•		
24 Trail of Two Forests	233	•			•

Hike	Trail Number	Hiker	Bike	Stock	Wheelchair
25 Kalama Springs	No number	•	•	•	
26 June Lake	216B	•	•		
27 Loowit Trail	216	•	•		
28 Ape Canyon	234	•	•		
29 Loowit Trail	216	•	•		
30 Pine Creek Shelter	216C	•	•		
31 Lahar Viewpoint	241	•			•
32 Lava Canyon	184	•			0.2 mile
33 Cedar Flats	32	•	•		
34 Smith Creek	225	•			
35 Truman Trail	207	•	•		
36 Plains of Abraham	216D, 216, 216E	•	•		
37 Harmony Trail	224	•	•		
38 Independence Pass (south segment)	227 (was 207)	•	•		
39 Independence Pass	227 (was 207)	•	•		
40 Independence Ridge	227A	•	•		
41 Meta Lake	210	•			•
42 Boundary Trail	1	•	•		
43 Ghost Lake	1H	•	•		
44 Boundary Trail	1	•	•		
45 Whittier Trail	214	•			
46 Lakes Trail	211	•	•		
47 Shovel Lake	211C	•	•		
48 Goat Mountain	217	•	•	•	
49 Deep Lake	217E	•	•	•	
50 Green River Trail	213	•	•	•	
51 Vanson Ridge	213A	•	•	•	
52 Ryan Lake Loop	222	•			
53 Vanson Peak Loop	217, 217A	•	•	•	
54 Vanson Lake	217B	•	•	•	
55 Goat Creek	205	•	•	•	
56 Tumwater Mountain	218	•	•	•	
57 Strawberry Mountain	220	•	•	•	
58 Strawberry Lake	No number	•	•	•	
59 Woods Creek Watchable Wildlife Loop	247, 247A	•			
60 Iron Creek Falls	91	•			
61 Monitor Ridge Climbing Route	216A, no number	•			

Trail Finder Table

	EASY	MODERATE	STRENUOUS
Along Streams	50 Green River 13 Toutle Trail	55 Goat Creek	32 Lava Canyon 34 Smith Creek
Alpine Country			9 Coldwater Peak 44 Boundary Trail 45 Mount Whittier 46 Lakes Trail 47 Shovel Lake 48 Goat Mountain 61 Monitor Ridge Summit Climb

Overnight backpacking	26 June Lake
	30 Pine Creek
	   Shelter
	43 Ghost Lake
	54 Vanson Lake
		10 Sheep Canyon–
		   Crescent Ridge
		   Loop
		15 Toutle Trail
		19 Butte Camp
		29 Loowit Trail
		50 Green River
		55 Goat Creek
		58 Strawberry Lake
			6 Boundary–Coldwater
			27 Loowit Trail
			34 Smith Creek
			44 Boundary Trail
			45 Mount Whittier
			46 Lakes Trail
			47 Shovel Lake
			48 Goat Mountain
			49 Deep Lake

Lakes	2 Birth of a Lake
	   Loop
	26 June Lake
	41 Meta Lake
	43 Ghost Lake
	52 Ryan Lake Loop
		4 Coldwater Loop
		12 Castle Lake
		15 Toutle Trail
		58 Strawberry
		   Lake
			46 Lakes Trail
			47 Shovel Lake
			49 Deep Lake

Mountain Tops		8 Harry's Ridge
		53 Vanson Peak Loop
		57 Strawberry
		   Mountain
			9 Coldwater Peak
			44 Boundary Trail
			45 Mount Whittier
			48 Goat Mountain
			61 Monitor Ridge
			   Summit Climb

Waterfalls	26 June Lake
	32 Lava Canyon
	   (first 0.3 mile)
	60 Iron Creek Falls
		42 Boundary Trail
		55 Goat Creek
		56 Tumwater
		   Mountain
			27 Loowit Trail
			32 Lava Canyon
			34 Smith Creek

Trail Finder Table

	EASY	MODERATE	STRENUOUS
Trails in Green Timber out of the Blast Zone	13 Toutle Trail 18 Goat Marsh 24 Trail of Two Forests 25 Kalama Springs 26 June Lake 30 Pine Creek Shelter 33 Cedar Flats Nature Loop 59 Woods Creek Watchable Wildlife Loop 60 Iron Creek Falls	14 Toutle Trail 15 Toutle Trail 16 Blue Horse Trail 17 Kalama Ski Trail 19 Butte Camp 23 Ptarmigan Trail 28 Ape Canyon 51 Vanson Ridge 53 Vanson Peak Loop 54 Vanson Lake 55 Goat Creek 56 Tumwater Mountain	32 Lava Canyon 49 Deep Lake 22 Upper Ape Cave
Trails in the Blast Zone	1 Hummocks Loop 2 Birth of a Lake Loop 7 Eruption Loop 41 Meta Lake 52 Ryan Lake Loop	3 Boundary Trail 4 Coldwater Loop 5 Elk Bench 6 Boundary–Coldwater 8 Harry's Ridge 11 Castle Ridge 12 Castle Lake 35 Truman Trail 36 Plains of Abraham Loop 37 Harmony Trail 38 Independence Pass (south segment) 39 Independence Pass 40 Independence Ridge 57 Strawberry Mountain 58 Strawberry Lake	9 Coldwater Peak 44 Boundary Trail 45 Mount Whittier 46 Lakes Trail 47 Shovel Lake

Trail Finder Table

	EASY	MODERATE	STRENUOUS
Trails on the Edge: Between the Blast Zone and Green Timber	43 Ghost Lake 50 Green River	10 Sheep Canyon–Crescent Ridge Loop 42 Boundary Trail	34 Smith Creek 48 Goat Mountain
Heavily Traveled Trails	1 Hummocks Loop 2 Birth of a Lake Loop 7 Eruption Loop 24 Trail of Two Forests 31 Lahar Viewpoint 33 Cedar Flats Nature Loop 41 Meta Lake 60 Iron Creek Falls	3 Boundary Trail 10 Sheep Canyon–Crescent Ridge Loop 21 Lower Ape Cave 23 Ptarmigan Trail 28 Ape Canyon 35 Truman Trail	32 Lava Canyon

South Coldwater Trail in April.

Western Region
Access from Washington Highway 504

The old twisting asphalt ribbon of Washington Highway 504, up the Toutle River Valley from Interstate 5, was used for decades as the main access route to Spirit Lake and the slopes of Mount St. Helens. The route endures today though its location and character are much changed.

As you approach the mountain the new highway leaves the valley floor. By the time you get to Coldwater Ridge Visitor Center, 43 miles from I-5, you are well within the Blast Zone and high above the debris-filled Toutle River Valley. **Hike 5 Elk Bench Trail** descends from Coldwater Ridge to the shore of Coldwater Lake.

Past Coldwater Ridge the route descends to the foot of Coldwater Lake, a lake that was formed when the Debris Avalanche dammed the mouth of Coldwater Creek Canyon. From trailheads near the foot of the lake **Hike 1 Hummocks Loop** explores the debris-filled Toutle River Valley and **Hike 2 Birth of a Lake Trail** takes you along the shore and out over the waters of Coldwater Lake.

The highway then follows the south fork of Coldwater Creek up to its headwaters, passing South Coldwater Trailhead where **Hike 4 Coldwater Loop** begins, before climbing the last couple of miles to the top of Johnston Ridge and the Johnston Ridge Observatory. The observatory parking area is the trailhead for **Boundary Trail Hikes 3 and 6.** The popular and sometimes crowded plaza next to the observatory is the trailhead for **Hike 7 Eruption Loop.**

Western Region Overview

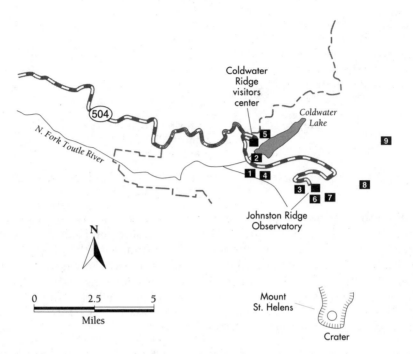

Coldwater Ridge visitors center

Coldwater Lake

N. Fork Toutle River

504

5

9

2

1 4

3

8

6 7

Johnston Ridge Observatory

N

0   2.5   5

Miles

Mount St. Helens

Crater

1 Hummocks Loop (Trail 229)

Type of hike:	Day hike, loop.
Total distance:	2.3 miles.
Difficulty:	Easy to moderate.
Best months:	April–October.
Elevation gain:	Minimal.
Trailhead elevation:	2,500 feet.
Permits:	None.
Maps:	MSHNVM. Elk Rock USGS quad covers the area but does not show this trail.
Starting point:	Hummocks Trailhead.

General description: A loop hike through a jumbled landscape which was formed by the eruption of Mount St. Helens.

Finding the trailhead: The Hummocks Trailhead is located 2.4 miles southeast of the Coldwater Ridge Visitor Center on Washington Highway 504. To reach it from Portland or Seattle take Exit 49 from Interstate 5 (49 miles north of the Columbia River Bridge or 120 miles south of Seattle). Drive east on WA 504, 45 miles to the trailhead on the right side of the highway. There is a sign marking the trailhead. There are really two trailheads for this loop trail. They are both at this parking area, about 50 yards apart. GPS coordinates are 46 17.176 N 122 16.306 W.

Parking & trailhead facilities: There is parking for several cars but no other facilities at the trailhead.

Key points:
- 0.2 Viewpoint of Coldwater Creek Canyon.
- 0.7 Marsh.
- 1.6 Junction with Boundary Trail.

The hike: To hike the loop in a counter-clockwise direction, as described here, leave the Hummocks Trail parking area at its west end. At first the trail climbs a few feet over the mudflow debris. The path then bears right 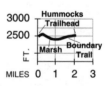 heading northwest and soon begins to descend. A couple of hundred yards from the parking area you make a switchback to the left in a grove of thick young alders. Note the damage caused by elk rubbing their antlers against and chewing on the young trees.

A short distance farther along there is a view to the right of the new canyon dug by Coldwater Creek. There is a short path to the right here but regulations require that hikers stay on the main trail. The trail passes a pond 0.3 mile past the viewpoint and soon comes alongside a cattail-filled marsh. After passing the marsh you cross a stream and the North Fork Toutle River comes into view, 150 yards to the right. The trail is now heading southeast with Mount St. Helens in view ahead.

Hummocks Loop (Trail 229)

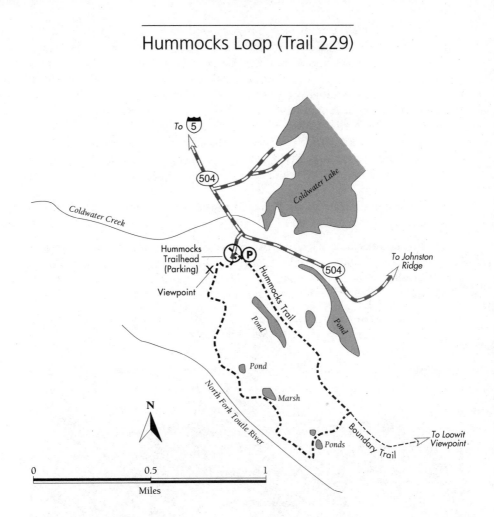

The trail follows the riverbank but goes well away from the river for 0.2 mile. It then bears left (northeast) and climbs past a couple of ponds. Watch for ducks in the ponds and for elk nearby. A small wooden bridge that may be flooded in spring eases the stream crossing between the ponds. The trail climbs gently after passing the ponds. It passes another pond and comes to the junction with the Boundary Trail 0.3 mile from the bridge.

At the junction, the Boundary Trail (Hike 3) leads off to the right. To continue on the Hummocks Trail, turn left and head northwest. Follow this route from the junction back 0.7 mile to the parking area. On the way, the tread passes a couple more ponds before reentering the parking area at its southeast corner.

Elk are very common along this trail in the spring. I saw more than 100 of them when I hiked this trail in April.

Camping & services: The nearest campgrounds to this trail are private and located on WA 504, 25 miles to the west. The closest gas is at Kid Valley, also 25 miles west on WA 504. There is a restaurant at Coldwater Ridge Visitor Center. Other services can be had at Toutle or Castle Rock.

For more information: Coldwater Ridge Visitor Center, 2.4 miles northwest of the trailhead on WA 504. See Appendix A.

Coldwater Creek Canyon from Hummocks Trail.

2   Birth of a Lake Loop (Trail 246)

Type of hike: Day hike, loop.
Total distance: 0.5 mile.
Difficulty: Easy.
Best months: March–October.
Elevation gain: Minimal.
Trailhead elevation: 2,500 feet.
Permits: None.
Maps: None required. Look at the map at the trailhead and the one in this book.
Starting point: Birth of a Lake Trailhead.

General description: A barrier-free interpretive loop path along the shore of and across Coldwater Lake.

Finding the trailhead: The Birth of a Lake Trailhead is located 2.2 miles southeast of the Coldwater Ridge Visitor Center on Washington Highway 504. To reach it from Portland or Seattle take Exit 49 off Interstate 5 (49 miles north of the Columbia River Bridge or 120 miles south of Seattle). Drive 45 miles east on WA 504 until you get to the sign pointing left to the Coldwater Recreation Area. Go left, then bear right at the Y intersection to reach the trailhead which is 0.1 mile from the highway. GPS coordinates at the trailhead are 46 17.204 N 122 15.895 W.

Parking & trailhead facilities: There are restrooms and adequate parking at the trailhead.

Key points:
  0.1   Junction with boardwalk.
  0.3   Path to boat launch.

The hike: The paved trail leaves the parking area at its north end, next to a signboard with a map of the area. Working your way along the lakeshore for 250 yards you will see several interpretive signs. These signs explain the formation of the lake which occurred after the 1980 eruption of Mount St. Helens. Take the time to turn right (north) at the junction and walk out on the boardwalk over the shallow waters of the lake to points of interest over the water.

When you return to the main trail, continue until you pass a viewpoint and the path to the boat launch area, then on to the south end of the parking area where you started. You will climb over a small rise between the path to the boat launch and the parking area.

Options: Hike this short loop after you have finished hiking Hike 1.

Camping & services: The nearest campgrounds to this trail are private and located on WA 504, 25 miles to the west. The closest gas is at Kid Valley, also

Birth of a Lake Loop (Trail 246)

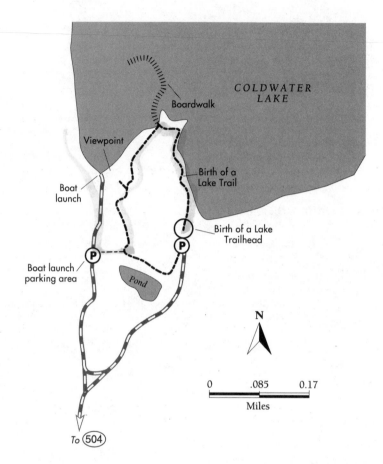

COLDWATER LAKE

Boardwalk

Viewpoint

Boat launch

Birth of a Lake Trail

Birth of a Lake Trailhead

Boat launch parking area

Pond

N

0   .085   0.17
Miles

To 504

25 miles west on WA 504. There is a restaurant at the Coldwater Ridge Visitor Center and emergency medical services can be called from there. You can find other services at Toutle or Castle Rock.

For more information: Coldwater Ridge Visitor Center, 2.4 miles northwest of the trailhead on WA 504. See Appendix A.

Boardwalk over Coldwater Lake.

Boundary Trail (Trail 1)

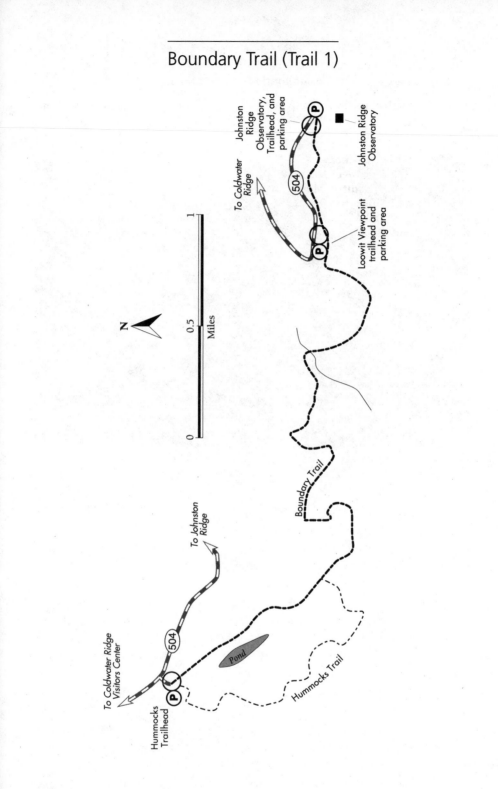

N

0   0.5   1

Miles

Johnston Ridge Observatory, Trailhead, and parking area

Johnston Ridge Observatory

To Coldwater Ridge

504

Loowit Viewpoint trailhead and parking area

Boundary Trail

To Johnston Ridge

504

To Coldwater Ridge Visitors Center

Hummocks Trailhead

Pond

Hummocks Trail

3 Boundary Trail (Trail 1, Johnston Ridge to Hummocks Trailhead)

Type of hike: Day hike, shuttle.
Total distance: 4.3 miles.
Difficulty: Moderate.
Best months: Mid-June–September.
Elevation loss: 1,680 feet.
Trailhead elevation: 4,200 feet.
Permits: Mount St. Helens National Volcanic Monument Visitors Pass.
Maps: MSHNVM. Spirit Lake West and Elk Rock USGS quads covers the area but do not show this trail.
Starting point: Johnston Ridge Observatory parking area.

General description: A downhill hike through the Blast Zone, along the lower end of Johnston Ridge.

Finding the trailhead: From Portland head north on Interstate 5, from Seattle head south on I-5. Take Exit 49 off I-5 (49 miles north of the Columbia River Bridge or 120 miles south of Seattle). Then follow Washington 504 for 52 miles east to the Johnston Ridge Observatory parking area. The observatory is at the end of WA 504. The trail leaves from the west corner of the large parking area. The GPS coordinates are 46 16.500 N 122 13.050 W.

Parking & trailhead facilities: There are restrooms, water, and adequate parking at the trailhead.

Key points::
- 0.6   Loowit Viewpoint. GPS 46 16.663 N 122 13.765 W.
- 3.6   Junction with Hummocks Trail.
- 4.3   Hummocks Trailhead. GPS 46 17.176 N 122 16.306 W.

The hike: The trail crosses the highway and then climbs a few feet to the ridgeline of Johnston Ridge. Lupine and fireweed grow from the pumice-covered landscape. The path soon descends along the south side of the ridge in full view of Mount St. Helens, the Pumice Desert, and the grassy benchlands along the North Fork Toutle River Valley. Small huckleberry and elder-

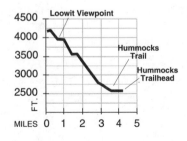

berry bushes grow up between the stumps. Penstemon blooms here in July and by August pearly everlasting blooms appear. Half a mile from the parking area you will reach an old borrow pit. Just past the pit is the Loowit

Trailhead and Viewpoint parking area. The route, which is paved for a short distance, skirts the parking area along its south side.

After it leaves the paved parking area at the Loowit Viewpoint, the Boundary Trail traverses the volcanically blasted slope to the west. You cross a spur ridge 0.3 mile from the Loowit Viewpoint Trailhead. Blacktail deer as well as elk frequent this spur ridge. You will probably see their tracks on the trail and may get a glimpse of them moving away at your approach. Castle Lake is in view ahead to the southwest. Castle Lake was formed by the eruption of Mount St. Helens in 1980 and the resulting mudflow that dammed the South Fork of Castle Creek.

After crossing the spur, the trail heads northwest. Soon Coldwater Lake, another lake that was formed by the eruption, comes into view ahead. The Coldwater Ridge Visitor Center can be seen on the far side of the lake on Coldwater Ridge. The path heads northwest for 0.2 mile, crosses a tiny stream that may be dry by summer, then bears to the left (west). The tread soon crosses a flat area; posts mark the trail here as it may be hard to spot on the ground. Past the flat area the trail continues gently down a stump and bracken fern–covered slope for 0.3 mile. The route then makes a switchback to the left, then one to the right at the edge of a steep canyon as it descends. The trail now follows a long-abandoned roadbed for a short distance. After it bears left off the roadbed the path crosses a gentle slope to another abandoned road. Follow this roadbed south for 0.1 mile then make a switchback to the left and descend east to the base of the ridge.

Once off the steep sided hill the trail crosses the mudflow debris southeast and south before turning west and going towards the junction with the Hummocks Trail. From here to the junction the trail is marked with posts. The route descends a gully then crosses a grassy meadow. It soon meets the Hummocks Trail after passing a pond to the left. Beyond the junction, at 2,520 feet elevation, the Hummocks Trail and the Boundary Trail share the same route. Bear right (really straight ahead to the northwest) on the Hummocks Trail and follow it 0.7 mile to the Hummocks Trailhead and parking area.

Options: You can make the return trip back up the same route to the Johnston Ridge Observatory, but it is better to make a car shuttle between the trailheads. Hiking the Hummocks Loop is a nice addition to this hike. See Hike 1 for directions to the Hummocks Trailhead and a description of the Hummocks Loop hike.

Camping & services: The closest camping is at private campgrounds about 33 miles west of the trailhead on WA 504. Gas can be obtained in Kid Valley, about 33 miles to the west. For other services you must go back on WA 504 to Toutle. Emergency medical help can be called from either of the visitor centers.

For more information: USDA Forest Service at Johnston Ridge Observatory or Coldwater Ridge Visitor Center. See Appendix A.

Grassy tablelands and hummocks looking south from Boundary Trail to Mount St. Helens.

4 Coldwater Loop (Trails 230A, 230, and 211)

Type of hike:	Day hike, loop, or very short shuttle.
Total distance:	10.8 miles.
Difficulty:	Moderate.
Best months:	June–October. The section of this trail along Coldwater Lake is usually snow free by April.
Elevation gain:	1,380 feet.
Trailhead elevation:	2,520 feet.
Permits:	None.
Maps:	MSHNVM. Elk Rock and Spirit Lake West USGS quads cover the area but don't show these trails.
Starting point:	South Coldwater Trailhead.

General description: Hike up a ridge from the South Coldwater Trailhead on the South Coldwater Trail past demolished logging equipment. Then descend into Coldwater Canyon on the Coldwater Trail. Once you reach the canyon bottom, hike along Coldwater Lake on the Lakes Trail to the Lakes Trailhead.

Finding the trailhead: To reach the South Coldwater Trailhead from Portland or Seattle, take Exit 49 off Interstate 5 (49 miles north of the Columbia River Bridge or 120 miles south of Seattle). Drive east on Washington 504, 46 miles to the trailhead, which is on the left side of the highway. The trailhead is 3.3 miles east of Coldwater Ridge Visitor Center. GPS coordinates at the trailhead are 46 17.144 N 122 15.239 W.

Parking & trailhead facilities: There is parking for several cars but no other facilities at the trailhead.

Key points:
- 3.4 Junction with Coldwater Trail.
- 5.0 Junction with Lakes Trail.
- 8.7 Junction with Elk Bench Trail.
- 9.4 Lakes Trailhead. GPS 46 17.481 N 122 16.018 W.
- 10.8 South Coldwater Trailhead.

The hike: The South Coldwater Trail leaves from the southwest corner of the parking area. The path climbs gently on a slope through scattered willows. Stumps between the willows and the general lack of downed trees show that this area was logged before the

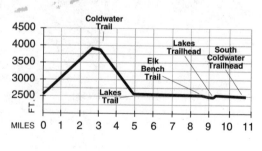

1980 eruption. Shortly, as you round a poorly defined ridge, the Coldwater Ridge Visitor Center and Coldwater Lake come into view to the northwest. If you hike this section of trail in late spring you will probably see elk. This is winter range for the large animals; by June most of them have left for the higher country to the northeast. The route that is marked with posts crosses an abandoned roadbed 0.5 mile from the trailhead. This roadbed, like all of the abandoned roads on this hill, is badly drifted in with pumice. The path makes a switchback to the right then crosses the rounded ridgeline. On the ridgeline you make a wide switchback to the left as you cross another roadbed.

As you climb along the ridge you will pass much evidence of pre-eruption logging in the form of roads and skid trails. You will pass an abandoned borrow pit 1.3 miles from the trailhead. This pit, at 3,150 feet elevation, was dug to furnish rock for the construction of the logging roads and is marked on the quad map. The tread passes the remains of a portable spar pole 0.8 mile after passing the borrow pit. This broken and twisted equipment shows the tremendous force of the 1980 eruption. A logging operation was in progress in this area at the time of the eruption. It is easy to pick out the sections that were not yet logged at the time of the blast by the thousands of logs that now lie on the ground. A short distance past the portable spar pole is a half-buried caterpillar tractor.

For the next mile the route generally follows another abandoned roadbed. The tread traverses along the left side of the ridgeline to the junction with the Coldwater Trail. This junction, at 3,830 feet elevation, is 3.4 miles from the South Coldwater Trailhead. This is the end of the South Coldwater Trail. To the right, on the Coldwater Trail at 0.3 mile, is a campsite. For a description of the Coldwater Trail see Hike 6.

From here to the Lakes Trailhead the Coldwater Loop and the Boundary–Coldwater hikes follow the same route. To continue on the Coldwater Loop bear left (almost straight ahead). You will first descend northeast along the slope of Coldwater Canyon. Then the trail makes several switchbacks as it drops down to Coldwater Creek. Partway down the switchbacks a path will turn off to your right. This path is a now-abandoned section of Coldwater Trail. Bear left at the junction and descend to the bridge over Coldwater Creek. A short distance after crossing the bridge you will come to the junction with the Lakes Trail. You are now at 2,600 feet elevation and 5 miles from the South Coldwater Trailhead.

Turn left and head west from the junction. In 0.6 mile the route reaches the head of Coldwater Lake. The lake was formed when the Debris Avalanche from the 1980 eruption blocked the mouth of Coldwater Creek Canyon. Coldwater Lake is within the Restricted Zone; therefore you must stay on the trail. There is, however, an access point to the lake at its head. The access point is marked with a sign. If you want to approach the lakeshore you can at the access point.

The trail parallels the lakeshore as it heads southwest. As you pass through the alder thickets look for trees that are scarred by elk where they rubbed their antlers and chewed the bark. When I hiked this section of trail in

Coldwater Loop (Trails 230, 230A, and 211)
Boundary–Coldwater (Trails 1, 230, and 211)

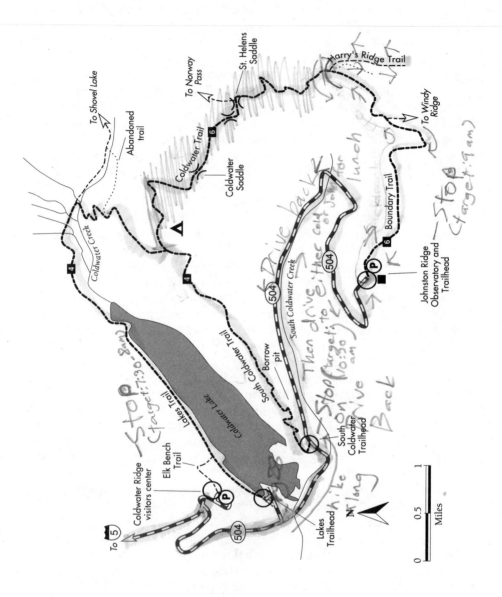

April, I had elk in sight all the way from the head of the lake to Lakes Trailhead. After hiking 1.9 miles along the lake you will cross a stream with a waterfall that drops in stages from the ridge above. This stream may be dry by midsummer as is true with many streams in the Blast Zone. Another 0.8 mile brings you to another lake access point. This access point is marked with signs. There is a restroom to the right of the trail. Reach the junction with Elk Bench Trail at 0.3 mile past the access point. At this junction, 8.7 miles from the South Coldwater Trailhead, the Elk Bench Trail turns to the right. See Hike 5 for the details of the Elk Bench Trail. The Lakes Trail continues southwest for another 0.7 mile to the Lakes Trailhead at the foot of Coldwater Lake.

From the trailhead, hike southwest along the access road to WA 504 then turn left on the highway and hike 1 mile to the South Coldwater Trailhead.

Options: To eliminate hiking along the road from the Lakes Trailhead to the South Coldwater Trailhead, arrange for a short car shuttle. The section of trail along Coldwater Lake from the Lakes Trailhead up to the head of the lake makes a great early season hike.

Camping & services: The closest developed campgrounds are private camps 26 miles to the west on WA 504. No camping is allowed in this part of the monument. There is a restaurant at the Coldwater Ridge Visitor Center, and emergency services can be obtained from there. The closest gas is at Kid Valley, 26 miles to the west.

For more information: USDA Forest Service at Coldwater Ridge Visitor Center. See Appendix A.

Half-buried tractor along South Coldwater Trail.

Elk Bench (Trail 211D)

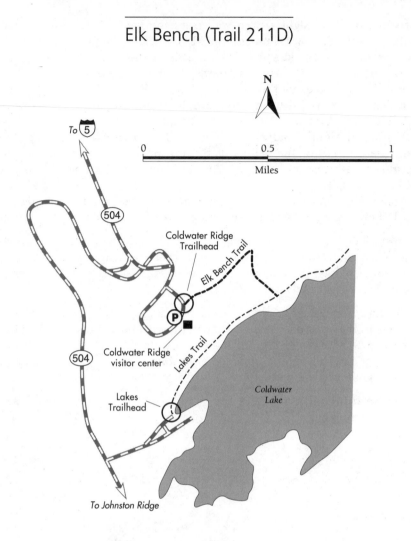

5 Elk Bench (Trail 211D)

Type of hike:	Day hike, out and back, with shuttle option.
Total distance:	1.4 miles.
Difficulty:	Moderate.
Best months:	April–October.
Elevation loss:	530 feet.
Trailhead elevation:	3,090 feet.
Permits:	Mount St. Helens National Volcanic Monument Visitors Pass.
Maps:	MSHNVM. Elk Rock USGS quad covers the area but this trail is not shown.
Starting point:	Coldwater Ridge Visitor Center.

General description: The Elk Bench Trail is a short access trail through logged forest from the Coldwater Ridge Visitor Center to a junction with the Lakes Trail near Coldwater Lake. In April and May there is an excellent chance of seeing elk from this trail.

Finding the trailhead: From Portland head north on Interstate 5, from Seattle head south on I-5. Take Exit 49 off I-5 (49 miles north of the Columbia River Bridge or 120 miles south of Seattle). Then follow Washington 504 east for 43 miles to the Coldwater Ridge Visitor Center. The Elk Bench Trail begins at the northeast end of the parking area. GPS coordinates at the trailhead are 46 17.856 N 122 15.945 W.

Parking & trailhead facilities: Restrooms, water and adequate parking at the trailhead.

Key points:
    0.7   Junction with Lakes Trail. GPS 46 17.925 N 122 15.463 W.

The hike: From the trailhead the trail immediately begins to descend. It makes a couple of tiny switchbacks then begins a long descending traverse to the northeast. This area was logged before the 1980 eruption, so there are many blasted stumps but very few downed trees. Much of this slope is covered with flowers. The varieties in bloom change with the time of year. A few cottonwood trees are growing up between the stumps. The route makes a wide switchback to the right 0.5 mile from the trailhead. It soon makes another switchback, this one to the left, as it continues its descent through the foxglove and fireweed. You will reach the junction with the Lakes Trail 0.7 mile from the trailhead.

There is no lake access at the junction, but if you turn left and hike 0.3 mile along the Lakes Trail there is an access point. The Elk Bench Trail is all within the Restricted Zone, so off-trail hiking is prohibited.

Options: If you wish to make a car shuttle to Lakes Trailhead, you can make a one-way hike. To do this turn right at the junction with the Lakes Trail and follow it to the Lakes Trailhead. See Hike 4 for a description of this section of the Lakes Trail.

Camping & services: The closest developed campgrounds are private camps 23 miles back toward I-5 on WA 504. No camping is allowed in this part of the monument. There is a restaurant at the Coldwater Ridge Visitor Center and emergency services can be obtained from there. For groceries and gas the closest place is Kid Valley, 23 miles west on WA 504.

For more information: USDA Forest Service at Coldwater Ridge Visitor Center. See Appendix A.

6 Boundary–Coldwater (Trails 1, 230, and 211)

See Map on Page 36

Type of hike:	Day hike or backpack, shuttle.
Total distance:	14 miles.
Difficulty:	Moderate to strenuous.
Best months:	Mid-June–mid-October.
Elevation gain/loss:	1,100 feet/2,600 feet. (See elevation profile).
Trailhead elevation:	4,200 feet.
Permits:	Mount St. Helens National Volcanic Monument Visitors Pass.
Maps:	MSHNVM. Spirit Lake West and Elk Rock USGS quads cover the area but don't show the trail.
Starting point:	Johnston Ridge Observatory.

General description: Hike from Johnston Ridge northeast on the Boundary Trail to St. Helens Saddle, then travel northwest into Coldwater Canyon on the Coldwater Trail. Follow Coldwater Creek to Coldwater Lake on the Lakes Trail. Then continue on the Lakes Trail along the shore of the lake to the Lakes Trailhead. This hike is all within the Blast Zone.

Finding the trailhead: To reach the Johnston Ridge Observatory from Portland or Seattle take Exit 49 off Interstate 5 (49 miles north of the Columbia River Bridge or 120 miles south of Seattle). Drive east on Washington 504 for 52 miles to the highway's end at the observatory. GPS coordinates are 46 16.505 N 122 13.040 W.

Parking & trailhead facilities: Water, restrooms, and more than adequate parking at the trailhead.

Key points:

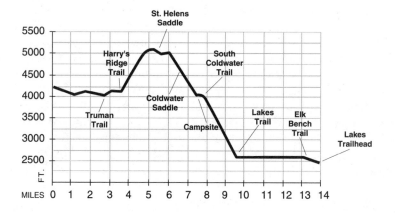

The hike: The Boundary Trail heads east from the east corner of the parking area for the first 250 yards the Boundary Trail and the Eruption Trail follow the same paved route. See Hike 7 for a description of the Eruption Trail. The path then bears left off of the Eruption Trail at a switchback to continue southeast. Here Mount St. Helens and the Pumice Plain come into full view to the south.

The Boundary Trail descends gently along the flower-covered ridge for a short distance. After losing about 150 feet in elevation the path flattens out and even climbs in a few spots. You will generally follow the ridgeline for the next 0.8 mile before the route makes a right turn to head south across a steep hillside. Hang on to children here if you have them along. This traverse crosses a very steep and loose slope. A slip off the side of the route could have disastrous results. The traverse lasts for 0.3 mile then the trail turns left to cross a spur ridge.

As it crosses the spur ridge the route turns to the northeast. You now traverse a gentler slope for 0.5 mile to the junction with the Truman Trail. Mount Adams and Spirit Lake are in view to the right along this traverse. The junction with the Truman Trail, at 4,150 feet elevation, is 2.5 miles from the Johnston Ridge Observatory. The Truman Trail crosses the Pumice Plain to the Windy Ridge Viewpoint which is 5.9 miles away. See Hike 35 for a description of the Truman Trail.

As you leave the junction with the Truman Trail, the path climbs to the northeast and reaches the ridgeline at Spillover Saddle. The Spillover is where the Debris Avalanche that immediately preceded the May 1980 eruption crossed over the top of Johnston Ridge and descended into South Coldwater Canyon. The hummocks on both sides of the trail were once part of the pre-1980 Mount St. Helens. The route crosses the Spillover Saddle then traverses around the head of a basin to the junction with Harry's Ridge Trail.

The junction with Harry's Ridge Trail at 4,380 feet elevation is 3.6 miles from Johnston Ridge Observatory. From the junction, a short hike brings you to an abandoned volcano-monitoring site on top of Harry's Ridge and a slightly longer hike to a viewpoint overlooking Spirit Lake. See Hike 8 for information about Harry's Ridge.

You will cross a saddle and leave the junction with Harry's Ridge Trail as the Boundary Trail heads to the north. Soon the route begins to climb. The path makes five switchbacks in the next 0.7 mile, gaining 600 feet in elevation as it climbs the ridge. As you climb higher, Mount Hood comes into view to the south. The now rough route continues to wind along the ridgeline. The path passes through a window in the rock wall ridgeline, 1.6 miles after leaving the junction with Harry's Ridge Trail. Along the ridge Mount Rainier and St. Helens Lake come into view. After going through the window another 0.3 mile of hiking brings you to St. Helens Saddle and the junction with the Coldwater Trail. At the saddle, you are at 5,080 feet elevation and 5.4 miles from Johnston Ridge Observatory; from here you can look down on sparkling St. Helens Lake with its many floating logs.

At St. Helens Saddle you turn left on the Coldwater Trail to head west toward Coldwater Lake. See Hike 44 if you wish to continue on the Boundary Trail toward Coldwater Peak or Mount Margaret. To continue on the loop turn left and traverse the slope covered with downed timber. The route reaches another saddle in 0.3 mile. The trail crosses the saddle then traverses the slopes of Coldwater Peak for 0.7 mile to Coldwater Saddle at 4,590 feet elevation. From Coldwater Saddle the route descends gradually, first west, then north, then west again, for 0.8 mile to a developed campsite. This campsite, in a north-facing cirque at about 4,000 feet elevation, is the only place to camp along this hike. A backcountry camping permit is required to camp here. There are tent platforms and a restroom at the camp.

The trail heads west from the campsite, reaching the junction with the South Coldwater Trail in another 0.3 mile. At the junction it's 3.4 miles to the left to the South Coldwater Trailhead. See Hike 4 for a description of the South Coldwater Trail. You are 7.5 miles from Johnston Ridge Observatory here. From this junction to the Lakes Trailhead this hike and Hike 4 follow the same route. To continue to the Lakes Trailhead turn right at the junction. You will first descend northeast along the slope of Coldwater Canyon. Then the trail makes several switchbacks as it drops down to Coldwater Creek. Partway down the switchbacks a path will turn off to your right. This path is a now abandoned section of the Coldwater Trail. Bear left at the junction and descend to the bridge over Coldwater Creek. A short distance after crossing the bridge you will come to the junction with the Lakes Trail, at 2,600 feet elevation.

To the right on the Lakes Trail are the high lakes of the Mount Margaret Backcountry. To hike to them see the trail description in Hike 46. To continue on this hike turn left (west) at the junction. The tread reaches the head of Coldwater Lake in 0.6 mile. Coldwater Lake is in the Restricted Zone, so access to the lakeshore is limited to a couple of marked places. Lake access is allowed just as you reach the lake. The route generally follows the lakeshore from here to the Lakes Trailhead 3.8 miles away. For more detailed information about the trail along Coldwater Lake see Hike 4.

Options: A shorter option would be to turn left on South Coldwater Trail and follow it to South Coldwater Trailhead.

Camping & services: The nearest campgrounds to this trail are private and located on WA 504, 33 miles to the west. There is a restaurant at Coldwater Ridge Visitor Center, and emergency services can be summoned from there or Johnston Ridge Observatory. The closest gas is at Kid Valley, 33 miles west on WA 504. Find other services at Toutle or Castle Rock.

For more information: USDA Forest Service at Johnston Ridge Observatory or Coldwater Ridge Visitor Center. See Appendix A.

Window in the rock ridge along Boundary Trail.

Eruption Loop (Trail 201)

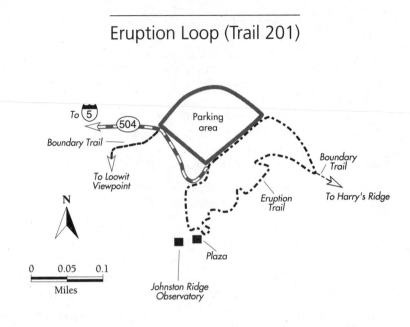

Johnston Ridge Observatory.

7 Eruption Loop (Trail 201)

Type of hike: Day hike, loop.
Total distance: 0.5 mile.
Difficulty: Easy.
Best months: June–September.
Elevation gain: Minimal.
Trailhead elevation: 4,200 feet.
Permits: Mount St. Helens National Volcanic Monument Visitors Pass.
Maps: No map is needed for this short paved trail. There is a map on a signboard at the beginning of the trail.
Starting point: Johnston Ridge Observatory Plaza.

General description: A short interpretive hike on a paved trail next to the Johnston Ridge Observatory.

Finding the trailhead: From Portland head north on Interstate 5, from Seattle head south on I-5. Take Exit 49 off I-5 (49 miles north of the Columbia River Bridge or 120 miles south of Seattle). Then follow Washington 504 for 52 miles to the Johnston Ridge Observatory at the end of the highway. Walk up the wide paved trail from the parking area to the observatory. The Eruption Trail will be to your left as you reach the observatory.

Parking & trailhead facilities: Water, restrooms, and plenty of parking at the observatory.

Key points:
0.2   Cul-de-sac at top of hill.
0.3   Junction with Boundary Trail.
0.4   Parking area.

The hike: The Eruption Trail starts at the east edge of the paved outdoor plaza next to the Johnston Ridge Observatory. The trail climbs gently, making three switchbacks, then winds up to an interpretive sign entitled "Stumps." Half-buried logs, penstemon and fireweed line the

route. You will shortly come to another interpretive sign, this one about the Debris Avalanche. There is a paved cul-de-sac to the left of the trail 0.2 mile from the trailhead where a third sign discusses "New Magma." This is the highest point on this trail, at 4,310 feet.

The trail descends from the cul-de-sac and passes another interpretive sign, "Change". Pearly everlasting flowers crowd this part of the trail in August. After the trail makes a switchback to the right Coldwater Peak looms ahead. The Spillover, where the Debris Avalanche crossed over the top of Johnston Ridge, is visible to the east. Beyond The Spillover is Harry's Ridge.

The trail makes a switchback to the left at the junction with the Boundary Trail, 0.3 mile from the trailhead. From here to the parking area 0.1 mile ahead, the Boundary Trail and the Eruption Trail are concurrent. The exit of the tunnel that now drains Spirit Lake is visible below, next to the highway. Once you have reached the parking area turn left to get back to the observatory.

Options: If you want to add some distance to your hike, walk out the Boundary Trail to the Spillover or Harry's Ridge. See Hike 6 for details about this section of the Boundary Trail. Take the time to check out the exhibits in the observatory and see the great movie about the eruption.

Camping & services: The nearest campgrounds to this trail are private and located on WA 504, 33 miles to the west. There is a restaurant at the Coldwater Ridge Visitor Center, and emergency services can be summoned from there or from Johnston Ridge Observatory. The closest gas is at Kid Valley, 33 miles west on WA 504. Find other services at Toutle or Castle Rock.

For more information: USDA Forest Service at Johnston Ridge Observatory or Coldwater Ridge Visitor Center. See Appendix A.

8 Harry's Ridge (Trail 1E)

Type of hike:	Day hike, out and back.
Total distance:	1.2 miles
Difficulty:	Easy to moderate.
Best months:	July–September.
Elevation gain:	Minimal, 240 feet on side path to highest point.
Trailhead elevation:	4,410 feet at junction with Boundary Trail.
Permits:	Mount St. Helens National Volcanic Monument Visitors Pass.
Maps:	MSHNVM. Spirit Lake West USGS quad covers the area but this trail is not shown.
Starting point:	Junction with Boundary Trail, 3.6 miles east of Johnston Ridge Observatory.

General description: An *internal* side hike, off the Boundary Trail, to two viewpoints overlooking the Blast Zone and Spirit Lake.

Finding the trailhead: Follow driving directions to Johnston Ridge Observatory in Hike 6. Then follow the Boundary Trail east and north for 3.6 miles to the junction with Harry's Ridge Trail. GPS coordinates are 46 16.900 N 122 10.370 W.

Author at abandoned monitoring site. MIKE BARSTAD PHOTO

Harry's Ridge (Trail 1E)
Coldwater Peak (Trail 1G)

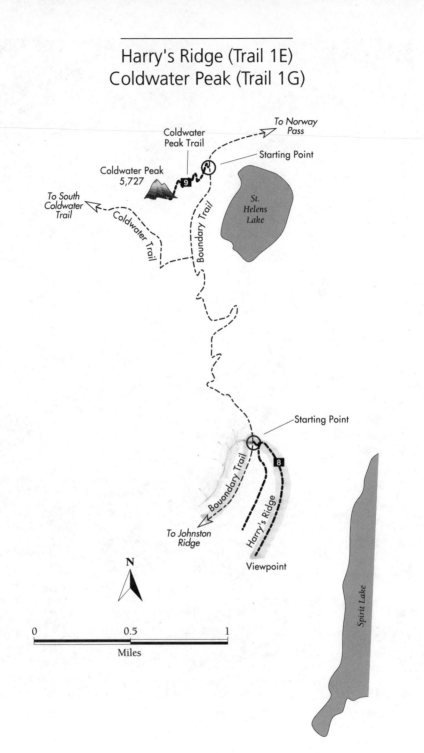

To Norway Pass

Coldwater Peak Trail

Starting Point

Coldwater Peak 5,727

9

Boundary Trail

Coldwater Trail

St. Helens Lake

To South Coldwater Trail

Starting Point

8

Boundary Trail

Harry's Ridge

To Johnston Ridge

Viewpoint

Spirit Lake

N

0   0.5   1
Miles

Key points:
   0.6   Viewpoint.

The hike: Harry's Ridge is named for Harry Truman, the lodge owner at the south end of Spirit Lake who died in the 1980 eruption. For the first 0.2 mile the cairn-marked trail winds up a hillside covered with flowers and blasted-off stumps. Here you have a choice: either follow the post-lined path across the ridgeline that traverses the east facing slope for 0.4 mile to a viewpoint or bear slightly right (south) on the now unmaintained path to follow the ridgeline to its highest point, 0.4 mile away.

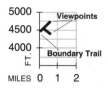

In either case Mount Adams is in view to the east. From either viewpoint the panoramic vista is spectacular in all directions. To the south is the crater of Mount St. Helens, with the nearly black Lava Dome bulging in its center. To the east are Spirit Lake and Windy Ridge. The rugged peaks of the Mount Margaret Backcountry are to the north, and to the west is the devastated area along the Toutle River.

Options: This hike can be done as a side trip off Hike 6 Boundary–Coldwater.

Camping & services: The nearest campgrounds to this trail are private and located on WA 504, 33 miles to the west of the Johnston Ridge Observatory. There is a restaurant at the Coldwater Ridge Visitor Center, and emergency services can be summoned from there or from the Johnston Ridge Observatory. The closest gas is at Kid Valley, 33 miles west on WA 504. Find other services at Toutle or Castle Rock.

For more information: USDA Forest Service at the Johnston Ridge Observatory or at the Coldwater Ridge Visitor Center. See Appendix A.

9 Coldwater Peak (Trail 1G)

See Map on Page 48

Type of hike: Day hike, out and back.
Total distance: 2 miles.
Difficulty: Moderate to strenuous.
Best months: July–September.
Elevation gain: 670 feet.
Trailhead elevation: 5,060 feet at junction with Boundary Trail.
Permits: None.
Maps: MSHNVM. Spirit Lake West USGS quad covers the area but does not show this trail.
Starting point: Junction with the Boundary Trail 6 miles northeast of the Johnston Ridge Observatory or 9.7 miles west of Norway Pass Trailhead.

General description: The Coldwater Peak Trail is an *internal* spur trail from the Boundary Trail to the summit of Coldwater Peak.

Finding the trailhead: From Portland head north on Interstate 5, from Seattle head south on I-5. Take Exit 49 off I-5 (49 miles north of the Columbia River Bridge or 120 miles south of Seattle). Follow Washington 504 east for 52 miles to the Johnston Ridge Observatory. Then hike 5.7 miles east and north on the Boundary Trail to the St. Helens Saddle, as described in Hike 6. From the saddle hike another 0.3 mile north on the Boundary Trail to the junction with the Coldwater Peak Trail.

St. Helens Saddle can also be reached via South Coldwater and Coldwater Trails. See Hikes 4 and 6 for details.

If you are coming from the Norway Pass Trailhead, follow the driving and hiking directions in Hike 44. The junction with the Coldwater Peak Trail is 0.3 mile before the end of the hiking description for Hike 44.

Key points:
1.0   Summit of Coldwater Peak.

The hike: Leaving the junction with the Boundary Trail, the Coldwater Peak Trail first climbs to the northwest. The lightly used trail quickly makes a switchback to the left and continues to climb the grassy slope. A couple more switchbacks bring you to the base of a cliff. As you climb through the lupine and col-

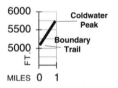

umbine watch for less common pasqueflower and spiraea. The trail makes eight more switchbacks as it climbs to the summit of Coldwater Peak, at 5,727 feet elevation. There are some antennas near the summit.

From the summit there is a great 360-degree view, reaching from Mount Hood in Oregon to Mount Rainier. Watch and listen for the whistle pigs (hoary marmots), that make a very loud, shrill, whistle to show their annoyance at your approach.

Coldwater Peak. MIKE BARSTAD PHOTO

Options: This hike is best done as a side trip when backpacking along the Boundary Trail.

Camping & services: The nearest campgrounds to this trail are private and located on WA 504, 33 miles to the west of the Johnston Ridge Observatory. There is a restaurant at the Coldwater Ridge Visitor Center, and emergency services can be summoned from there or from the Johnston Ridge Observatory. The closest gas is at Kid Valley, 33 miles west on WA 504. Find other services at Toutle or Castle Rock.

For more information: USDA Forest Service at Johnston Ridge Observatory or Coldwater Ridge Visitor Center. See Appendix A.

Creek along Loowit Trail.

Southern Region
Access from Washington 503– Forest Road 90

This lush side of Mount St. Helens National Volcanic Monument was little affected by the 1980 eruption. Old and second growth forests cover most of the area.

The Southern Region however has no lack of volcanic features. Over the centuries lava flows have streamed from the mountain in many places. In some of these flows lava tube caves were formed. **Hikes 21 and 22** explore the largest of these caves.

Lahars did rush down several of the canyons on the south side of the mountain during the 1980 eruption, wiping out nearly everything in their path. **Hike 10 Sheep Canyon–Crescent Ridge Loop, Hike 28 Ape Canyon and Hike 31 Lahar Viewpoint** take you to the largest of these Lahars. **Hike 32 Lava Canyon**, descends through a canyon that was scoured by one of the lahars to expose some of the prettiest waterfalls to be found anywhere.

The Southern Region of Mount St. Helens National Volcanic Monument is used in all seasons. Marked cross-country ski trails as well as snowmobile trails crisscross this region. Cougar and Marble Mountain snoparks are maintained throughout the winter to provide easier access.

Dispersed camping is permitted in many areas on this side of the monument, allowing the hiker to camp close to the trailheads.

Southern Region Overview

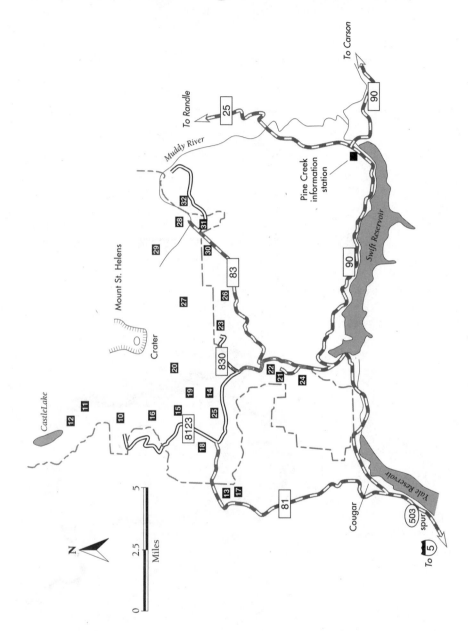

Sheep Canyon–Crescent Ridge Loop (Trails 240, 216, and 238)

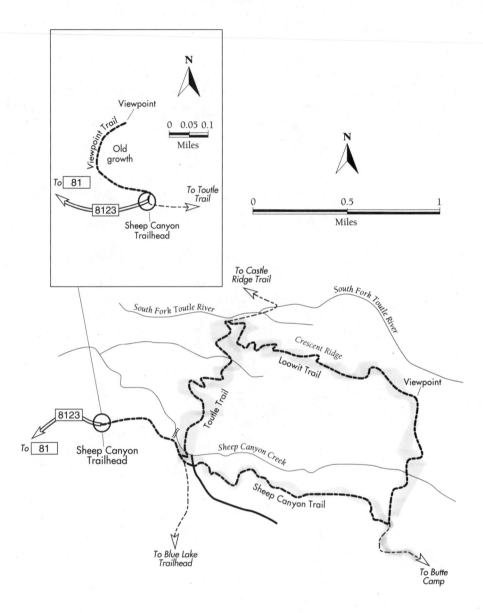

10 Sheep Canyon–Crescent Ridge Loop (Trails 240, 216, and 238)

Type of hike:	Day hike or backpack, loop.
Total distance:	7 miles.
Difficulty:	Moderate.
Best months:	Late June–September.
Elevation gain:	1,260 feet.
Trailhead elevation:	3,420 feet.
Permits:	None.
Maps:	MSHNVM. Goat Mountain and Mount St. Helens USGS quads cover the area but do not show these trails.
Starting point:	Sheep Canyon Trailhead.

General description: The Sheep Canyon–Crescent Ridge Loop offers the hiker as wide a variety of views and terrain as any hike in the monument. Starting in large, old-growth forest it climbs to near timberline. As you descend down Crescent Ridge you can see the destructive power of a volcanic eruption in the form of blasted trees and lahars. Much of the more open terrain is covered with flowers through the summer.

Finding the trailhead: From Portland or Seattle take Interstate 5 to Exit 21 at Woodland (21 miles north of the Columbia River Bridge or 150 miles south of Seattle). Then drive east for 26.5 miles on Washington 503 (which becomes WA 503 spur) to the junction with Forest Road 81. Turn left (north) and follow FR 81 for 11.3 miles to the junction with FR 8123. Turn left on FR 8123 and drive north 6.5 miles to the Sheep Canyon Trailhead at the end of the road.

Parking & trailhead facilities: Parking for several cars but no other facilities at the trailhead.

Key points:
0.6 First junction with Toutle Trail. GPS 46 12.001 N 122 15.586 W.
2.3 Junction with Loowit Trail.
4.9 Junction with Toutle Trail in South Fork Toutle River Canyon. GPS 46 12.607 N 122 15.179 W.
6.4 Junction with Sheep Canyon Trail.

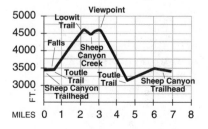

The hike: As you leave the trailhead the route climbs gently through a brushy area. Lupine and other flowers add color along the trail. Soon the tread enters old-growth forest. The trail skirts the edge of Sheep Canyon 0.5 mile from the trailhead. Here a side path goes to the left a short distance to the viewpoint of a waterfall in Sheep Canyon Creek.

Just past the viewpoint is the first junction with the Toutle Trail. Bear right at the junction and continue to climb. For a short distance here the Toutle Trail and the Sheep Canyon Trail follow the same route. The Toutle Trail splits off to the right 0.7 mile from the trailhead. Bear left (almost straight ahead) at this junction and cross a single log bridge. A few yards after crossing the bridge there is a good campsite on the right side of the trail.

For the next 0.9 mile the trail winds its way up the ridge on the south side of Sheep Canyon. When you are away from the edge of the canyon you climb through old-growth forest, but close to the canyon rim the forest was stripped away by the mudflow from the 1980 eruption. The route bears to the right away from the canyon 1.7 miles from the trailhead. Now, at about 4,200 feet elevation, the composition of the forest begins to change. The trees are smaller and spaced farther apart. Huckleberries grow thickly between the trees. If you are here in late August you may want to take the time to enjoy their fruit.

Two-tenths mile after leaving the rim of Sheep Canyon the trail crosses a gully. It then climbs out onto an old lava flow. From here the route winds its way up through thinning timber to the junction with the Loowit Trail at 4,600 feet elevation, 2.3 miles from the Sheep Canyon Trailhead. If you turn right at this junction, the trail goes to Butte Camp.

This section of the Loowit Trail is also covered in Hike 20. Turn left on the Loowit Trail and head north. In a short distance the trail descends a little and crosses Sheep Canyon. Sheep Canyon Creek flows down the center of the canyon. The canyon is much broader here than it was down below. The route climbs a flower-covered slope and leaves the canyon. Shortly after leaving the canyon the trail enters the Blast Zone. One mile from the junction with the Sheep Canyon Trail a great viewpoint on the right side of the trail overlooks the South Fork Toutle River Canyon.

At the viewpoint the trail turns to the northwest and begins the long descent of Crescent Ridge. The route winds and switchbacks its way down, losing 1,400 feet in elevation in the next 1.6 miles. The descent route down Crescent Ridge is along the edge of the Blast Zone. At times you walk through blown-down timber and at others through old-growth forest.

The route reaches another junction with the Toutle Trail 4.9 miles from the trailhead at the bottom of Crescent Ridge. At this junction near the South Fork Toutle River, the Loowit Trail turns to the right. Turn left and follow the Toutle Trail climbing to the southwest. This section of the Toutle Trail is also covered in Hike 15. The trail climbs for 1.5 miles to the junction with the Sheep Canyon Trail, completing the loop. At the junction with the Sheep Canyon Trail turn right (northwest) and retrace your steps for 0.6 mile to Sheep Canyon Trailhead.

Falls in Sheep Canyon.

Options: For a more extended hike follow the Toutle Trail to the Blue Lake Trailhead or even to Redrock Pass. Either of these possibilities requires a car shuttle. See Hikes 14 and 15 for more information. Another option is to camp near the South Fork Toutle River and day hike from there along the Loowit Trail to Studebaker Ridge. See Hike 20 for a description of this section of the Loowit Trail.

Another, much shorter option is to hike from the trailhead to the Sheep Canyon Viewpoint. The viewpoint trail leaves from the north side of the parking area directly across from the Sheep Canyon Trail. Reach the viewpoint in 0.3 mile, after passing through a short section of open old growth forest. See map insert.

Camping & services: Disbursed camping is permitted along FR 8123 and the upper part of FR 81. There is a campground at Merrill Lake off FR 81, 5 miles north of WA 503 spur. Gas, groceries, restaurant, and motel are available in Cougar. Emergency medical facilities are in Woodland.

For more information: USDA Forest Service at Mount St. Helens National Volcanic Monument Headquarters in Chelatchie or at Jack's Restaurant at the junction of WA 503 and WA 503 spur, 5 miles west of Cougar. See Appendix A.

11 Castle Ridge (Trail 216G)

Type of hike:	Day hike, out and back.
Total distance:	3 miles.
Difficulty:	Moderate.
Best months:	July–September.
Elevation gain:	360 feet.
Trailhead elevation:	3,840 feet at the junction with the Loowit Trail.
Permits:	None.
Maps:	MSHNVM. Mount St. Helens and Goat Mountain USGS quads cover the area but do not show this trail.
Starting point:	Junction with Loowit Trail, 3.5 miles from Sheep Canyon Trailhead.

General description: The Castle Ridge Trail, an *internal* trail, used to be known as the Fairview Trail. It follows a silvered snag and flower-covered ridge northwest from the Loowit Trail. It is the main access route to the Castle Lake Trail and Castle Lake.

Finding the trailhead: The Castle Ridge Trail begins at a junction with the Loowit Trail on the north rim of the South Fork Toutle River Canyon. The easiest way to reach this junction is from the Sheep Canyon Trailhead. Follow the driving directions in Hike 10 to the Sheep Canyon Trailhead. Then hike east on the Sheep Canyon Trail for 0.6 mile (also described in Hike 10).

Castle Ridge (Trail 216G)
Castle Lake (Trail 221)

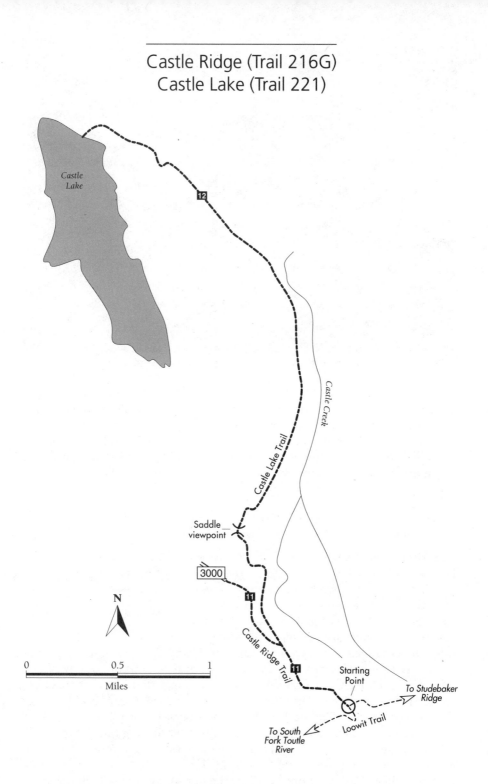

Loowit Trail near the junction with Castle Ridge Trail. ERIC VALENTINE PHOTO

Next turn left and hike north on the Toutle Trail for 1.5 miles to the junction with the Loowit Trail in the bottom of the South Fork of the Toutle River Canyon. Turn left on the Loowit Trail (described in Hike 20) and continue 1.4 miles north to the junction with the Castle Ridge Trail. The sign at this junction may still call it the Fairview Trail.

Key points:
    0.8   Junction with Castle Lake Trail.
    1.5   Junction with Weyerhaeuser Road 3000.

The hike: The Castle Ridge Trail leaves the Loowit Trail just below the rim of the South Fork Toutle River Canyon. The route heads west from the junction, climbing at a moderate rate. After a short distance, make a switchback as you climb to the rounded ridgeline. Along the

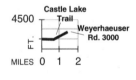

ridge the path leads northwest through snags and downed timber. Flowers grow between the downed logs creating beautiful gardens in this devastated area. If you happen to reach this ridge in the fog, don't be disappointed; certain light conditions caused by the fog seem to enhance this area rather than detract from it. The flowers are at their peak in early July.

The route reaches a small saddle 0.7 mile after leaving the Loowit Trail. At the saddle the path turns to the northwest to traverse a slope for 0.1 mile to the junction with the Castle Lake Trail. See Hike 12 for a description of the Castle Lake Trail. Continuing on to the northwest the path climbs to its end at the junction with Weyerhaeuser Road 3000. The junction is 1.5 miles from the Loowit Trail at about 4,200 feet elevation. It is difficult but not impossible to reach this junction by road. A Weyerhaeuser Mount St. Helens Tree Farm map is as big of a help as a road map but it does not show this trail.

Options: The Castle Ridge Trail is a good day hike from a camp near the South Fork Toutle River. See Hike 20 to locate this campsite. If you are ambitious, turn right 0.8 mile after leaving the Loowit Trail and hike down to Castle Lake. See Hike 12 for details.

Camping & services: Disbursed camping is permitted along FR 8123 and the upper part of FR 81. There is a campground at Merrill Lake off FR 81, 5 miles north of WA 503 spur. Find gas, groceries, restaurant, and motel in Cougar. Emergency medical facilities are in Woodland.

For more information: USDA Forest Service at Mount St. Helens National Volcanic Monument Headquarters in Chelatchie. See Appendix A.

12 Castle Lake (Trail 221)

See Map on Page 61

Type of hike:	Day hike or backpack, out and back.
Total distance:	8 miles.
Difficulty:	Moderate.
Best months:	July–September.
Elevation loss:	1,490 feet.
Trailhead elevation:	3,980 feet at junction with the Castle Ridge Trail.
Permits:	None.
Maps:	MSHNVM. Goat Mountain, Mount St. Helens, and Spirit Lake West USGS quads cover the area but do not show this trail.
Starting point:	Junction with Castle Ridge Trail 0.8 mile from Loowit Trail and 4.3 miles from Sheep Canyon Trailhead.

General description: Hike from the junction with Castle Ridge to a saddle overlooking Castle Lake. Then descend to the foot of Castle Lake.

Finding the trailhead: Follow the driving and hiking directions in Hike 10 to reach the Sheep Canyon Trailhead. Then hike east for 0.6 mile along the Sheep Canyon Trail to the junction with the Toutle Trail. Turn left and hike north on the Toutle trail for 1.5 miles to the junction with the Loowit Trail. Bear left on the Loowit Trail and cross the South Fork Toutle River. Then climb out of the South Fork Toutle River Canyon on the Loowit Trail to the junction with the Castle Ridge Trail. Turn left on the Castle Ridge Trail and hike northwest for 0.8 mile to the junction with the Castle Lake Trail. See Hike 11 for a description of the Castle Ridge Trail.

The junction of the Castle Ridge and the Castle Lake Trails can also be reached from Weyerhaeuser Road 3000. This out-of-the-way trailhead is difficult to find. If you are going to start your hike from Road 3000, get a Weyerhaeuser Mount St. Helens Tree Farm map; it's about the only map that shows these timber company roads, although it doesn't show the trails. From Road 3000 the junction is 0.7 mile to the southeast.

Key points:
- 0.4 Saddle with view of Castle Lake.
- 4.0 Castle Lake.

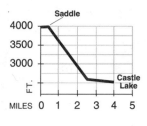

The hike: As you leave the junction with the Castle Ridge Trail the route traverses north across an open slope. You will reach an abandoned roadbed 0.2 mile from the Castle Ridge Trail. Turn right on the roadbed and continue north. The route along the roadbed is marked with posts. The path reaches a saddle 0.2 mile farther along. Walk a few feet west in the saddle for a view of Castle Lake. Take the time to admire the view and watch the elk that are common here.

The wide, well-maintained path begins its descent from the saddle to Castle Creek. The route follows the abandoned roadbed and descends at a moderate grade for a couple of miles. It then levels out and heads northwest to the foot of Castle Lake, 4 miles from the junction with Castle Ridge Trail.

Saddle overlooking Castle Lake. ERIC VALENTINE PHOTO

There are some possible campsites at the foot of the lake in the alder brush. The lake, at 2,510 feet elevation, was formed by a mudflow that dammed the South Fork Castle Creek. The mudflow was the result of the 1980 eruption.

Options: A good option if you want a shorter hike is to stop at the saddle 0.4 mile from the junction with the Castle Ridge Trail.

Camping & services: Disbursed camping is permitted along FR 8123 and the upper part of FR 81. There is a campground at Merrill Lake off FR 81, 5 miles north of Washington Highway 503 spur. Find gas, groceries, restaurant, and motel in Cougar. Emergency medical facilities are in Woodland.

For more information: USDA Forest Service at Mount St. Helens National Volcanic Monument Headquarters in Chelatchie. See Appendix A.

13 Toutle Trail (Trail 238, Kalama Horse Camp to Redrock Pass)

Type of hike: Day hike, shuttle.
Total distance: 5.6 miles.
Difficulty: Easy to moderate.
Best months: June–October.
Elevation gain: 1,070 feet.
Trailhead elevation: 2,020 feet.
Permits: None.
Maps: MSHNVM. Goat Mountain and Mount St. Helens USGS quads cover the area but don't show this trail.
Starting point: Kalama Horse Camp.

General description: The trail first follows the Kalama River with its moss-covered banks and splashing pools to McBride Lake. Then it climbs along a forested slope to Redrock Pass.

Finding the trailhead: To reach Kalama Horse Camp, take Exit 21 off Interstate 5 at Woodland (21 miles north of the Columbia River Bridge or about 150 miles south of Seattle). Drive east on Washington 503 (which becomes WA 503 spur at a junction 23 miles from I-5) for 26.5 miles to the junction with Forest Road 81. Turn left (north) on FR 81 and follow it 8.6 miles to the Kalama Horse Camp. The horse camp is on the right side of FR 81. GPS coordinates at the horse camp and trailhead are 46 08.518 N 122 19.413 W.

Parking & trailhead facilities: There is a campground for horse packers at the trailhead, with restrooms and horse facilities.

Toutle Trail (Trail 238, Kalama Horse Camp to Red Rock Pass)

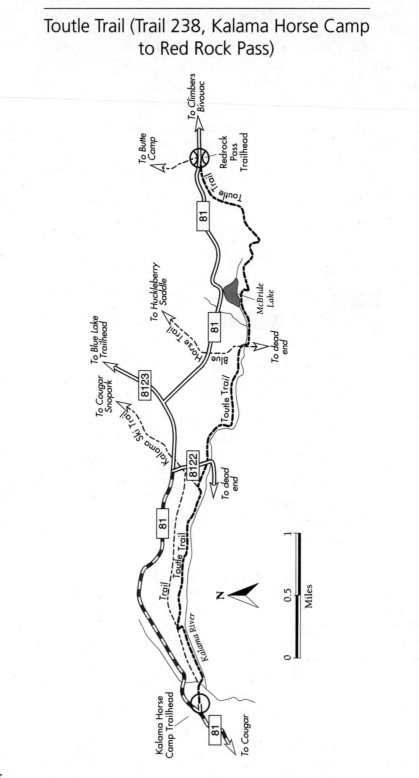

Kalama River.

Key points:

- 0.2   Kalama Ski Trail and Toutle Trail separate.
- 2.0   Last junction with Kalama Ski Trail.
- 2.3   FR 8122. GPS 46 08.527 N 122 17.132 W.
- 3.6   Junction with Blue Horse Trail.
- 4.0   McBride Lake.
- 5.6   Redrock Pass. GPS 46 08.682 N 122 14.087 W.

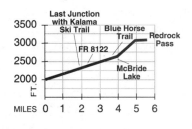

The hike: The Kalama Ski Trail and the Toutle Trail leave the Kalama Horse Camp along the same route, heading east. The ski trail is marked with blue diamond cross-country ski markers, so in the places where the trails follow the same route these markers will be visible, well up in the trees, along the trail. The path descends slightly through mixed forest for a few yards to a wooden bridge over a small stream. A short distance past the bridge the wide trail forks. Kalama Ski Trail with its cross-country ski markers turns to the left (northeast). Bear right (southeast) at the junction and cross another wooden bridge over a usually dry streambed.

The trail then follows the Kalama River upstream. The well-maintained tread makes a switchback to the left 0.7 mile from the trailhead then climbs out of the riverbed. After climbing for 0.1 mile the path switches back to the right, well above the river, on the rim of the canyon. As the trail switches back the Kalama Ski Trail briefly rejoins the Toutle Trail.

Heading on to the east the route generally follows the rim of the canyon for about 0.8 mile. The path then gets close to the river again. At the signed junction, 2 miles from the trailhead, the Kalama Ski Trail leaves this section of the Toutle Trail for the last time. Here the blue diamond marked Kalama Ski Trail turns to the left. The Toutle Trail goes straight ahead to the east-southeast. In another 0.3 mile you will cross FR 8122. Just to the left, at the crossing, is a nice campsite which can be reached by car.

The trail, which is well maintained and cleared for skiers in this section, climbs very gently on to the east after crossing FR 8122. This part of the Toutle Trail is marked with blue diamonds. The tread follows the Kalama River upstream for another 1.3 miles to the junction with the Blue Horse Trail. The Blue Horse Trail, which is an abandoned road at this point, turns to the left and heads north. See Hike 16 for a description of the Blue Horse Trail.

At the junction turn right and follow the abandoned road for a few yards, crossing the Kalama River. Just across the river the Toutle Trail turns to the left off the road and heads east. There is a path to the left 0.1 mile after leaving the roadbed, which goes to another campsite. Shortly after passing the campsite there is a small waterfall on the right side of the trail. The trail passes beneath moss-covered cliffs for a short distance. Look for beaver dams in the river to the left. The tread crosses a couple of tiny steep streams and soon starts to climb above the south shore of McBride Lake. The lake, which is 4 miles from the trailhead, contains a healthy population of brook and cutthroat trout. The access to the lake from the trail is difficult, but there is easy access from FR 81 on the north side of the lake. See Hike 25 for the details.

The trail climbs away from the lake through old-growth forest. It follows a long-abandoned roadbed for a short distance 0.3 mile after leaving the lake. The path leaves the old-growth forest 4.6 miles from the trailhead. It then traverses mostly brush-covered slopes, covered with vine maple and huckleberry bushes. The trail crosses several tiny streams that may dry up in late summer as it traverses these slopes. In this more open area elk are common. Watch for their tracks on the trail. Just before reaching Redrock Pass the trail re-enters old-growth forest, with devils club in some of the wetter spots. The pass, elevation 3,110 feet, is 5.6 miles from the Kalama Horse Camp where this hike begins.

Options: For a loop hike follow the Toutle Trail north from Redrock Pass to the junction with the Kalama Ski Trail. Then take the Kalama Ski Trail back to the Kalama Horse Camp to complete the 12.4 mile loop. See Hikes 14 and 17 for details.

Camping & services: Disbursed camping is allowed in this part of the Mount St. Helens National Volcanic Monument. The closest developed campground except for the horse camp is at Merrill Lake, 4 miles back toward WA 503 spur. Find gas, groceries, restaurant, and motel in Cougar. Medical services are in Woodland.

For more information: USDA Forest Service at Monument Headquarters in Chelatchie or at Pine Creek Information Station. See Appendix A.

14 Toutle Trail (Trail 238, Redrock Pass to Blue Lake Trailhead)

Type of hike:	Day hike, shuttle, with loop option.
Total distance:	3.1 miles.
Difficulty:	Moderate.
Best months:	June–October.
Elevation gain:	370 feet.
Trailhead elevation:	3,110 feet.
Permits:	None.
Maps:	MSHNVM. Mount St. Helens and Goat Mountain USGS quads cover the area but do not show this trail.
Starting point:	Redrock Pass Trailhead.

General description: This section of the Toutle Trail crosses a lava flow for the first 0.5 mile. Then you hike through old growth forest around the base of the Butte Camp Dome to cross a lahar. Past the lahar, the rest of the hike to Blue Lake Trailhead is through open forest. There are great views of Mount St. Helens from the lava flow and the lahar.

Finding the trailhead: Drive on Interstate 5 to Exit 21 at Woodland (21 miles north of the Columbia River Bridge or about 150 miles south of Seattle). Then drive east on Washington 503 (which becomes WA 503 spur). Turn left (north) off WA 503 spur, 26.5 miles from I-5, onto Forest Road 81. Follow FR 81 for 13.5 miles to Redrock Pass Trailhead. GPS 46 08.682 N 122 14.087 W.

Parking & trailhead facilities: There is parking for several cars but no other facilities at the trailhead.

Key points:
- 0.5 Junction with Kalama Ski Trail.
- 1.2 Junction with Butte Camp Trail. GPS 46 09.409 N 122 13.971 W.
- 2.8 Junction with Blue Horse Trail.
- 3.1 Blue Lake Trailhead. GPS 46 10.114 N 122 15.678 W.

The hike: The trail leaves Redrock Pass heading north. It first makes a switchback, then climbs out on top of a flow of a lava. The tread crosses this rough, chunky flow for 0.3 mile then enters an older smoothed-off flow covered with beargrass and small timber. The well-used path crosses an abandoned roadbed 0.4 mile from the trailhead and reaches the junction with the Kalama Ski Trail 0.1 mile farther along.

Toutle Trail (Trail 238, Red Rock Pass to Blue Lake Trailhead)

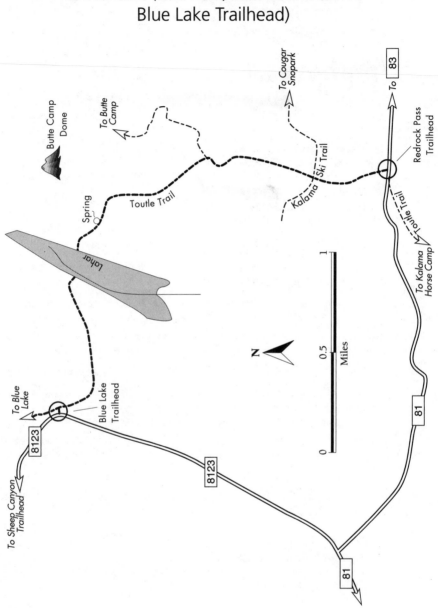

The Toutle Trail crosses the Kalama Ski Trail at the signed junction and continues north. After passing the junction the tread enters old-growth timber. The path crosses a dry wash 0.5 mile after crossing the ski trail. Reach the junction with the Butte Camp Trail 0.2 mile farther along. The junction with the

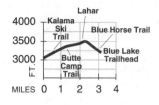

Butte Camp Trail is 1.2 miles from Redrock Pass and at 3,340 feet elevation. The Butte Camp Trail connects with the Loowit Trail and is used by climbers doing routes on the southwest side of Mount St. Helens. See Hike 19 for a description of the Butte Camp Trail.

The Toutle Trail leaves the junction with the Butte Camp Trail and turns to the northwest. The tread traverses around the base of the Butte Camp Dome for 0.7 mile to a small stream crossing. The stream flows from a spring a short distance above the trail. This may be the only source of water along this trail.

Lava flow north of Redrock Pass.

Past the stream the trail climbs gently along the base of the dome, then heads west to cross a lahar. The trail may disappear temporarily in the main wash of the lahar. If it does, look for a cairn on the far side and pick up the trail again. This section of the Toutle Trail reaches its highest elevation, 3,480 feet, as it crosses this lahar.

Once you have crossed the lahar the trail heads west through smaller forest of mostly lodgepole and white pine. You will reach the junction with Blue Horse Trail 0.5 mile after crossing the lahar. This signed junction is 2.8 miles from the trailhead at Redrock Pass. See Hike 16 for information about the Blue Horse Trail. Another 0.3 mile northwest along the path brings you to the Blue Lake Trailhead. A side trail leads a few yards west to the parking area at 3,210 feet elevation.

Options: A loop hike can be made by turning left (south) on Blue Horse Trail and following it to the Kalama Ski Trail. Then turn left (southeast) on the Kalama Ski Trail and follow it to the junction with the Toutle Trail 0.5 mile north of Redrock Pass. Turn right on the Toutle Trail here and retrace your steps back to the trailhead.

Camping & services: Disbursed camping is allowed in this part of the Mount St. Helens National Volcanic Monument. The closest developed campground except for the Kalama Horse Camp is at Merrill Lake, 9 miles back on FR 81 toward WA 503 spur. Beaver Bay and Cougar, Pacific Power campgrounds, are located east of Cougar on WA 503 spur. Find gas, groceries, restaurant, and motel in Cougar. Medical services are in Woodland.

For more information: USDA Forest Service at Monument Headquarters in Chelatchie or at Pine Creek Information Station. See Appendix A.

15 Toutle Trail (Trail 238, Blue Lake Trailhead to South Fork Toutle River)

Type of hike: Day hike or backpack, out and back, with loop option.
Total distance: 8.6 miles.
Difficulty: Moderate.
Best months: Late June–October.
Elevation gain/loss: 750 feet each direction.
Trailhead elevation: 3,210 feet.
Permits: None.
Maps: MSHNVM. Goat Mountain USGS quad covers the area but does not show this trail.
Starting point: Blue Lake Trailhead.

General description: This section of the Toutle Trail takes you past Blue Lake and over Huckleberry Saddle before descending into Sheep Canyon. Past Sheep Canyon you traverse around a point then descend to the lahar at the bottom of the South Fork Toutle River Canyon.

Finding the trailhead: Drive on Interstate 5 to Exit 21 at Woodland (150 miles south of Seattle or 21 miles north of the Columbia River Bridge). Head east from the freeway on Washington 503 (which becomes WA 503 spur). Turn left (north) off WA 503 spur, 26.5 miles from I-5, onto Forest Road 81. Follow FR 81 for 11.3 miles to the junction with FR 8123. Turn left on FR 8123 and drive north 1.7 miles to Blue Lake Trailhead. The trailhead is on the right side of FR 8123. GPS coordinates are 46 10.114 N 122 15.678 W.

Parking & trailhead facilities: Parking for several cars but no other facilities at the trailhead.

Key points:
0.3   Blue Lake.
2.1   Junction with Blue Horse Trail.
2.8   Junction with Sheep Canyon Trail. GPS 46 12.001 N 122 15.586 W.
4.3   Junction with Loowit Trail. GPS 46 12.607 N 122 15.179 W.

The hike: From the parking area at Blue Lake Trailhead a broad path leads a few yards east to the Toutle Trail. Turn left (north) on the Toutle Trail. In a short distance cross a wooden bridge over Coldspring Creek. The tread climbs gently along the west bank of Coldspring Creek for 0.3 mile to Blue Lake. As you

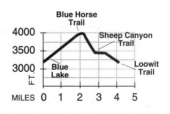

climb, look to the right for a view of Mount St. Helens. There are two side

Toutle Trail (Trail 238, Blue Lake Trailhead to South Fork Toutle River)

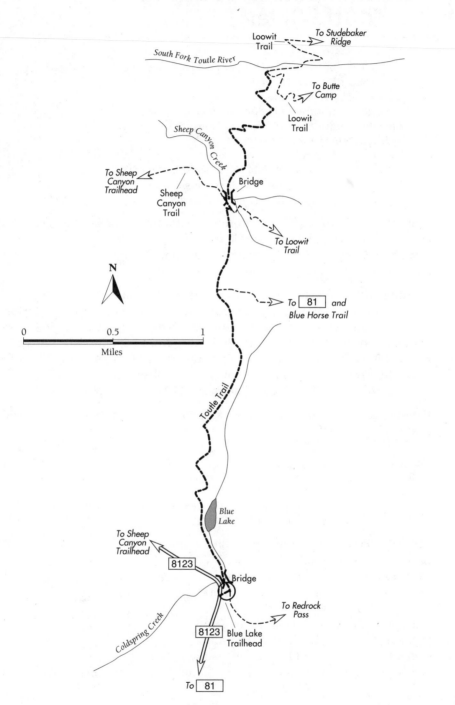

Blue Lake.

paths leading down to the lake. Once past the lake the trail winds up through the large timber. The path enters a more open area with another view of the mountain, 1.1 miles above the lake. Seven-tenths mile farther along is the junction with Blue Horse Trail, at 3,960 feet elevation. This junction, in Huckleberry Saddle, is 2.1 miles from Blue Lake Trailhead. See Hike 16 for a description of the Blue Horse Trail. There are several possible campsites in the area. Please don't camp in the meadows.

The Toutle Trail goes straight ahead (north) at the junction. As you head north through the large timber you may notice a faint trail to the right. This trail follows a now abandoned route through Huckleberry Saddle and should not be used. The tread leaves the broad saddle and descends at a moderate grade. Half a mile after leaving the saddle the trail makes a switchback to the right along the side of a semi-open canyon. A few yards past the switchback is the upper junction with the Sheep Canyon Trail. The Sheep Canyon Trail turns to the right and climbs to the Loowit Trail. See Hike 10 for a description of the Sheep Canyon Trail. For a short distance the Toutle Trail and the Sheep Canyon Trail follow the same route.

At the junction turn left. A few yards farther is the lower junction with the Sheep Canyon Trail at a switchback. Here the Sheep Canyon Trail turns left and heads northwest to the Sheep Canyon Trailhead. Turn right at this junction and descend the last few yards to the bridge over Sheep Canyon Creek. The bridge, at 3,560 feet elevation, is 2.9 miles from the Blue Lake Trailhead.

After it crosses the bridge the path traverses out of Sheep Canyon and still heads generally north. It descends in and out of draws and through stands of old growth timber for 0.7 mile to the edge of the Blast Zone. Once in the Blast Zone nearly all the large trees are either blown down or stripped and broken off. The trail follows the edge of the Blast Zone, sometimes in large timber and sometimes on brushy slopes. It crosses a stream on a wooden bridge in a side draw and rounds a point. Then it descends a brushy slope into the canyon of the South Fork Toutle River. As you approach the river you come to the junction with the Loowit Trail, 4.3 miles from the Blue Lake Trailhead, at 3,180 feet elevation. This is the end of the Toutle Trail. For a description of this section of the Loowit Trail see Hike 20. Water is available from the river a short distance east along the Loowit Trail.

Options: A nice loop hike can be made by turning right on the Blue Horse Trail 2.1 miles north of Blue Lake Trailhead. Follow the horse trail back to the Toutle Trail 0.3 mile east of the Blue Lake Trailhead. Then take the Toutle Trail west to the parking area. See Hikes 16 and 14 for details.

Camping & services: Disbursed camping is permitted along FR 8123 and the upper part of FR 81. There is a campground at Merrill Lake off FR 81, 5 miles north of WA 503 spur. Gas, groceries, restaurant, and motel are in Cougar. Emergency medical facilities are in Woodland.

For more information: USDA Forest Service at Mount St. Helens National Volcanic Monument Headquarters in Chelatchie or at Pine Creek Information Station. See Appendix A.

16 Blue Horse Trail (Trail 237)

Type of hike:	Day hike, shuttle, with loop option.
Total distance:	5.3 miles.
Difficulty:	Moderate.
Best months:	Late June–October.
Elevation loss:	1,280 feet.
Trailhead elevation:	3,960 feet at junction with Toutle Trail in Huckleberry Saddle.
Permits:	None.
Maps:	MSHNVM. Goat Mountain USGS quad covers the area but this trail is not shown.
Starting point:	Junction with Toutle Trail at Huckleberry Saddle.

General description: A downhill hike from the junction with the Toutle Trail in the Huckleberry Saddle passing the Blue Lake Lahar to another junction with the Toutle Trail. After crossing the Toutle Trail, continue to descend. Cross the Kalama Ski Trail and FR 81 to yet another junction with the Toutle Trail near McBride Lake.

Finding the trailhead: The Blue Horse Trail begins *internally* at a junction with the Toutle Trail in the Huckleberry Saddle, 2.1 miles north of the Blue Lake Trailhead. See Hike 15 for directions to the Blue Lake Trailhead. Then hike 2.1 miles north on the Toutle Trail (also described in Hike 15).

Key points:
0.7 Leave roadbed.
1.5 Cross Blue Lake Lahar.
2.8 Junction with Toutle Trail near Blue Lake Trailhead.
3.0 Junction with Kalama Ski Trail.
5.0 Cross FR 81. GPS 46 08.535 N 122 16.053 W.
5.3 Junction with Toutle Trail west of McBride Lake.

The hike: The Blue Horse Trail heads east from the Toutle Trail in Huckleberry Saddle. It crosses through small meadows and stands of trees for a few yards, and then it becomes evident that you are following an abandoned roadbed. The wide, sandy road continues to the east for 0.5 mile then crosses Coldspring Creek. The creek may be dry by midsummer. After crossing the

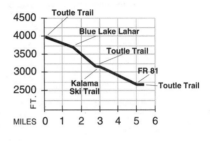

creek the trail (still a roadbed) heads southwest for another 0.2 mile. Here the trail leaves the roadbed. The path turns left off the road and soon makes a turn to the right to head south.

The trail continues south for 0.5 mile then skirts the west side of Blue Lake Lahar. Mount St. Helens is in full view to the left as you skirt this 1980 mudflow. Before long the trail turns a bit to the left and gets out on the lahar. You descend the lahar for some distance, then bear left and cross to its southeast side. There may be a stream flowing down the lahar, but don't count on it for water.

As the trail leaves the lahar it continues to descend, now through mostly lodgepole pine forest. You may notice the orange diamonds marking the trail as you descend. These are snowmobile trail markers. The section of the Blue Horse Trail from here to FR 81 is used by snowmobiles in the winter.

Slightly more than 1 mile after leaving the lahar the junction with the Toutle Trail is reached. This junction, elevation 3,320 feet, is 2.8 miles from where you left the Toutle Trail in the Huckleberry Saddle. To the right at this signed junction Blue Lake Trailhead is only 0.3 mile away.

Cross the Toutle Trail and continue to descend gently through the small lodgepole pine timber. As you descend, the hill you see to the left is Butte Camp Dome. The Blue Horse Trail crosses the Kalama Ski Trail 0.3 mile after crossing the Toutle Trail. Continue south at the four-way junction. Seven-tenths of a mile after passing the Kalama Ski Trail the path forks in an inverted Y. Continue south at the Y, following the orange diamond markers.

Blue Horse Trail crosses FR 81, 2 miles after crossing the Kalama Ski Trail. This road crossing is 5 miles from Huckleberry Saddle. If you are a

Blue Horse Trail (Trail 237)

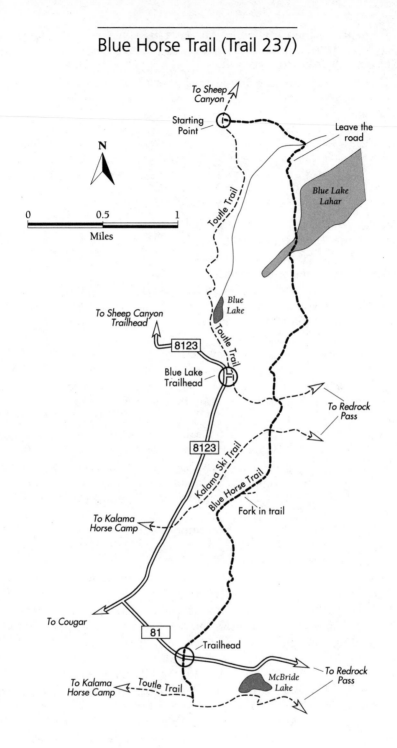

hiker this will probably be the end of your hike. A car shuttle can easily be made to here from Blue Lake Trailhead. There is parking for one or two cars on the south side of the road.

To continue on Blue Horse Trail, something that few hikers will do, cross FR 81 and follow the abandoned and blocked roadbed of FR 600 to the south. After following FR 600 for 0.3 mile you come to another junction with the Toutle Trail. The roadbed continues but this is the end of the Blue Horse Trail. If you turn right (west) on the Toutle Trail it is 3.6 miles to Kalama Horse Camp. To the left (east) it's 0.4 mile to McBride Lake and 2 miles to Redrock Pass. See Hike 13 for a description of this section of the Toutle Trail.

Options: The Blue Horse Trail is usually used as a return trip when you have hiked a section of the Toutle Trail. See Hikes 13, 14, and 15 for the details on the Toutle Trail.

Camping & services: Disbursed camping is permitted along FR 8123 and the upper part of FR 81. There is a campground at Merrill Lake off FR 81, 5 miles north of WA 503 spur. Gas, groceries, restaurant, and motel are in Cougar. Emergency medical facilities are in Woodland.

For more information: USDA Forest Service at Mount St. Helens National Volcanic Monument Headquarters in Chelatchie or at Pine Creek Information Station. See Appendix A.

Scouts on Blue Horse Trail. ERIC VALENTINE PHOTO

17 Kalama Ski Trail (Trail 231)

Type of hike: Day hike, shuttle, with loop option.
Total distance: 10.9 miles.
Difficulty: Moderate.
Best months: June–October.
Elevation gain: 1,240 feet.
Trailhead elevation: 2,020 feet.
Permits: None.
Maps: Goat Mountain and Mount St. Helens USGS quads cover the area but this trail is not shown.
Starting point: Kalama Horse Camp.

General description: This trail is seldom hiked its whole length at one time. The Kalama Ski Trail connects with several other trails and is used as an access trail or to combine with other trails to make loops. The trail is almost always in the woods, so good views are rare. This is, however, a popular ski trail and gets some horse use.

Finding the trailhead: To reach Kalama Horse Camp, take Exit 21 off Interstate 5 at Woodland (21 miles north of the Columbia River Bridge or aobut 150 miles south of Seattle) Then drive east on Washington 503 (which becomes WA 503 spur at a junction 23 miles from I-5) for 26.5 miles to the junction with Forest Road 81. Turn left (north) on FR 81 and follow it 8.6 miles to Kalama Horse Camp. The horse camp is on the right side of FR 81. There is a sign marking the entrance to the horse camp. GPS coordinates at the horse camp and trailhead are 46 08.518 N 122 19.413 W.

Parking & trailhead facilities: There is water for horses, as well as restrooms and adequate parking at the trailhead.

Key points:
- 0.2 Leave Toutle Trail.
- 0.8 Join Toutle Trail.
- 2.0 Leave Toutle Trail.
- 2.2 Cross FR 8122.
- 2.3 Cross FR 81.
- 3.1 Junction with Goat Marsh Trail.
- 3.3 Cross FR 8123. GPS 46 09.295 N 122 16.115 W.
- 4.3 Junction with Blue Horse Trail.
- 6.3 Junction with Toutle Trail. GPS 46 08.993 N 122 14.116 W.
- 8.5 Cross FR 830 (Climbers Bivouac Road).
- 10.3 Junction with Loop B.
- 10.9 Cougar Snopark. GPS 46 07.126 N 122 12.382 W.

The hike: Leaving Kalama Horse Camp Trailhead the wide, well-marked Kalama Ski Trail and the Toutle Trail follow the same route. The trail heads east descending a few yards through the forest. In about 0.2 mile after crossing a

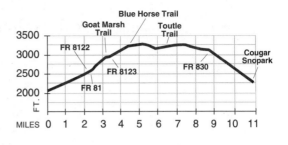

wooden bridge the trail forks. Kalama Ski Trail bears left (northeast) and climbs gently, while the Toutle Trail follows the Kalama River. For the next 0.6 mile the trails parallel each other. The ski trail, which is marked with blue diamond cross-country ski markers, climbs a gentle rounded ridge away from the river.

Just before rejoining the Toutle Trail a path bears left off the ski trail. This path is easy to follow and rejoins the Kalama Ski Trail a couple miles farther east, close to FR 8122. The unmarked path makes an excellent return route for hikers wishing to make 5.6 mile loop.

For the next 1.2 miles the Kalama Ski Trail and the Toutle Trail follow the same route along the bank of the Kalama River. At first the trail is well above the river, but by the time the trails split again the route is only a few feet above river level. See Hike 13 for more information. At the well-marked junction 2 miles from Kalama Horse Camp Trailhead, the Kalama Ski Trail turns to the left again off the Toutle Trail. Follow the trail marked with blue diamonds to the northeast. In about a quarter-mile you come to the unmarked junction with the path mentioned earlier. At the junction bear right if you wish to continue on the Kalama Ski Trail. If you are going to make the 5.6 mile loop mentioned above turn left (west).

A couple hundred yards farther along the ski trail you will cross FR 8122, at 2,540 feet elevation. Continue northeast after crossing the road for a short distance and cross FR 81. Once across FR 81 the ski trail follows FR 590, which is the old roadbed, for a few yards to the northeast to a large parking area. At the northeast edge of the parking area, piles of dirt and stumps block FR 590. The ski trail continues around the obstacles and follows the roadbed, which is reverting to a trail.

The route climbs gently for the next 0.8 mile to the junction with Goat Marsh Trail. See Hike 18 for details about Goat Marsh Trail. At the junction the ski route turns to the right (east) and reaches FR 8123 in 0.2 mile. Cross FR 8123 and climb gently to the northeast through semi-open lodgepole pine forest for 1 mile to the junction with Blue Horse Trail. See Hike 16 for information about Blue Horse Trail. At the junction follow the blue diamonds and head east. Past this junction the route is not well maintained for hiking, but it is easy to follow. There is another path to the left 0.3 mile past the junction with the horse trail, but stay off this path. Instead, follow the route marked with diamonds, heading southeast.

In another 0.3 mile you will come to an open area. There may be no trail across the open area. Head southeast and the route will show up again as

Kalama Ski Trail (Trail 231)

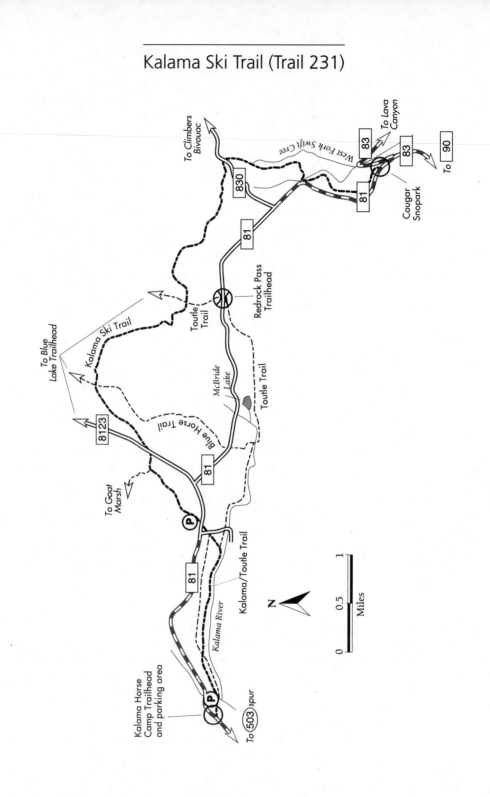

To Climbers Bivouac

West Fork Swift Cree

To Lava Canyon

83

83

To 90

830

81

81

Cougar Snopark

Redrock Pass Trailhead

Toutle Trail

Kalama Ski Trail

To Blue Lake Trailhead

McBride Lake

Toutle Trail

Blue Horse Trail

8123

81

To Goat Marsh

P

81

Kalama/Toutle Trail

Kalama River

N

0   0.5   1

Miles

Kalama Horse Camp Trailhead and parking area

P

503 spur

To

you enter the timber. The route continues through large timber and semi-open areas for another 1.4 miles to the junction with Toutle Trail. The route may be hard to spot in the open areas; watch for the blue diamonds.

At the junction, elevation 3,210 feet, the Toutle Trail crosses the Kalama Ski Trail for the last time. If you turn right on the Toutle Trail, Redrock Pass Trailhead is about half a mile to the south. To continue on the Kalama Ski Trail head east at the junction, through the young forest of fir and hemlock. A quarter of a mile from the junction the route bears left (northeast) along the side of an area of dead trees. Soon the trail heads east again, then gradually bends around to the southeast as it descends gently, crossing an old lava flow.

One and a half miles from the last junction with the Toutle Trail the route enters an area that was logged many years ago. The old skid roads in this area can be confusing. The ski trail follows sections of these old roads as it winds its way through this semi-open area. If it were not for the blue diamonds it would be easy to lose the route here. Mount St. Helens looms above to the north. After leaving the logged area the ski trail follows an abandoned roadbed to FR 830. FR 830 is the road to the Climbers Bivouac.

Kalama Ski Trail crosses FR 830, at 3,150 feet elevation, and soon descends to the south. The route crosses another road in about a quarter of a mile, then drops gently along a logged section. From here on, the ski trail follows an abandoned road all the way down to Cougar Snopark. Along the way you will pass three marked ski trails which turn to the right and lead to FR 81. Shortly before reaching the snopark the trail narrows along a ridge; the roadbed has washed away at this point. Reach Cougar Snopark, elevation 2,300 feet, 2.4 miles after crossing FR 830.

Options: The loop mentioned above makes a good return for the lower section of Kalama Ski Trail. Another loop option is to return on the Toutle Trail from the junction 6.3 miles from Kalama Horse Camp. By turning south on the Toutle Trail and following it back you will have a 0.2 mile shorter return trip.

Camping & services: Disbursed camping is allowed in this part of the Mount St. Helens National Volcanic Monument. The closest developed campground except for the horse camp (which is reserved for horse campers) is at Merrill Lake, 4 miles back toward WA 503 spur. Gas, groceries, restaurant, and motel are available in Cougar. Emergency medical help can be found in Woodland.

For more information: USDA Forest Service at Monument headquarters in Chelatchie or at Pine Creek Information Station. See Appendix A.

Goat Marsh (Trail 237A)

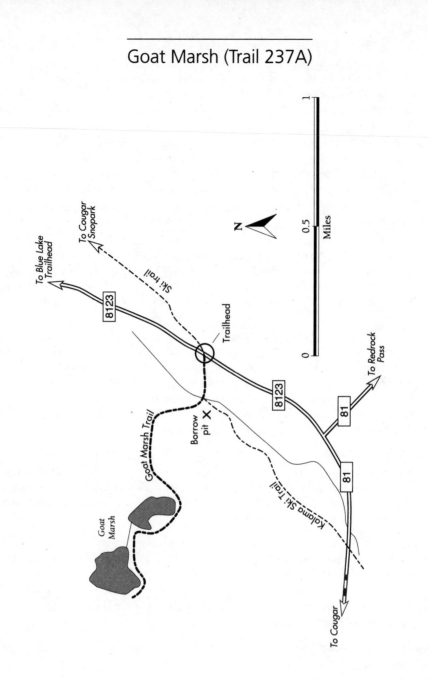

18 Goat Marsh (Trail 237A)

Type of hike: Day hike, out and back.
Total distance: 2.8 miles.
Difficulty: Easy.
Best months: May–October.
Elevation gain: Minimal.
Trailhead elevation: 2,880 feet.
Permits: None.
Maps: Goat Mountain USGS quad.
Starting point: The junction of Kalama Ski Trail and FR 8123.

General description: A hike through the forest to a marsh containing two lakes with a beaver-dammed stream between them. Goat Marsh is a research area.

Finding the trailhead: From Interstate 5 Exit 21 at Woodland (about 150 miles south of Seattle or 21 miles north of the Columbia River Bridge), drive east on Washington 503 (which becomes WA 503 spur). Turn left (north) off WA 503 spur, 26.5 miles from I-5, onto Forest Road 81. Follow FR 81 for 11.3 miles to the junction with FR 8123. Turn left on FR 8123 and drive north 0.6 mile to the point where Kalama Ski Trail crosses the road. There is a sign at the junction.

Goat Marsh Lake.

Parking & trailhead facilities: There is parking for one or two cars at the trailhead but no other facilities.

Key points:
   0.2   Leave Kalama Ski Trail and join Goat Marsh Trail. GPS 46 09.251 N 122 16.251 W.
   0.9   First lake.
   1.4   End of trail next to second lake.

The hike: Much of Goat Marsh Trail is really an abandoned roadbed that is reverting nicely to a trail. Hike west on the Kalama Ski Trail for 0.2 mile to the junction with Goat Marsh Trail. Turn right at the junction and head northwest through hemlock forest. The route passes an abandoned borrow pit and soon comes to a wooden fence with a gate. The fence and gate are here to prevent motor vehicles

from continuing to Goat Marsh. The route climbs very gently at first, then levels out. For the first 0.9 mile the route is marked with blue diamond cross-country ski trail markers.

As you near the first lake the hiking trail bears left off the marked ski trail. The roadbed soon ends and the poorly marked trail traverses around the south side of the lake. As the trail leaves the first lake it passes a beaver dam. The path soon reaches the south side of another shallow lake. It works its way around to the southeast corner of this second lake and ends in the forest near the shore.

Many elk inhabit Goat Marsh. Watch for them in the open areas north of the lakes in the early morning and evening. The return trip is made via the same route.

Options: The options are very limited on this hike.

Camping & services: Disbursed camping is permitted along FR 8123 and the upper part of FR 81. There is a campground at Merrill Lake off FR 81, 5 miles north of WA 503 spur. Gas, groceries, restaurant, and motel are available in Cougar. Emergency medical facilities are in Woodland.

For more information: USDA Forest Service at Mount St. Helens National Volcanic Monument Headquarters in Chelatchie or at Jack's Restaurant at the junction of WA 503 and WA 503 spur, 5 miles west of Cougar. See Appendix A.

19 Butte Camp (Trail 238A)

Type of hike: Day hike, out and back.
Total distance: 5.2 miles.
Difficulty: Moderate.
Best months: July–September.
Elevation gain: 1,410 feet.
Trailhead elevation: 3,340 feet at junction with Toutle Trail.
Permits: None.
Maps: MSHNVM. Mount St. Helens USGS quad covers the area but this trail is not shown.
Starting point: Junction with Toutle Trail 1.2 miles north of Redrock Pass Trailhead.

General description: A moderate hike from the Toutle Trail to the Loowit Trail at timberline on Mount St. Helens. This is an *internal* trail.

Finding the trailhead: Follow the directions to Redrock Pass Trailhead in Hike 14, then take the Toutle Trail for 1.2 miles north, passing the junction with Kalama Ski Trail to the junction with Butte Camp Trail. GPS coordinates at this junction are 46 09.409 N 122 13.971 W.

Butte Camp Trail near Loowit Trail.

Butte Camp (Trail 238A)

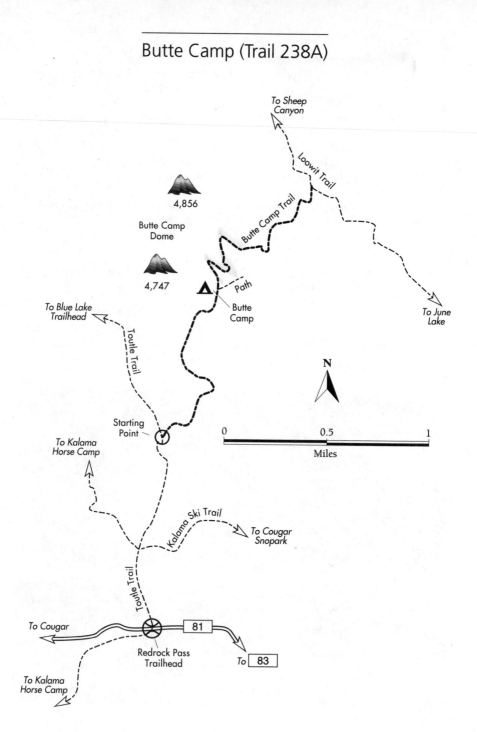

To Sheep Canyon

Loowit Trail

4,856

Butte Camp Dome

Butte Camp Trail

4,747

Path

Butte Camp

To Blue Lake Trailhead

Toutle Trail

To June Lake

N

Starting Point

0   0.5   1

Miles

To Kalama Horse Camp

Kalama Ski Trail

To Cougar Snopark

Toutle Trail

To Cougar

81

Redrock Pass Trailhead

To 83

To Kalama Horse Camp

Key points:
1.2   Butte Camp (lower).
2.0   Viewpoint
2.6   Loowit Trail. GPS coordinates 46 10.527 N 122 13.023 W.

The hike: After it leaves the marked junction with the Toutle Trail, the Butte Camp Trail climbs to the northeast, through open forest on an old lava flow. Lupine and paintbrush dot the sides of the trail as you climb. A little over 1 mile from the junction Mount St. Helens comes into view ahead. A little farther along, 1.2 miles from the junction, the trail passes Butte Camp. The camp, elevation 3,990 feet, is on the left side of the trail and has several good campsites. There is usually water in a small stream a few yards to

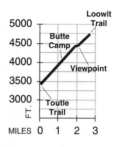

the west. Monkeyflowers and false hellebore brighten the meadows around the campsites. A path turns to the right as you pass Butte Camp. This path is part of an older, now abandoned trail. There are really two Butte Camps, Lower and Upper. The one mentioned above is Lower Butte Camp. The upper camp is now closed for research.

The trail makes a switchback to the right shortly after passing the camp. Here it enters an area where the lava is much older and has had more time to develop a layer of soil so the trees here are much larger. Butte Camp Trail climbs at a steady grade for another 0.6 mile, then flattens out and soon comes to a viewpoint. The viewpoint has a great view to the south, with Mount Hood in the distance. At the viewpoint, 2 miles from the Toutle Trail, the trail makes a hard left turn. From the viewpoint the tread heads north and northeast, climbing gently through small alpine firs and lodge-pole pines. Lupine and phlox almost cover the ground in spots. The trail climbs above timberline 0.5 mile past the viewpoint. Another 0.1 mile and the junction with Loowit Trail is reached at 4,750 feet elevation.

Options: If you turn left on Loowit Trail you can make a loop by following it to Sheep Canyon Trail. Then turn left and descend Sheep Canyon Trail back down to Toutle Trail. Turn left again on the Toutle Trail and follow it back to the junction where you started up Butte Camp Trail. See Hikes 14, 15 and 20 for details.

Camping & services: Disbursed camping is permitted along Forest Road 8123 and the upper part of FR 81. There is a campground at Merrill Lake off FR 81, 5 miles north of WA 503 spur. Gas, groceries, restaurant, and motel are available in Cougar. Emergency medical facilities are in Woodland.

For more information: USDA Forest Service at Mount St. Helens National Volcanic Monument Headquarters in Chelatchie or at Jack's Restaurant at the junction of WA 503 and WA 503 spur, 5 miles west of Cougar. See Appendix A.

20 Loowit Trail (Trail 216, Butte Camp Trail to Studebaker Ridge)

Type of hike: Backpack, shuttle, with out and back and loop options.

Total distance: 7.8 miles.

Difficulty: Strenuous.

Best months: July–September.

Elevation loss: About 1,500 feet.

Trailhead elevation: 4,750 at junction with Butte Camp Trail.

Permits: None.

Maps: MSHNVM. Mount St. Helens and Goat Mountain USGS quads cover the area but do not show this trail.

Starting point: Junction with Butte Camp Trail, 3.8 miles north of Redrock Pass Trailhead.

General description: This section of the Loowit Trail, an *internal* trail, contours very close to the timberline on Mount St. Helens for the first 3 miles. It then dives down Crescent Ridge to the South Fork Toutle River. After crossing the South Fork Toutle River the route climbs back above timberline and crosses the pumice-covered slopes to Studebaker Ridge.

Finding the trailhead: See Hike 14 for driving directions to the Redrock Pass Trailhead. Then hike the Toutle and Butte Camp Trails to the junction with the Loowit Trail. See Hike 19 for the details on the Butte Camp Trail. GPS coordinates at the junction are 46 10.527 N 122 13.023 W.

Key points:

2.0 Junction with Sheep Canyon Trail.
3.0 Viewpoint.
4.6 Junction with Toutle Trail. GPS 46 12.607 N 122 15.179 W.
6.0 Junction with Castle Ridge Trail.
7.8 Studebaker Ridge.

The hike: If you are reaching this junction via the Butte Camp Trail, turn left. If this is a continuation of a hike along the Loowit Trail, go straight ahead. In any case, the Loowit Trail heads northwest from the junction with the Butte Camp Trail. A few yards after leaving the junction you will cross a tiny stream, which is usually dry by

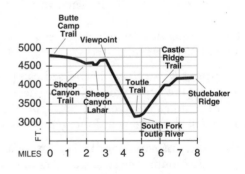

midsummer. This section of the Loowit Trail is just above timberline. In spots the sandy ground is covered with heather that blooms in July. Many

Crossing the lava on the Loowit Trail. ERIC VALENTINE PHOTO

Loowit Trail (Trail 216)

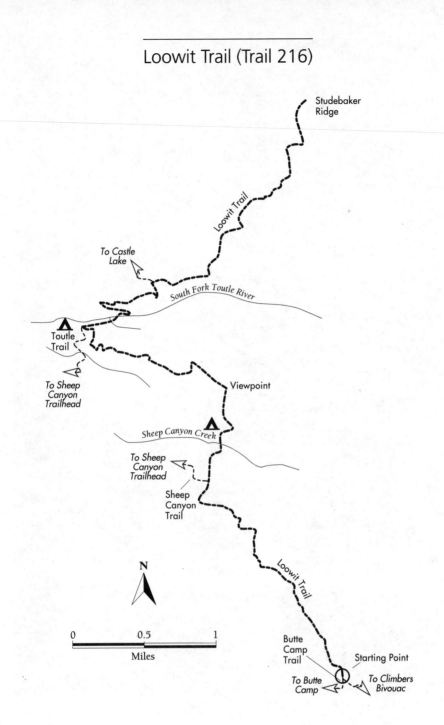

Studebaker Ridge

Loowit Trail

To Castle Lake

South Fork Toutle River

Toutle Trail

To Sheep Canyon Trailhead

Viewpoint

Sheep Canyon Creek

To Sheep Canyon Trailhead

Sheep Canyon Trail

Loowit Trail

N

0   0.5   1
Miles

Butte Camp Trail

Starting Point

To Butte Camp

To Climbers Bivouac

other alpine flowers also dot the landscape. Mount St. Helens looms above to the right.

The trail crosses a lahar 0.8 mile from the junction. After crossing the mudflow the path passes through an open stand of stunted lodgepole pines. The tread crosses a small canyon 0.7 mile farther along. Penstemon and paintbrush bloom here in profusion in July. The trail traverses out of the canyon, then descends through open fir, white pine, and lodgepole pine woods. Soon the path makes a switchback to the right as it descends into another canyon. The remains of Blue Lake Lahar can be seen far below in this canyon. Loowit Trail climbs steeply out of the canyon and reenters the woods.

Another 0.3 mile and the junction with Sheep Canyon Trail is reached. The junction with Sheep Canyon Trail, elevation 4,600 feet, is 2 miles from the junction with Butte Camp Trail. Sheep Canyon Trail turns left (west) and descends to the Sheep Canyon Trailhead. See Hike 10 for a description of the Sheep Canyon Trail. The Loowit Trail goes straight ahead (north) at the junction.

The trail continues through the woods for a short distance then descends slightly to cross the Sheep Canyon Lahar. Sheep Canyon Creek flows down this lahar. As you leave the lahar, look for a pond below the trail to the left. There are a few campsites along this section of Loowit Trail. Camp carefully and don't trample any more flowers than necessary.

The trail passes the pond and skirts a small basin before making an ascending traverse to a flat-topped ridgeline. Once on the ridge the path heads north through snags and beargrass. Huckleberries and small firs are growing up between the snags. This area is part of the Singe Zone, which is marked by standing dead trees. Soon the trail enters the Blast Zone. Here nearly all the trees were knocked down by the eruption.

Three miles from the Butte Camp Trail junction there is a rocky outcropping on the right side of the trail. This outcropping, on Crescent Ridge, is an excellent viewpoint overlooking the South Fork Toutle River Canyon. From the viewpoint Coldwater Ridge Visitor Center can be seen to the north, across both forks of the Toutle River. Also in view to the north are Mount Margaret and even Mount Rainier.

Leaving the viewpoint the Loowit Trail begins its 1,400-foot descent of Crescent Ridge. The trail winds and switchbacks its way down the ridge at the edge of the Blast Zone. Some of the time the trail is in large old-growth timber and at other times it is in the Blast Zone. After descending Crescent Ridge for 1.6 miles you come to the junction with the Toutle Trail. See Hike 15 for a description of the Toutle Trail.

At the junction, 3,180 feet in elevation and 4.6 miles from Butte Camp Trail, the Loowit Trail turns to the right. The path descends a few more feet, crosses a stream, then heads up the river bottom to a crossing. This crossing could be difficult at times of high water. Ford the river, then follow the cairn-marked trail on up the river bottom for 300 yards. Here the trail climbs steeply to the northeast for a short distance. It then makes a switchback to the left and the grade moderates. The tread climbs through the vine maple and silver snags making three more switchbacks. Then the path traverses an open sandy slope for 0.3 mile. The trail then makes a switchback to the left and continues to climb the sandy slope another 350 yards to the junction with the Castle Ridge Trail, at 3,840 feet elevation. At this junction 6 miles from the Butte Camp Trail, the Loowit Trail turns to the right. See Hike 11 for the details on the Castle Ridge Trail.

From the junction with the Castle Ridge Trail the route climbs gently for 0.5 mile. It then heads northeast, traversing the open gentle slope. These slopes are devoid of trees and brush, but there are a few hardy flowers. The path crosses several washes before reaching Studebaker Ridge. Studebaker Ridge is 1.8 miles from the junction with Castle Ridge Trail and 7.8 miles from the Butte Camp Trail junction where this description started.

At the publication of this book, the Loowit Trail is closed and washed out between here and Windy Trail, 4 miles to the east. This section of the Loowit Trail may be reopened in 1999 if volcanic and mudflow activity remains low. The reopening of this part of the Loowit Trail would make hiking around the mountain possible once again.

Options: A good option is to camp near the South Fork Toutle River and day hike from there to Studebaker Ridge and back.

By turning left on the Toutle Trail 6 miles into this hike you can make a loop back to the Butte Camp Trail. Then you can follow the Toutle Trail to the Redrock Pass Trailhead.

Camping & services: Disbursed camping is permitted along Forest Road 8123 and the upper part of FR 81. There is a campground at Merrill Lake off FR 81, 5 miles north of WA 503 spur. Gas, groceries, restaurant, and motel are available in Cougar. Emergency medical facilities are in Woodland.

For more information: USDA Forest Service at Mount St. Helens National Volcanic Monument Headquarters in Chelatchie or at Jack's Restaurant at the junction of Washington 503 and WA 503 spur, 5 miles west of Cougar. See Appendix A.

21 Lower Ape Cave (Trail 239B)

Type of hike:	Day hike, out and back.
Total distance:	1.7 miles.
Difficulty:	Easy by caving standards, moderate for the average hiker.
Best months:	Mid-April–October.
Elevation loss:	Minimal.
Trailhead elevation:	2,120 feet.
Permits:	Mount St. Helens National Volcanic Monument Visitors Pass.
Maps:	MSHNVM and Mount Mitchell USGS quad show the main entrance to the cave.
Starting point:	Ape Cave parking area.

General description: A short walk down a lava tube cave that has many interesting formations.

Finding the trailhead: Head north from Portland on Interstate 5 to Exit 21 at Woodland, Washington, from Seattle drive south on I-5 to Exit 21 (about 150 miles). Then follow Washington 503 (which becomes WA 503 spur) for 27.5 miles east to Cougar. From Cougar drive east on WA 503 spur (which becomes Forest Road 90) for 6.8 miles. Then turn left (north) on FR 83. Follow FR 83 for 2 miles then turn left again on FR 8303. Follow FR 8303 for 1 mile north to the parking area and trailhead. The parking area is on the right side of the road and there is a sign marking it. Trailhead GPS coordinates are 46 06.336 N 122 12.782 W.

Parking & trailhead facilities: There is ample parking and restrooms at the trailhead. Ape's Headquarters located at the trailhead is an information station and a rental shop for the lanterns that most hikers use inside Ape Cave.

Key points:
- 0.1   Cave entrance.
- 0.6   The Meatball.
- 0.8   Crawl space at end of cave.

The hike: This is a very popular cave, so traffic may be heavy. The main hazard in this cave is the darkness. Two good sources of light are recommended for each person entering the cave. Because hiking this section of Ape Cave requires little or no use of the hands a lantern makes a good light source. I personally like to wear a headlamp as well as carry a lantern. The cave floor is generally fairly smooth, but there are rocks lying on it that can be real shin busters and one spot where you must step down about 1.5 feet. In one spot very tall hikers may have to duck for a low ceiling. The temperature inside the cave

Lower Ape Cave (Trail 239B)
Upper Ape Cave (Trails 239A and 239)

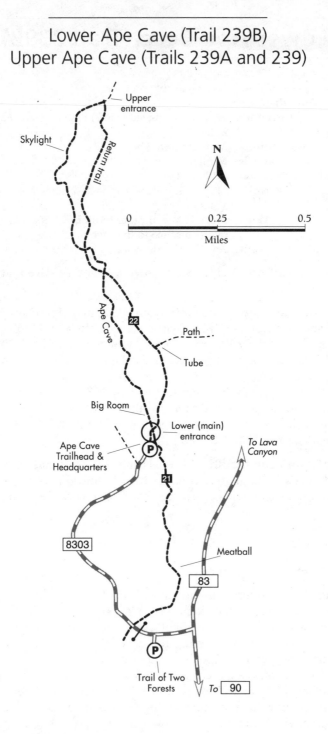

Descending into Ape Cave. SUZI BARSTAD PHOTO

is about 42 degrees F year-round and water drips from the ceiling at times, so dress accordingly.

Leave the paved parking area and head north on the paved trail between Ape's Headquarters and the restrooms. In 175 yards you will reach the main entrance to Ape Cave. Before entering the cave stop and read the information signs in the gazebo. This information will help you to know what to look for in the cave.

Descend the steps and enter the cave. It is a good idea to stop at the top of the second set of steps and let your eyes adjust to the lack of light before climbing down to the cave floor. This is also the spot to turn on your headlamp and make sure your lantern is running. At the bottom of the second set of steps the upper and lower cave routes split. A sign here points you south into the lower cave. See Hike 22 for information on the more difficult upper section of the cave to the north.

About 150 yards into the lower cave, if you are walking close to the left wall as most hikers do here, there will be a step down of 1.5 feet. For most people this is the only place in the cave where you will want to use your hand for balance. Half a mile from the cave entrance, The Meatball comes into view overhead. The Meatball is the last and largest of several boulders stuck in an opening in the cave ceiling.

The cave divides into upper and lower passages 0.2 mile past The Meatball. Continue on a short distance in the lower passage. The passage quickly gets smaller and lower; soon you will be on your hands and knees. This is as far as most people go in the cave. If you crawl and slither any farther be very careful not to go too far and get stuck. Do not crawl into the last section if you are alone. A person who gets stuck here could easily die from hypothermia. Retracing your steps makes the return trip.

Options: Hike the trail to the upper exit of Upper Ape Cave. See Hike 22.

Camping & services: Beaver Bay and Cougar Campgrounds located along WA 503 spur, just east of Cougar, are the closest developed campsites. Gas and groceries can be obtained in Cougar. The closest medical services are in Woodland.

For more information: USDA Forest Service at Ape's Headquarters. See Appendix A.

22 Upper Ape Cave (Trails 239A and 239)

See Map on Page 96

Type of hike:	Cave scramble, day hike, loop.
Total distance:	2.5 miles.
Difficulty:	Strenuous cave, easy return trail.
Best months:	Mid-April–October.
Elevation gain:	360 feet.
Trailhead elevation:	2,120 feet.
Permits:	Mount St. Helens National Volcanic Monument Visitors Pass.
Maps:	MSHNVM and Mt Mitchell USGS quad show the main entrance to Ape Cave but nothing else.
Starting point:	Ape Cave parking area.

General description: An underground scramble up the longest lava tube cave in North America, returning via an interesting trail through forests and lava flows.

Finding the trailhead: Head north from Portland on Interstate 5 to Exit 21 at Woodland, Washington, from Seattle drive south on I-5 to Exit 21 (about 150 miles). Then follow Washington 503 (which becomes WA 503 spur) for 27.5 miles east to Cougar. From Cougar drive east on WA 503 spur (which becomes Forest Road 90 at the Skamania County line) for 6.8 miles. Then turn left (north) on FR 83. Follow FR 83 for 2 miles then turn left again on FR 8303. Follow FR 8303 for 1 mile north and turn right into the parking area. There is a sign marking the parking area. Trailhead GPS coordinates are 46 06.336 N 122 12.782 W.

Parking & trailhead facilities: There is ample parking and restrooms at the trailhead. Ape's Headquarters located at the trailhead is an information station and a rental shop for the lanterns that most hikers use inside Ape Cave.

Key points:

0.2   The Big Room.
0.8   Lava Falls.
1.0   The Skylight.
1.2   Upper Ape Cave entrance. GPS coordinates 46 07.424 N 122 12.977 W.
2.3   Side path to small lava tube.
2.5   Main Ape Cave entrance.

The hike: From the parking area walk north between the restrooms and Ape's Headquarters. In 175 yards along the paved trail, you will reach the main entrance to Ape Cave. This is the lower entrance for Upper Ape

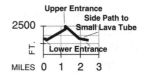

Cave and the only entrance to Lower Ape Cave. Stop at the open-air shelter and read the informational signs inside before descending into the cave.

Descend the two sets of stairs into the cave. At the bottom of the second set of stairs is a sign that points north to the upper cave and south to the lower. This is the point to stop if you are not sure of your caving skills or your lights. For the next 1.2 miles you hike through a lava tube cave where there is no trail, and where you must climb over and through several piles of fallen boulders. Crawling is necessary in at least one spot. An 8-foot-high vertical lava falls must also be negotiated. There is no natural light in the cave; therefore each person should carry at least two good sources of light. Headlamps are best because in many places the use of both hands is necessary. Without light, getting through this cave is virtually impossible. The temperature of the cave is about 42 degrees F year-round. Much of the time the cave drips almost everywhere making the humidity nearly 100%, so

Upper exit from Ape Cave.

dress for cool, damp conditions. If you wear glasses, be sure to put an anti-fog solution on the lenses or they will be steamed up most of the time. Unless you have experience exploring unlit caves, do not try this one without a competent leader. Don't attempt Upper Ape Cave alone. Less ambitious cavers can explore the lower cave without many problems, but the upper cave is a different story. See Hike 21 for information about Lower Ape Cave.

If you decide to hike the upper cave, turn on your headlamp and head north over the rough cave floor. About 400 feet into the upper cave is the Big Room, the largest open area in the upper cave. The Big Room is the turnaround point for the inexperienced. From here you climb over, under, and through the boulder-strewn cave floor for about 0.6 mile to the Lava Falls. The Lava Falls is a vertical 8-foot climb. There are hand and foot holds but they can be hard to find. A quarter of a mile farther up the twisting cave you come to The Skylight. The Skylight is 1 mile from the trailhead with 0.2 mile to go before reaching the upper entrance, the point where you exit from the cave. The light from the outside descending through the opening in the cave ceiling is a welcome sight for hikers who are unused to being in the absolute darkness of a cave. There is no exit from the cave here, so head on up the cave and plunge back into the darkness. More light is seen ahead in about another 300 yards, and soon you reach the Upper Ape Cave entrance. The upper entrance, at 2,480 feet elevation, is not the end of the cave, but it is your exit point. Climb the two metal ladders and reenter the outside world.

Above the ladders, climb the moss-covered lava for a few feet, then head south on the return trail. The path soon passes a small collapsed lava tube and enters a young forest of fir, red cedar, hemlock, and vine maple, with a scattering of white pine. The tread descends gently and follows an abandoned roadbed for a short distance. Soon the path bears right off the roadbed and enters a semi-open area that was logged long ago. The ground in the open area is nearly covered with beargrass. In many places the trail crosses short sections of ropey lava.

About a mile from the upper entrance and 2.3 miles from the starting point, the trail rounds the end of a lava flow. Soon you enter a flat sandy area. A couple hundred yards into the sandy area a side path turns to the left (east). The side path goes a few feet to the entrance of another small lava tube then continues along the side of a lava flow for a short distance before ending.

The main trail continues south past the path and across the sand. The trail may be hard to see here but there are usually human tracks on it. Shortly, the trail enters an area that was burned by arson in 1998. The tread then crosses a couple of streambeds that are usually dry. The main entrance of Ape Cave and the parking area is just a few yards farther. Upper Ape Cave Trail is maintained by the Oregon Grotto of the National Speleological Society.

Options: To hike to the upper entrance of the cave without scrambling through it, you can hike up and back on the return trail leaving from the main entrance to Ape Cave.

Camping & services: Beaver Bay and Cougar campgrounds, located along WA 503 spur just east of Cougar, are the closest developed campsites. Gas, Groceries, restaurant, and motel are available in Cougar. The closest medical services are in Woodland.

For more information: USDA Forest Service at Ape's Headquarters. See Appendix A.

23 Ptarmigan Trail (Trail 216A)

Type of hike:	Day hike, out and back.
Total distance:	4.2 miles.
Difficulty:	Moderate.
Best months:	July–September.
Elevation gain:	850 feet.
Trailhead elevation:	3,750 feet.
Permits:	None up to Loowit Trail; climbing permit required to go above 4,800 feet elevation.
Maps:	MSHNVM. Mount St. Helens USGS quad covers the area but this trail is not shown.
Starting point:	Climbers Bivouac Trailhead.

General description: Hike first through dense forest then cross an open slope with a great view to a junction with the Loowit Trail. This trail is the access route for the popular Monitor Ridge climbing route to the summit of Mount St. Helens.

Finding the trailhead: Head north from Portland or south from Seattle on Interstate 5 to Exit 21 at Woodland, Washington (21 miles from the Columbia River Bridge or about 150 miles from Seattle). Then drive east on Washington 503 (which becomes WA 503 spur then Forest Road 90) for 34.3 miles, passing Cougar, to the junction with FR 83. Turn left on FR 83 and follow it for 3.1 miles north to the junction with FR 81. Turn left on FR 81 and drive northwest 1.6 miles to the junction with FR 830. Turn right and head northeast on FR 803 for 2.6 miles to Climbers Bivouac Trailhead. GPS coordinates are 46 08.799 N 122 10.991 W.

Parking & trailhead facilities: There are restrooms and adequate parking at the trailhead. Camping is allowed at Climbers Bivouac Trailhead.

Key points:
2.1   Junction with Loowit Trail. GPS 46 09.865 N 122 11.433 W.

Heading for the summit above the end of the Ptarmigan Trail. ERIC VALENTINE PHOTO

The hike: Ptarmigan Trail begins to climb gently to the north as it leaves the parking area at Climbers Bivouac. The route is marked with blue diamond cross-country ski markers. The wide, well-maintained trail heads north through a fir forest, and huckleberry bushes. Avalanche lilies dot the ground between the bushes and trees. A sign marks the boundary of Mount St. Helens National Volcanic Monument 0.3 mile from the trailhead.

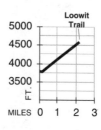

The first good view of Mount St. Helens past the parking area is at 1.3 miles. Now beargrass shares the openings with the huckleberries. The tread gets close to a lava flow 0.3 mile farther along. As you climb, Mount Hood and Mount Adams come into view to the south and east. Two miles from the trailhead the trail makes a switchback to the left. Reach the junction with the Loowit Trail, at 4,600 feet elevation, 0.1 mile after passing the switchback.

Options: The Ptarmigan Trail is used as an approach trail for climbers ascending the Monitor Ridge Climbing Route to the summit of Mount St. Helens. If the summit is your goal, get your climbing permit and see Hike 61 Monitor Ridge Summit Climb in this book.

The Ptarmigan Ridge Trail provides one of the easiest access routes to the Loowit Trail. For a description of this section of the Loowit Trail, see Hike 27.

Camping & services: Beaver Bay and Cougar Campgrounds, located along WA 503 spur just east of Cougar, are the closest developed campsites. Gas , groceries, restaurant, and motel are available in Cougar. The closest medical services are in Woodland.

For more information: USDA Forest Service at Mount St. Helens National Volcanic Monument Headquarters at Chelatchie or Ape's Headquarters at the Ape Cave parking area. See Appendix A.

Ptarmigan Trail (Trail 216A)

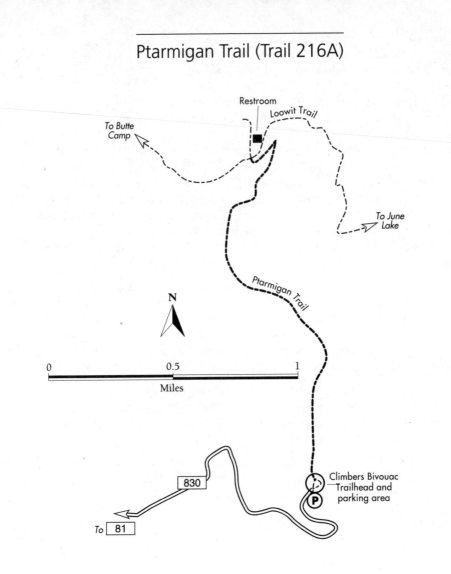

Restroom

Loowit Trail

To Butte Camp

To June Lake

Ptarmigan Trail

N

0   0.5   1

Miles

830

To 81

Climbers Bivouac
Trailhead and
parking area

P

24 Trail of Two Forests (Trail 233)

Type of hike:	Day hike, loop.
Total distance:	0.3 mile.
Difficulty:	Easy.
Best months:	April–October.
Elevation gain:	Minimal.
Trailhead elevation:	1,840 feet.
Permits:	None.
Maps:	The one on the signboard at the trailhead is more than adequate.
Starting point:	Trail of Two Forests parking area.

General description: A short, barrier-free boardwalk loop trail through lava flows and old growth forest, with a side trip consisting of a short crawl through a tree mold. This is an excellent short hike for small children with adult supervision.

Finding the trailhead: Drive Interstate 5 to Exit 21 at Woodland (21 miles north of the Columbia River Bridge or about 150 miles south from Seattle). Then drive east on Washington 503 (which becomes 503 spur) for 27.5 miles to Cougar. From Cougar drive east on WA 503 spur (which becomes Forest Road 90 at the Skamania County line) for 6.8 miles to the junction with FR 83. Turn left (north) on FR 83 and follow it for 2 miles to FR 8303. Turn left again on FR 8303 and follow it 0.2 mile to the trailhead. A sign marks the parking area and trailhead on the left side of FR 8303.

Parking & trailhead facilities: There are restrooms and adequate parking at the trailhead.

Key points:

45 yards	Boardwalk starts at junction.
85 yards	Forest returns sign.
120 yards	Cushions of life sign.
175 yards	Path to The Crawl exit.
190 yards	Tree molds sign.
205 yards	Rim of rock sign.
220 yards	Entrance to The Crawl.
260 yards	Lava log dam sign.
360 yards	The Tunnel sign.
425 yards	Junction with paved trail back to parking area.

The hike: Leave the trailhead and walk south 45 yards on the paved trail to a junction and the beginning of the boardwalk. Bear left at the junction and go another 40 yards to the sign explaining the return of the forest after an eruption 2,000 years ago. Next come to a sign with information about the moss breaking down the lava so that other plants can take root.

A bit farther along, a paved path to the right leads 10 yards to the exit from The Crawl. The Crawl is a horizontal tree mold about 50 feet long and

Trail of Two Forests (Trail 233)

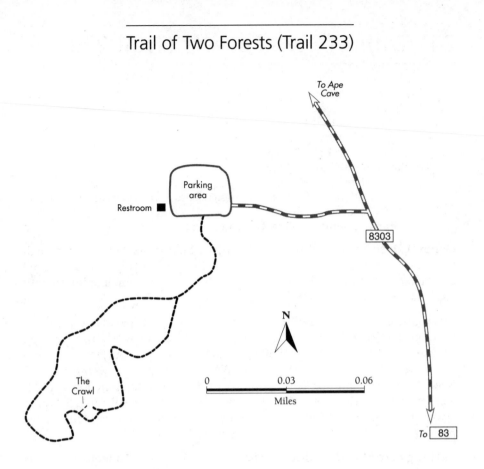

about 2.5 feet in diameter. It was formed when hot lava engulfed a fallen tree. The tree burned and rotted away after the lava solidified, leaving a round hole through the rock. Read the Tree Molds signs just ahead for more information about this process.

The Crawl will probably be the high point of this hike if you have children along. The entrance for the Crawl is about 50 yards ahead on the trail. It can easily be seen across the lava flow, to your left, from the end of the side path. If you have small children it is best to leave an adult at the exit and send the children with another adult ahead to the entrance. This way the children can be talked through the short cave. You can see through the straight opening, so lights are not necessary. Be very careful at the entrance and exit since there is the possibility of falling from the metal steps to the rocks below.

When you are finished with The Crawl, continue another 40 yards past the entrance to a sign explaining a lava log dam. One hundred yards after passing the log dam, a lava tube cave can be seen to your right, out on the moss-covered lava flow. A short distance more brings you to the junction where you got on the boardwalk. Turn left and walk the 45 yards back to the parking area on the paved trail.

Lava tube on Trail of Two Forests.

Allow plenty of time to read the very informative signs along this trail. If you quietly hike this path very early in the morning, you may see one or more of the many cottontail rabbits that inhabit the area.

Camping & services: Beaver Bay and Cougar Campgrounds, located along WA 503 spur just east of Cougar, are the closest developed campsites. Gas, groceries, restaurant, and motel are available in Cougar. The closest medical services are in Woodland.

For more information: USDA Forest Service at Ape's Headquarters at the Ape Cave parking area. See Appendix A.

25 Kalama Springs

Type of hike:	Day hike, out and back.
Total distance:	0.6 mile.
Difficulty:	Easy.
Best months:	May–October.
Elevation gain:	Minimal.
Trailhead elevation:	2,700 feet.
Permits:	None.
Maps:	MSHNVM. Goat Mountain USGS quad covers the area but does not show this trail.
Starting point:	An unmarked parking spot on Forest Road 81 just west of McBride Lake.

General description: A short hike to the spot where the Kalama River emerges from beneath an ancient lava flow.

Finding the trailhead: Drive on Interstate 5 to Exit 21 at Woodland (21 miles north of the Columbia River Bridge or about 150 miles south of Seattle). Then drive east on Washington 503 (which becomes WA 503 spur). Turn left (north) off WA 503 spur, 26.5 miles from I-5, onto Forest Road 81. Follow FR 81 for 12.1 miles to an unmarked parking spot on the north side of the road. GPS coordinates are 46 08.497 N 122 15.719 W.

Parking & trailhead facilities: There is parking for one or two cars at the unmarked trailhead.

Key points:
0.3   Kalama Springs. GPS 46 08.663 N 122 15.423 W.

The hike: The route to Kalama Springs leaves FR 81 heading north. First you will climb over a couple of mounds of dirt that are there to block vehicle access. After walking a few yards through the alder brush the path enters a sandy area. Hike across the sand

Kalama Springs

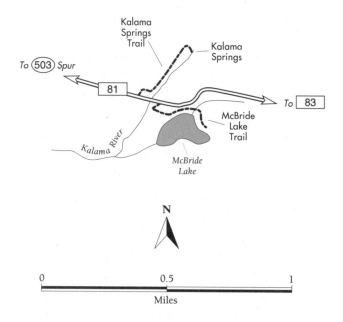

To (503) Spur

Kalama
Springs
Trail

Kalama
Springs

81

To 83

Kalama River

McBride
Lake
Trail

McBride
Lake

N

0   0.5   1
Miles

Kalama Springs.

for a short distance and reenter the brush and trees. The route makes a hard right turn, close to the base of a hill, 0.3 mile from the trailhead. It then goes a few yards east to Kalama Springs. At the wide springs, the cold, clear waters of the Kalama River bubble out from beneath an old lava flow.

The trail to Kalama Springs is a little vague in spots. It stays about 50 yards away from the river most of the way to the springs.

Options: The short but steep hike to McBride Lake is a good addition to the hike to Kalama Springs. To reach McBride Lake walk or drive 100 yards east on FR 81 to a place where there is parking for two or three cars on the south side of the road. From the road descend the steep but short bank to the south on a poor path. At the bottom of the bank you will reach a junction with another path. Turn left at the junction and head east for 150 yards to McBride Lake. The rough path follows the lake's north shore around to the east side of the lake. Brook and cutthroat trout can be caught in the lake, and there is a lot of beaver activity at its west end.

Camping & services: Disbursed camping is allowed in this part of the Mount St. Helens National Volcanic Monument. Kalama Horse Camp is located 3.8 miles west of the trailhead on FR 81. The horse camp is generally reserved for horse users. The closest developed campground except for the horse camp is at Merrill Lake, 4 miles back toward WA 503 spur. Gas , groceries, restaurant, and motel are available in Cougar.

For more information: USDA Forest Service at Monument Headquarters at Chelatchie or at Pine Creek Information Station. See Appendix A.

26 June Lake (Trail 216B)

Type of hike: Day hike or backpack, out and back.
Total distance: 2.8 miles.
Difficulty: Easy to June Lake, moderate above there.
Best months: June–October.
Elevation gain: 660 feet.
Trailhead elevation: 2,710 feet.
Permits: None.
Maps: MSHNVM. Mount St. Helens USGS quad covers the area but does not show this trail.
Starting point: June Lake Trailhead.

General description: A short hike to beautiful June Lake and an access route to the Loowit Trail.

Finding the trailhead: From Portland take Interstate 5 north to Exit 21 at Woodland, Washington; from Seattle drive I-5 south to Exit 21 (about 150 miles). Then follow Washington 503 (which becomes WA 503 spur) east for 27.5 miles to Cougar. From Cougar drive east on WA 503 spur (which becomes Forest Road 90) for 6.8 miles to the junction with FR 83. Turn left (north) on FR 83 and follow it 5.6 miles to the marked turnoff to June Lake Trailhead. The trailhead is a short distance north of FR 83 on a paved side road. Trailhead GPS coordinates are 46 08.237 N 122 09.442 W.

Parking & trailhead facilities: There is parking for several cars but no other facilities at the trailhead.

Key points:
1.1   June Lake.
1.4   Junction with Loowit Trail. GPS 46 09.865 N 122 11.433 W.

The hike: Leave the trailhead and head north on a trail marked with blue diamond cross-country ski markers. You are a few yards to the right of a creek as you begin your hike. As you ascend gently through the second-growth forest of fir and hemlock, glimpses of the smooth south slopes of

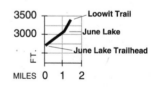

Mount St. Helens appear ahead. The path winds up through the woods, sometimes close to the creek and sometimes a distance away.

A lava flow comes into view to the left across the creek, 0.8 mile from the trailhead. Here the view of the mountain really opens up. Soon you cross a tiny stream then climb over a small rise before descending a few feet to a sandy area. Once past the sandy area the trail climbs a few yards to a bridge over the outlet of June Lake. The lake is in view to the right only a few yards away.

Steep hills and cliffs surround June Lake, elevation 3,130 feet, on three sides. The hills next to the lake have never been logged, so beautiful old-

June Lake (Trail 216B)

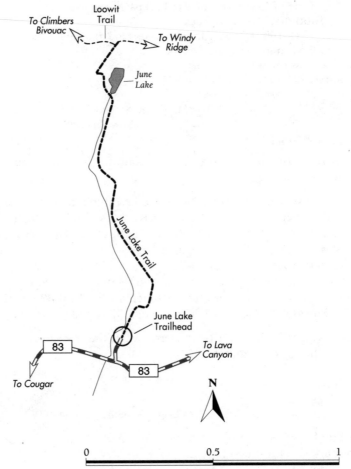

To Climbers Bivouac

Loowit Trail

To Windy Ridge

June Lake

June Lake Trail

June Lake Trailhead

83

To Cougar

83

To Lava Canyon

N

0   0.5   1

Miles

growth forest remains around much of the shoreline. A waterfall plunges into the lake on the northeast side. Smaller falls enter the lake in a couple of other spots. June Lake is the destination of most of the people who use this trail. The trail continues to climb on the west side of June Lake. It winds its way up another 0.3 mile, gaining 270 feet in elevation, to the junction with the Loowit Trail.

Options: The return trip is generally made by retracing your steps back to the June Lake Trailhead. A more interesting alternate hike can be done by turning left (west) on the Loowit Trail and following it to the Ptarmigan Trail, then descending that trail to the Climbers Bivouac Trailhead. This alternate return requires a car shuttle to the Climbers Bivouac Trailhead. See Hike 27 and Hike 23 for information on this alternate return hike.

Camping & services: Beaver Bay and Cougar Campgrounds are located along WA 503 spur just east of Cougar and are the closest developed campsites. Gas, groceries, restaurant, and motel are available in Cougar. The closest medical services are in Woodland.

For more information: USDA Forest Service at Pine Creek Information Station or Mount St. Helens Volcanic Monument Headquarters at Chelatchie. See Appendix A.

Waterfall into June Lake.

27 Loowit Trail (Trail 216, June Lake to Butte Camp)

Type of hike:	Day hike or backpack, shuttle option.
Total distance:	5.8 miles.
Difficulty:	Strenuous.
Best months:	July–September.
Elevation gain:	1,400 feet.
Trailhead elevation:	3,390 feet at junction with June Lake Trail.
Permits:	None. If you intend to climb higher than 4,800 feet elevation on Mount St. Helens a climbing permit is required.
Maps:	MSHNVM. Mount St. Helens USGS quad covers this area but does not show this trail.
Starting point:	Junction of June Lake Trail and Loowit Trail north of June Lake, 1.4 miles from June Lake Trailhead.

General description: Much of the hike from the junction with the June Lake Trail to the Butte Camp Trail along the Loowit Trail is above timberline. The views along this *internal* section of trail are among the best in the monument. However, the lava flow crossings between the Ptarmigan Trail and the Butte Camp Trail can be difficult for all but agile hikers.

Finding the trailhead: Follow the driving directions in Hike 26, then follow the June Lake Trail described there to its end at the junction with the Loowit Trail. GPS coordinates at the junction are 46 09.865 N 122 11.433 W.

Key points:
3.3   Junction with Ptarmigan Trail. GPS 46 09.865 N 122 11.433 W.
5.8   Junction with Butte Camp Trail. GPS 46 10.527 N 122 13.023 W.

The hike: The Loowit Trail climbs gently to the northwest as it leaves the junction with the June Lake Trail. The rough, rocky path skirts the lower edge of a lava flow for a short distance. Then, with cairns marking the route, it climbs onto the flow. Shortly the rough tread crosses a boulder-strewn gully and a possibly dry

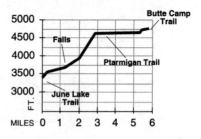

creek. Once across the creek you climb back onto the lava. The trail is marked with cairns and posts as it crosses this rough flow.

The path enters a small pocket of green timber 1.1 miles from the junction with the June Lake Trail. As you leave the timber, a waterfall splashes into a canyon, to the left of the trail. The path crosses the East Fork Swift Creek above the falls. You climb out of the creekbed and then turn right to follow the rim of the gully up for a short distance. The path soon turns away

Waterfall in Swift Creek.

Loowit Trail (Trail 216)

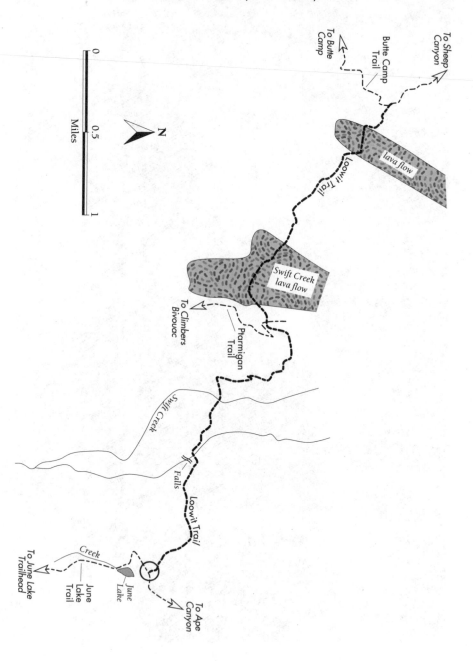

from the creekbed and continues to climb to the northwest. A line of posts marking a cross-country ski trail heads to the north as you turn away. Follow the trail and not this line of posts.

The route crosses a small creekbed, Swift Creek, which may be dry, and enters large, well-spaced timber 0.3 mile after leaving the line of posts. Here, 1.9 miles from the junction with the June Lake Trail, the route begins to climb more steeply. The path makes a switchback 0.2 mile farther along as it continues its steep climb. As you gain elevation the view improves. Mount Adams stands alone to the east across the lava flows. Part of this climb is on a slope that has avalanched in the past, knocking down the large timber. In the spaces between the downed logs, flowers cover the steep slope.

The route switches back to the left and soon leaves the avalanched area. After getting back into the forest the trail passes what appears to be a weather station. The equipment is 50 yards to the left of the path. In the open spots in the woods lupine and false hellebore add a bit of color. The route follows the upper edge of the timber, traversing steep, green slopes, and soon flattens out at about 4,500 feet elevation. Phlox, beargrass, and spiraea bushes line the trail.

The route enters a patch of small fir trees 3.2 miles from the junction with the June Lake Trail. After another 0.1 mile you will come to the junction with the Ptarmigan Trail. The Ptarmigan Trail is the access to the popular Monitor Ridge climbing route to the summit of Mount St. Helens. If you turn left on the Ptarmigan Trail it's 2.1 miles down to the Climbers Bivouac Trailhead. To the right it's a 3,700-foot climb to the summit. Climbing permits are required above 4,800 feet elevation on Mount St. Helens. For the details on the Ptarmigan Trail, see Hike 23. See Hike 61 if you are planning to climb above the Loowit Trail.

The Loowit Trail continues west from the junction with the Ptarmigan Trail. At first you hike through subalpine forest with huckleberries growing between the trees. Soon the route traverses a sandy side hill, where the path is marked with posts. Then the trail becomes very rough and a bit hard to follow as you enter the Swift Creek lava flow. As you cross the flow on the vague path, which is still marked with posts, Mount Hood is in view on the southern horizon. You will do a lot of boulder-hopping to work your way across this flow. In spots between the rocks, heather, which blooms in early July, grows in abundance.

After crossing the aa lava for nearly a mile the route descends a few feet and enters a lightly wooded area of small subalpine fir and lodgepole pine. A couple of tiny streams that will dry up by midsummer cross the path in these woods. For the next 0.6 mile the route is a little smoother and easier to follow. Then, 5.1 miles from the June Lake Trail, you will cross a stream with a series of small waterfalls. Once across the stream the tread climbs onto another aa lava flow. Here the post-marked route becomes rough and vague again. This flow is much narrower than the one you crossed earlier. In about 0.3 mile the path leaves the flow and crosses an open boulder-strewn slope for another 0.3 mile to the junction with the Butte Camp Trail.

The junction with the Butte Camp Trail, at 4,750 feet elevation, is 5.8 miles from the junction with the June Lake Trail. At the junction with the Butte Camp Trail, a climbing route up the southwest side of Mount St. Helens leaves the trail.

Options: If you are going to end your hike along the Loowit Trail here turn left (south) and descend the Butte Camp and Toutle Trails the 3.8 miles to the Redrock Pass Trailhead. See Hikes 19 and 14 for trail descriptions of these trails. If you want a shorter hike you can descend the Ptarmigan Trail 2.1 miles to the Climbers Bivouac Trailhead.

To continue along Loowit Trail see the description in Hike 20.

Camping & services: Disbursed camping is allowed in most areas on this side of the monument. The closest developed campsites are at Beaver Bay and Cougar Campgrounds. These Pacific Power campgrounds are east of Cougar on WA 503 spur. Gas, groceries, restaurant, and motel are available in Cougar. Emergency medical facilities are in Woodland.

For more information: USDA Forest Service at Mount St. Helens National Volcanic Monument Headquarters at Chelatchie. See Appendix A.

28 Ape Canyon (Trail 234)

Type of hike: Day hike, out and back.
Total distance: 9.6 miles.
Difficulty: Moderate.
Best months: Late June–September.
Elevation gain: 1,340 feet.
Trailhead elevation: 2,850 feet.
Permits: Mount St. Helens National Volcanic Monument Visitors Pass.
Maps: MSHNVM. Mount St. Helens and Smith Creek Butte USGS quads cover the area but this trail is not shown.
Starting point: Ape Canyon Trailhead.

General description: Ape Canyon Trail climbs along the edge of the Muddy River Lahar to a junction with the Loowit Trail at the top of a gorge in upper Ape Canyon.

Finding the trailhead: From Seattle drive south on Interstate 5 for about 150 miles to Woodland. From Portland take I-5 to Woodland. Then take Exit 21 off I-5 and drive east on Washington 503 (which becomes WA 503 spur then Forest Road 90) through Cougar. Turn left off FR 90, 34.8 miles east of I-5 (6.8 miles east of Cougar), onto FR 83. Follow FR 83 for 11.5 miles to the Ape Canyon Trailhead. The trailhead is on the left side of the road. GPS coordinates at the trailhead are 46 09.917 N 122 05.536 W.

Ape Canyon (Trail 234)

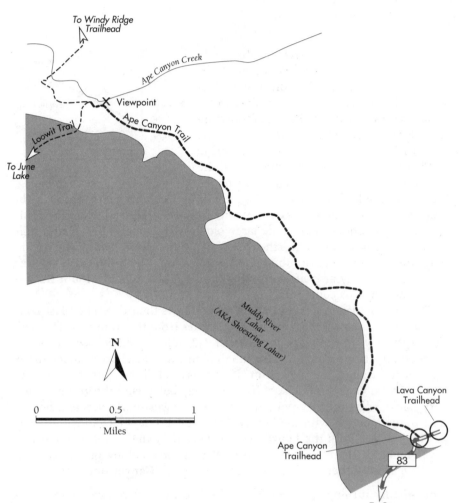

To Windy Ridge
Trailhead

Ape Canyon Creek

Viewpoint

Ape Canyon Trail

Loowit Trail

To June
Lake

Muddy River
Lahar
(AKA Shoestring Lahar)

N

0   0.5   1
Miles

Lava Canyon
Trailhead

Ape Canyon
Trailhead

83

To Cougar

Parking & trailhead facilities: There is parking for several cars but no other facilities at the trailhead.

Key points:
    2.6   Cross ridgeline.
    4.7   Viewpoint of Ape Canyon.
    4.8   Junction with Loowit Trail.

The hike: Ape Canyon Trail climbs gently as it leaves the trailhead. After a short distance the path turns right along the bank of the Muddy River Lahar. Four-tenths of a mile from the trailhead the trail follows an abandoned roadbed for a short distance. Soon the route leads up a small, open, ridge with great views. The path traverses off the left side of the ridge, through vine maple,

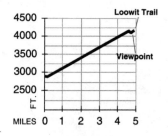

alder, and huckleberry bushes. You continue to climb gently through the small forest until you are about 0.9 mile from the trailhead. Here the route enters larger timber, with some large old-growth Douglas-firs. Half a mile farther along, the trail makes the first of five switchbacks taking you up to a ridgeline. The path crosses the ridge 2.6 miles from the trailhead. The tread traverses a brushy area after crossing the ridge. Here both Mount Rainier and Mount Adams come into view.

Continuing to climb, the trail generally follows the ridge. The Blast Zone across Ape Canyon comes into view 3.5 miles from the trailhead. The path makes its way up the ridge for another 1.2 miles to the viewpoint of the gorge in upper Ape Canyon. Take the time to walk the short distance to the right of the trail to the viewpoint. If you have children with you be very careful at the viewpoint. The cliffs drop away below and the ground is not very stable. From the viewpoint the route heads west-northwest another 0.1 mile to the junction with the Loowit Trail, at 4,190 feet elevation.

The junction with the Loowit Trail is very near the timberline. Flowers cover much of the open area in July. Watch for a colony of whistle pigs (hoary marmots) that inhabit the upper part of Ape Canyon above the gorge.

Options: By turning right (north) on the Loowit Trail you can hike across the Plains of Abraham to the Windy Ridge Viewpoint and Trailhead, about 6 miles away. Hiking to Windy Ridge would, however, require a long car shuttle. See Hike 36 for details.

If you turn left on the Loowit Trail you will be heading for the June Lake Trail, 4.9 miles away. Along the June Lake Trail it is 1.4 miles to the June Lake Trailhead. This hike requires a much shorter car shuttle. See Hikes 26 and 27 for trail descriptions and driving directions.

Camping & services: Dispersed camping is allowed in many areas on this side of the monument. The closest developed campgrounds are Beaver Bay and Cougar, east of Cougar on WA 503 spur. Gas, groceries, restaurant, and motel are available in Cougar. Emergency medical facilities are in Woodland.

For more information: USDA Forest Service at Mount St. Helens National Volcanic Monument Headquarters in Chelatchie or at Ape's Headquarters at the Ape Cave parking area. See Appendix A.

29 Loowit Trail (Trail 216, Ape Canyon to June Lake)

Type of hike:	Day hike or backpack, out and back, shuttle option.
Total distance:	4.9 miles.
Difficulty:	Moderate.
Best months:	July–September.
Elevation loss:	820 feet.
Trailhead elevation:	4,190 feet at junction with Ape Canyon Trail.
Permits:	None.
Maps:	MSHNVM. Mount St. Helens USGS quad covers the area but does not show this trail.
Starting point:	Junction of Ape Canyon Trail and Loowit Trail, 4.8 miles from Ape Canyon Trailhead.

General description: This section of the Loowit Trail, an *internal* trail, first crosses the mile-wide Muddy River Lahar and then a wide lava flow before descending to meet the June Lake Trail.

Finding the trailhead: See Hike 28 for directions to the Ape Canyon Trailhead. Then follow the the Ape Canyon Trail 4.8 miles to the junction with the Loowit Trail.

Key points:
- 0.3 Start across Muddy River Lahar.
- 1.3 Leave Muddy River Lahar.
- 2.2 Cross Pine Creek Lahar.
- 4.9 Junction with June Lake Trail.

The hike: As it leaves the junction with the Ape Canyon Trail, at 4,190 feet elevation, the Loowit Trail heads southwest. Watch for whistle pigs (hoary marmots) near the junction. The path crosses an area of scattered, stunted, alpine trees for 0.3 mile. Mount Hood can be seen ahead in the distance.

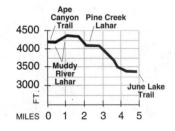

The tread then begins its crossing of the Muddy River Lahar (AKA Shoestring Lahar), which is 0.8 mile wide at this point. This large lahar was formed by the 1980 eruption, when much of the snow and ice of the Shoestring Glacier melted and combined with rock, sand, and ash. This mixture flowed down

Ape Canyon.

the mountainside, wiping out nearly everything in its path. Part of this flow made a sharp left turn, about 3 miles downstream from the trail, and scoured out the timber lining Lava Canyon (AKA Muddy River Gorge).

After crossing this lahar the Loowit Trail crosses an open slope that may be nearly covered with flowers in July. It then crosses the smaller Pine Creek Lahar. Heading south and leaving the Pine Creek Lahar the trail soon crosses a streambed that may or may not have water. The path then starts across a rough lava flow. The Loowit Trail stays on the flow for about 1 mile.

The tread then descends off the lava, making a couple of switchbacks as it leaves the flow. The trail soon crosses a finger of mostly small timber. It then follows the lower edge of the lava flow nearly to the junction with June Lake Trail. Shortly before reaching the junction a spring flows from beneath the lava flow below the trail. The junction with the June Lake Trail is at 3,370 feet elevation and is 4.9 miles from the junction with the Ape Canyon Trail.

Options: At the junction, turn left to go to June Lake or bear right to continue on the Loowit Trail. June Lake is 0.3 mile south of Loowit Trail and about 200 feet lower elevation. See Hike 26 for the details on the June Lake Trail and directions to the June Lake Trailhead. June Lake Trailhead is 1.1 miles south of June Lake.

To continue your hike on the Loowit Trail see Hike 27.

Camping & services: Beaver Bay and Cougar Campgrounds located along WA 503 spur just east of Cougar are the closest developed campsites. Gas, groceries, restaurant, and motel are available in Cougar. The closest medical services are in Woodland.

Whistle pig (hoary marmot).

Loowit Trail (Trail 216)

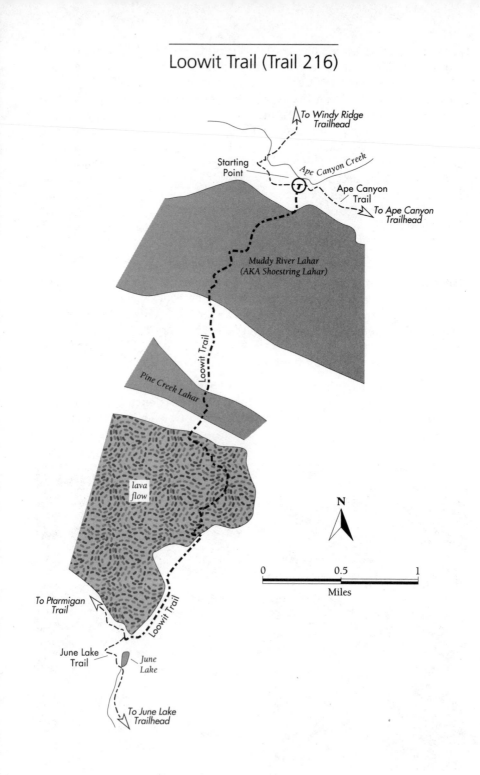

To Windy Ridge
Trailhead

Starting
Point

Ape Canyon Creek

Ape Canyon
Trail

To Ape Canyon
Trailhead

Muddy River Lahar
(AKA Shoestring Lahar)

Loowit Trail

Pine Creek Lahar

lava
flow

N

0   0.5   1
Miles

To Ptarmigan
Trail

Loowit Trail

June Lake
Trail

June
Lake

To June Lake
Trailhead

For more information: USDA Forest Service at Pine Creek Information Station or Mount St. Helens National Volcanic Monument Headquarters in Chelatchie. See Appendix A.

30 Pine Creek Shelter (Trail 216C)

Type of hike: Day hike, out and back.
Total distance: 0.8 mile.
Difficulty: Easy.
Best months: June–September.
Elevation gain: Minimal.
Trailhead elevation: 2,930 feet.
Permits: None.
Maps: MSHNVM or Smith Creek Butte USGS quad.
Starting point: Pine Creek Shelter Trailhead on Forest Road 83.

General description: A short hike to a historical shelter.

Finding the trailhead: From Seattle drive south on Interstate 5 for about 150 miles to Woodland. From Portland take I-5 to Woodland. Then take Exit 21 off I-5 and drive east on Washington 503 (which becomes WA 503 spur, then Forest Road 90) through Cougar. Turn left off FR 90, 34.8 miles east of I-5 (6.8 miles east of Cougar), onto FR 83. Then follow FR 83 for 10.5 miles to the poorly marked trailhead on the left side of the road. GPS coordinates at the trailhead are 46 09.197 N 122 06.159 W.

Parking & trailhead facilities: There is parking for a couple of cars on a side road across from the trailhead but no other facilities.

Key points:
0.4 Pine Creek Shelter.

The hike: The Pine Creek Shelter Trail was once a feeder trail for the Loowit Trail. The 1980 eruption and resulting Muddy River Lahar removed a large part of the trail above the shelter. This portion of the trail was never rebuilt, and now the Ape Canyon Trail has replaced it. The trail to the shelter is marked with blue diamond cross-country ski markers and receives considerable use during the winter season.

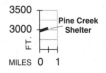

The trail climbs a few feet as it leaves FR 83, then heads northwest, through a mature fir and hemlock forest. A quarter of a mile from the trailhead the route leaves the mature forest for the younger woods of an old clearcut.

Pine Creek Shelter (Trail 216C)

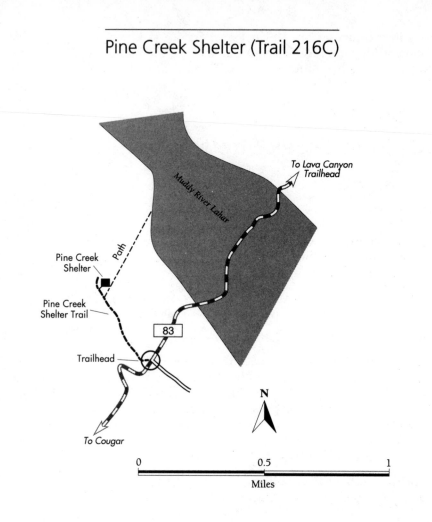

A short distance farther along you will reach **Pine Creek Shelter.** The three-sided shelter was originally built in 1922; volunteers reconstructed it in 1991. The shelter has a good roof and bunks inside. A fire pit is out front.

Options: If you want to continue another 0.3 mile on a vague path to the northeast you will reach the edge of the Muddy River Lahar.

Camping & services: Dispersed camping is permitted in much of this section of the monument. The closest developed campgrounds are east of Cougar along WA 503 spur. Gas, groceries, restaurant, and motel are available in Cougar. Medical facilities are in Woodland.

For more information: USDA Forest Service at Ape's Headquarters at the Ape Cave parking area or the Mount St. Helens National Volcanic Monument Headquarters in Chelatchie. See Appendix A.

Pine Creek Shelter.

31 Lahar Viewpoint (Trail 241)

Type of hike: Day hike, out and back.
Total distance: 0.4 mile.
Difficulty: Easy.
Best months: June–September.
Elevation gain: Minimal.
Trailhead elevation: 2,970 feet.
Permits: Mount St. Helens National Volcanic Monument Visitors Pass.
Maps: None needed for this short trail.
Starting point: Lahar Viewpoint parking area.

General description: A short interpretive hike on the Muddy River Lahar, with a tremendous view of Mount St. Helens.

Finding the trailhead: From Seattle drive south on Interstate 5 for about 150 miles to Woodland. From Portland take I-5 north to Woodland. Then take Exit 21 off I-5 and drive east on Washington 503 (which becomes WA 503 spur then Forest Road 90) through Cougar. Turn left off FR 90, 34.8 miles east of I-5 (6.8 miles east of Cougar), onto FR 83. Follow FR 83 for 10.9 miles northeast to Lahar Viewpoint. The parking area and trailhead are on the right side of FR 83. There is a sign marking the entrance to the parking area. The trail leaves from the northeast side of the parking area.

Lahar Viewpoint (Trail 241)

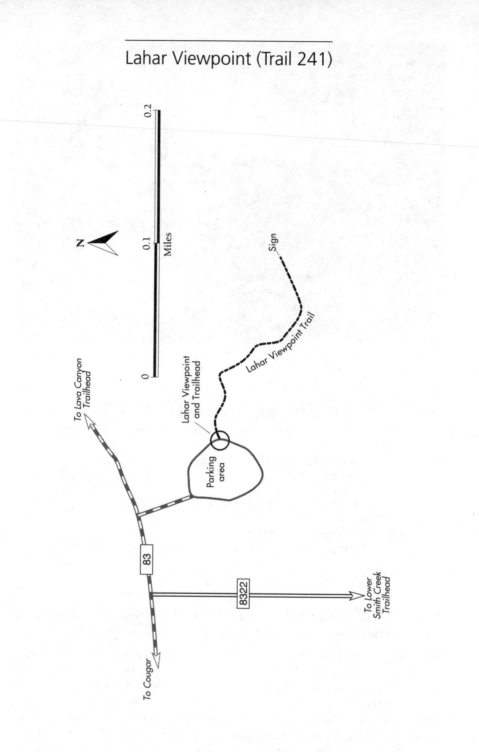

N

0   0.1   0.2
Miles

To Lava Canyon Trailhead

Lahar Viewpoint and Trailhead

Parking area

Lahar Viewpoint Trail

Sign

83

8322

To Cougar

To Lower Smith Creek Trailhead

Parking & trailhead facilities: There is parking for several cars but no other facilities at the trailhead.

Key points:
0.2   Sign at end of trail.

The hike: The wide gravel trail first goes a few yards northeast, then turns southeast across the mud-flow debris. Scattered small firs and willows dot the desert-like area. Two-tenths of a mile from the trailhead you reach an interpretive sign at the end of the trail. The sign, entitled "What Happened Here," describes the events that took place here during the 1980 eruption of Mount St. Helens. As you read this sign, look up the mountain and imagine what happened when the volcano blew.

Options: Hike this trail on the way out after you have hiked Lava Canyon. See Hike 32 for a description of Lava Canyon Trail.

Camping & services: Dispersed camping is allowed in many areas on this side of the monument. The closest developed campgrounds are Beaver Bay and Cougar, east of Cougar on WA 503 spur. Gas, groceries, and restaurant and motel are available in Cougar.

For more information: USDA Forest Service at Mount St. Helens National Volcanic Monument Headquarters in Chelatchie or at Ape's Headquarters at Ape Cave parking area. See Appendix A.

Muddy River Lahar (AKA Shoestring Lahar).

32 Lava Canyon (Trail 184)

Type of hike:	Day hike, out and back, with shuttle option and/or loop option.
Total distance:	6 miles.
Difficulty:	Easy to moderate loop, strenuous out and back.
Best Months:	Mid-June–October.
Elevation loss:	1,130 feet, loop 300 feet.
Trailhead elevation:	2,840 feet.
Permits:	Mount St. Helens National Volcanic Monument Visitors Pass.
Maps:	MSHNVM. USGS Smith Creek Butte quad covers the area but this trail is not shown.
Starting point:	Lava Canyon Trailhead.

General description: A short loop past some of the best waterfalls at Mount St. Helens or a difficult descent down the Muddy River Gorge. The first 0.3 mile is paved and barrier-free.

Finding the trailhead: From Seattle drive south on Interstate 5 for about 150 miles to Woodland. From Portland take I-5 north to Woodland. Then take Exit 21 off I-5 and drive east on Washington 503 (which becomes WA 503 spur) through Cougar. WA 503 spur becomes Forest Road 90 east of Cougar at the Skamania County line. Turn left off FR 90, 34.8 miles east of I-5 (6.8 miles east of Cougar), onto FR 83. Follow FR 83 for 11.7 miles to the Lava Canyon Trailhead. GPS coordinates at the trailhead are 46 09.912 N 122 05.286 W.

To reach the Lower Smith Creek Trailhead, where Lava Canyon Trail ends, follow the driving directions in Hike 31 to Lahar Viewpoint Trailhead. Just before reaching the parking area turn right on FR 8322, a rough, narrow, gravel road. Follow it 4.8 miles to Lower Smith Creek Trailhead.

Parking & trailhead facilities: There is adequate parking and restrooms at Lava Canyon Trailhead. At Lower Smith Creek Trailhead there is parking for several cars.

Key points:
- 0.3 Junction with Loop Trail near end of barrier-free trail.
- 0.7 Junction with Loop Trail at suspension bridge.
- 1.4 Ladder.
- 1.7 Junction with trail to The Ship viewpoint.
- 2.0 Junction with Smith Creek Trail, new bridge.
- 3.0 Lower Smith Creek Trailhead. GPS 46 10.926 N 122 03.302 W.

The hike: The Loop Trail is rough and slippery in spots. Below the Loop Trail the main trail is very rough, exposed, and slippery in spots. A steel ladder, which must be descended to continue down to the Smith Creek Trail and The Ship, can be slippery if wet. The trail to The Ship is also very difficult and exposed.

The paved trail leaves the south side of the parking area, descending gently. You will make a couple of switchbacks and pass some benches before reaching an interpretive viewpoint. The viewpoint is a wooden platform with a handrail and information sign. Past the viewpoint the trail continues to descend gently to the upper junction with the Loop Trail. A

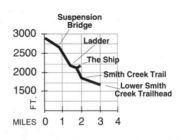

short distance ahead is the end of the barrier-free trail and another interpretive viewpoint.

The rough Loop Trail turns to the right (southeast) and drops to cross a bridge over the Muddy River. This alternate route then descends, sometimes steeply, for 0.5 mile to rejoin the main trail at the suspension bridge.

The main trail now becomes steeper and rougher as it works its way down from the upper junction with the Loop Trail. In 0.4 mile you will reach the lower junction with the Loop Trail at the suspension bridge. The bridge is suspended over a narrow gorge; it sways and bounces as you walk across it. If you want to return from here cross the bridge and climb back up the Loop Trail.

The suspension bridge is the turnaround point for the casual hiker. Below here the trail is steep, very rough, and exposed in some places. To continue down, descend north and northeast from the suspension bridge, crossing a stream with a cable handrail. The route makes several switchbacks in the 0.7 mile to a 30-foot steel ladder, passing wonderful falls and beautiful pools along the way. The slippery-when-wet ladder allows the trail to drop over a cliff of basalt and must be descended to continue down. Once down the ladder the rough path heads farther down and crosses another stream to the junction with a side trail to The Ship viewpoint.

The side trail turns to the right (southeast) and climbs very steeply to The Ship viewpoint 0.2 mile away. The Ship is a large rock outcropping above the riverbed. The view from The Ship is well worth the effort it takes to get there, but the trail is very steep and exposed. There is another steel ladder on the path to The Ship viewpoint. Do not send children up the trail to The Ship viewpoint alone. Below the junction with the path to The Ship viewpoint, the Lava Canyon Trail continues down, crossing a couple more exposed spots.

Two miles from Lava Canyon Trailhead is the new junction with the Smith Creek Trail. The Lava Canyon Trail used to continue another 0.9 mile east to the banks of Smith Creek, where it met the Smith Creek Trail, but now that lower 0.9 mile has become part of the Smith Creek Trail. See Hike 34 for a description of Smith Creek Trail. At this junction the Lava Canyon Trail turns to the right and crosses a bridge over the Muddy River (this bridge should be in place by early 1999). It then descends for 1 mile to Lower Smith Creek Trailhead, making a couple of switchbacks along the way. Lower Smith Creek Trailhead is at 1,700 feet elevation, 3 miles from Lava Canyon Trailhead.

Lava Canyon (Trail 184)

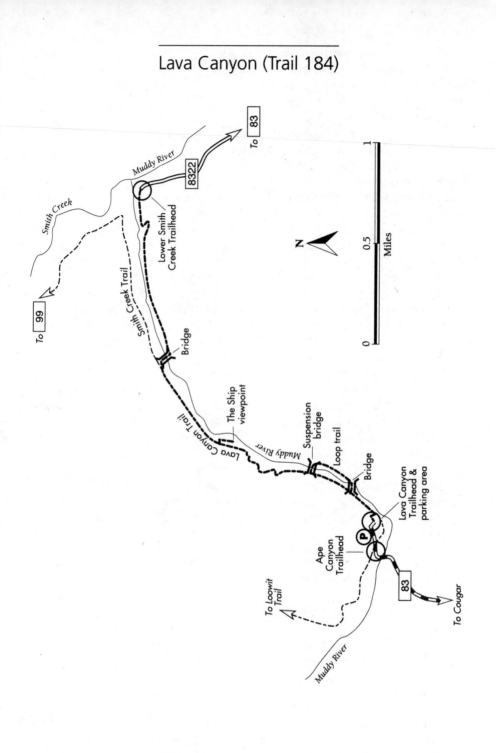

Options: The loop trail is an excellent option for a family hike. Retracing your steps can make the return from Lower Smith Creek Trailhead. A car shuttle can also be made.

Camping & services: Dispersed camping is allowed in many areas on this side of the monument. The closest developed campgrounds are Beaver Bay and Cougar, east of Cougar on WA 503 spur. Gas, groceries, a restaurant and motel are available in Cougar. Medical facilities are in Woodland.

For more information: USDA Forest Service at Mount St. Helens National Volcanic Monument Headquarters in Chelatchie or Ape's Headquarters next to Ape Cave parking area. See Appendix A.

Muddy River in Lava Canyon.

Eastern Region
Access from Forest Roads 25, 26, and 99

The Eastern Region of Mount St. Helens National Volcanic Monument is mostly within the Blast and Singe Zones caused by the 1980 eruption. Much of this region is covered with wildflowers between the broken stumps, blown-down trees, and beautiful silver snags.

As you start west up Forest Road 99, from FR 25, you will drive through large old-growth forest. First you will reach Bear Meadows Trailhead, where **Hike 42 Boundary Trail** begins. Shortly after passing Bear Meadows you will begin to enter the Blast Zone. Mount St. Helens soon comes into view between the denuded trees.

Continuing on FR 99, you soon arrive at the junction with FR 26, which bears right off FR 99 and leads to Norway Pass Trailhead and the trailheads along the upper Green River. The easiest access into the Mount Margaret Backcountry is from Norway Pass Trailhead. The Miner's Car Exhibit, which is also the trailhead for **Hike 41 Meta Lake,** is located next to the junction of FR 99 and FR 26.

FR 99 soon bears to the southwest, passing Independence Pass, Harmony and Smith Creek Trailheads, the starting points for **Hikes 39, 37, and 34,** before reaching Windy Ridge Viewpont and Trailhead at the end of the road. Windy Ridge Viewpoint is the trailhead for **Hikes 35 and 38** and offers the best view of the Mount St. Helens crater to be had on this side of the monument.

Mount St. Helens over Spirit Lake (note the floating logs on the right).

Eastern Region Overview

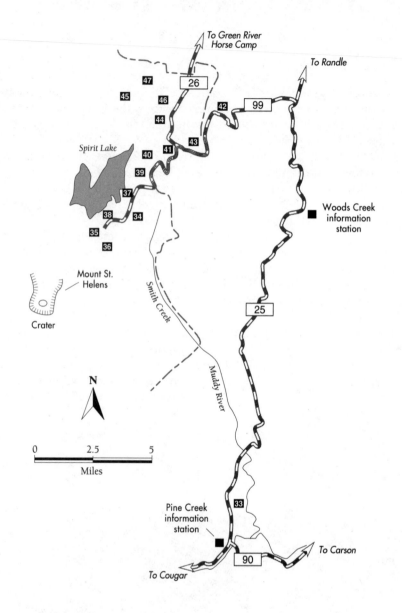

33 Cedar Flats Nature Loop (Trail 32)

Type of hike: Day hike, loop.
Total distance: 0.9 mile.
Difficulty: Easy.
Best months: April–October.
Elevation loss: Minimal.
Trailhead elevation: 1,350 feet.
Permits: None.
Maps: Cedar Flats USGS quad.
Starting point: Cedar Flats Trailhead.

General description: A short loop walk through magnificent old growth forest. This is an excellent hike for small children, with adult supervision.

Finding the trailhead: Head north from Portland on Interstate 5 to Exit 21 at Woodland (21 miles north of the Columbia River Bridge). Then drive east for 27.5 miles on Washington 503 (which becomes WA 503 spur) to Cougar. Continue east through Cougar on WA 503 spur (which becomes Forest Road 90 at the Skamania County line) for another 18.6 miles to the junction with FR 25. Bear left (nearly straight ahead) and head northeast on FR 25 for 3.6 miles to Cedar Flats Trailhead.

From Seattle take I-5 south to Exit 133 at Tacoma and then follow WA 7 for 55 miles to Morton. From Morton drive east on U.S. Highway 12 for 17 miles to Randle. Turn right and take WA 131 then FR 25 south for 41 miles to the Cedar Flats Trailhead. Cedar Flats Trailhead is on the east side of the road. GPS coordinates at the trailhead are 46 06.729 N 122 01.019 W.

Parking & trailhead facilities: There is parking for several cars but no other facilities at the trailhead.

Key points:
0.1   Wooden bridge and trail forks.
0.6   Viewpoint overlooking Muddy River.

The hike: Descending a few feet from the east side of the parking area, Cedar Flats Nature Trail enters the old-growth forest. The broad trail passes an interpretive sign and reaches a wooden bridge 0.1 mile from the trailhead. In the spring, when the new leaves are just out on the understory of vine

maple, the light green light that filters down through the canopy makes these deep woods especially beautiful. Just past the bridge the trail forks.

Bear right at the fork and continue along the well-maintained trail. You will pass some large cedar trees and in a few yards there will be two very large douglas-firs to the left of the trail. This seems to be a favorite picture-taking spot, as there is a path to the base of the largest tree.

Cedar Flats Nature Loop (Trail 32)

Author next to huge Douglas-fir.

The trail reaches the high bank of the Muddy River 0.4 mile farther along, after passing many more large trees. A lahar flowed down the Muddy River during the 1980 eruption. The evidence of the deluge is still present in the form of logs and stumps scattered along the river bottom. The trail follows the riverbank for a couple hundred yards to a viewpoint with a short rail fence. At the viewpoint the route turns away from the river and heads back through the woods. In about 300 yards you will reach the fork in the trail next to the bridge. Turn right and walk the last 0.1 mile to the trailhead.

Options: Take your time and enjoy the old-growth forest.

Camping & services: The closest campground is Swift Campground 4.5 miles south of the trailhead on FR 90. Groceries, cabins, and campsites can be had at Eagle Cliff Resort on FR 90, 1 mile east of the junction of FR 90 and FR 25. There is a sheriffs station across FR 90 from the Pine Creek Information Station 4 miles south of the trailhead.

For more information: USDA Forest Service at Pine Creek Information Station, 4 miles south of the trailhead on FR 90. See Appendix A.

34 Smith Creek (Trail 225)

Type of hike:	Day hike or backpack, shuttle.
Total distance:	10.9 miles.
Difficulty:	Strenuous.
Best months:	June–October.
Elevation loss:	2,620 feet.
Trailhead elevation:	4,340 feet.
Permits:	None.
Maps:	Spirit Lake East and Smith Creek Butte USGS quads. Part of the trail is missing on the Smith Creek Butte quad.
Starting point:	Smith Creek Trailhead.

General description: The Smith Creek Trail descends a long ridge through the Blast Zone to Smith Creek. Then it follows Smith Creek to the Muddy River. The last 2.5 miles of Smith Creek Trail are out of the Blast Zone.

Finding the trailhead: Head north from Portland on Interstate 5 to Exit 21 at Woodland (21 miles north of the Columbia River Bridge). Then drive east for 27.5 miles on Washington 503 (which becomes WA 503 spur) to Cougar. Continue east through Cougar on WA 503 spur (which becomes Forest Road 90 at the Skamania County line) for another 18.6 miles to the junction with FR 25. Bear left (nearly straight ahead) and head northeast on FR 25 for 24.3 miles to the junction with FR 99.

Smith Creek (Trail 225)

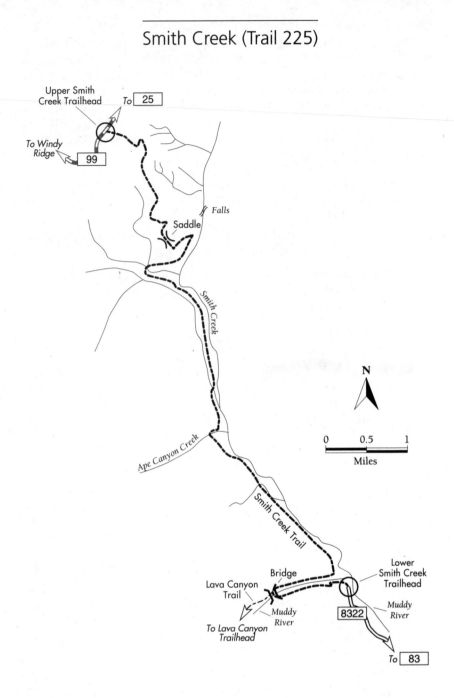

Upper Smith Creek Trailhead

To 25

To Windy Ridge

99

Falls

Saddle

Smith Creek

Ape Canyon Creek

N

0   0.5   1
Miles

Smith Creek Trail

Bridge

Lava Canyon Trail

Muddy River

To Lava Canyon Trailhead

Lower Smith Creek Trailhead

Muddy River

8322

To 83

From Seattle take I-5 south to Exit 133 at Tacoma and then follow WA 7 for 55 miles to Morton. From Morton drive east on U.S. Highway 12 for 17 miles to Randle. Turn right and take WA 131 then FR 25 south for 20 miles to the junction with FR 99.

Turn west on FR 99 and drive 14.4 miles to the Upper Smith Creek Trailhead. There is a sign marking the trailhead. GPS coordinates are 46 15.499 N 122 07.027 W.

To reach the the Lower Smith Creek Trailhead, follow the driving directions in Hike 31 to the Lahar Viewpoint Trailhead. Just before reaching the parking area turn right on FR 8322, a rough, narrow, gravel road. Follow it 4.8 miles to the Lower Smith Creek Trailhead.

Parking & trailhead facilities: There is parking for several cars but no other facilities at either of the trailheads.

Key points:
4.0	Creek crossing.
5.9	Creek crossing.
6.5	Ape Canyon Creek.
9.9	Junction with Lava Canyon Trail.
10.9	Lower Smith Creek Trailhead. GPS 46 10.926 N 122 03.302 W.

The hike: The first 5 miles of this trail are vague and hard to follow in spots. Leaving the high and sometimes windy trailhead on FR 99, Smith Creek Trail traverses to the east following an abandoned roadbed. After about a quarter of a mile the trail bears right

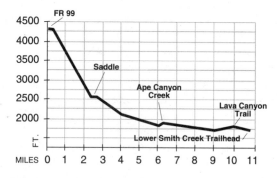

off the roadbed to begin its descent. Just after leaving the roadbed there is a large rock outcropping above the trail. The route soon turns left (north) and crosses a ridgeline. For the next 0.5 mile, snowdrifts may cover the path into June, making the trail hard to follow. The route is on a steep side hill here and if the drifts are hard there is some danger of sliding. The tread soon makes three descending switchbacks then traverses south back to the ridgeline. After getting back across the ridgeline and out onto a south-facing slope, the snow problem usually ends.

On the south side of the ridgeline the vague route heads down a pumice-covered ridge. Watch for elk as you descend these open slopes. The trail winds and switchbacks its way down for 1.2 miles, south-southeast, to a broad saddle. The path crosses the saddle and soon turns left and heads northeast on a relatively flat bench. The route descends off the bench to reach another abandoned roadbed. As you reach the roadbed a waterfall will come into view ahead.

Turn right on the roadbed and follow it to the southwest. From here to the first creek crossing the trail generally follows the remains of this old roadbed. This is not to say that this section of trail is easy however. The road has washed and slid away in several spots and getting across these gullies can be difficult. The route generally drops below the road grade to cross the washouts then climbs back to it.

Reach the first creek crossing (really two streams) 4 miles from the trailhead at 2,080 feet elevation. To reach the crossing you have to lose over 2,200 feet in elevation. The hard-to-see route fords the stream then turns left and heads southeast between the stream you crossed and another stream to the south. The route is marked with wood posts as it gently descends the semi-open peninsula between the streams. The trail follows the peninsula for 1.9 miles then turns right (west) and drops steeply to the streambed. A post on the west side of the stream marks the place where the trail crosses, but it is hard to spot in the brush. Cross the stream either by fording it or crossing a log. When I hiked this trail in May 1998 there was a cedar log, 4 feet in diameter, to cross on.

After crossing the creek the trail turns left (south-southeast) and heads downstream. The vague tread soon crosses a single log bridge over a small side stream. Half a mile down, the route bears southwest into Ape Canyon. The trail disappears as it enters the mudflow debris in the canyon bottom. Head south across the boulders and cross the fairly large Ape Canyon Creek. This crossing could be difficult during times of heavy runoff. As you cross Ape Canyon you leave the Eruption Impact Zone. From here on, the forest was not heavily affected by the 1980 eruption of Mount St. Helens.

On the south side of Ape Canyon the trail reappears. It climbs a short distance to reach another abandoned roadbed. The route generally follows this roadbed from here to the Muddy River, but many small sections of the roadbed have been washed away. In these spots the path makes detours into the woods. The route crosses a gully and then a nearly washed-out road bridge over a side stream, 1.6 miles after leaving Ape Canyon. Soon after crossing the bridge you will enter a flat, semi-open area. In the semi-open area the trail follows the roadbed along the riverbank to the old junction with Lava Canyon Trail, allowing for washouts along the way.

You will reach the old junction with Lava Canyon Trail, at 1,710 feet elevation, 9.9 miles from the trailhead on FR 99. Smith Creek Trail used to continue another 0.1 mile southeast from here, crossing a bridge over the Muddy River to Lower Smith Creek Trailhead. The bridge is being moved about 1 mile up the Muddy River. Turn right on what used to be the Lava Canyon Trail and follow it up the gentle open slope for 0.9 mile, to the new junction with the Lava Canyon Trail. Turn left on the Lava Canyon Trail and cross the bridge. (This construction should be completed in 1999.) Then descend the Lava Canyon Trail for 1 mile to the Lower Smith Creek Trailhead. See Hike 32 for a description of the Lava Canyon Trail.

Options: To hike the 2 miles to Lava Canyon Trailhead, turn right and climb west at the junction before reaching the Muddy River Bridge. Lava Canyon Trailhead is a 61-mile car shuttle from Smith Creek Trailhead.

Waterfall in Smith Creek.

Camping & services: The closest developed campground to the trailhead is Iron Creek Campground on FR 25, 9.7 miles south of Randle. Other services can be obtained in Randle or Morton.

For more information: USDA Forest Service at Woods Creek or Pine Creek Information Stations. See Appendix A.

35 Truman Trail (Trail 207)

Type of hike:	Day hike, out and back, with a very long shuttle option.
Total distance:	11.8 miles.
Difficulty:	Moderate.
Best months:	Mid June–September.
Elevation gain:	650 feet.
Trailhead elevation:	4,110 feet.
Permits:	Mount St. Helens National Volcanic Monument Visitors Pass.
Maps:	MSHNVM. Mount St. Helens and Spirit Lake West USGS quads cover the area but this trail is not shown.
Starting point:	Windy Ridge Viewpoint and Trailhead.

General description: The Truman Trail first heads south along Windy Ridge with views of Mount Adams to the east. It then crosses a saddle and descends to the Pumice Plain and crosses it before climbing up to Johnston Ridge at The Spillover. Much of the Truman Trail is in full view of the crater of Mount St. Helens.

Finding the trailhead: Head north from Portland on Interstate 5 to Exit 21 at Woodland (21 miles north of the Columbia River Bridge). Then drive east for 27.5 miles on Washington 503 (which becomes WA 503 spur) to Cougar. Continue east through Cougar on WA 503 spur (which becomes Forest Road 90 at the Skamania County line) for another 18.6 miles to the junction with FR 25. Bear left (nearly straight ahead) and head northeast on FR 25 for 24.3 miles to the junction with FR 99.

From Seattle take I-5 south to Exit 133, then follow WA 7 to Morton. From Morton drive east 17 miles to Randle on U.S. Highway 12. Turn right and take WA 131, which soon becomes FR 25, south for 20 miles to the junction with FR 99.

From the junction turn west on FR 99 and drive 15.8 miles to the trailhead. GPS coordinates are 46 15.990 N 122 08.200 W.

Parking & trailhead facilities: There are restrooms and adequate parking at the trailhead.

Truman Trail. SUZI BARSTAD PHOTO

Key points:
1.7 Junction with Abraham Trail.
2.0 Junction with Windy Trail.
2.8 Brushy oasis.
5.9 Junction with Boundary Trail.
       GPS 46 16.458 N 122 11.014 W.

The hike: The Truman Trail, which is really a closed section of FR 99 at this point, heads south from the Windy Ridge Viewpoint and Trailhead. The route travels along the east side of Windy Ridge through the severely blasted forest. Penstemon and paint-

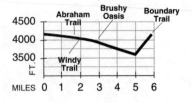

brush color the slopes between the alder and huckleberry bushes. Mount Adams is in view to the east across Smith Creek Canyon. About 1.5 miles from the trailhead a wet spot on the right side of the trail produces a patch of Lewis monkeyflowers.

The Abraham Trail turns to the left at Truman-Abraham Saddle 1.7 miles from the trailhead. See Hike 36 for a description of the Abraham Trail. The Truman Trail crosses the ridgeline at the saddle. It then makes a descending traverse to the flatter ground below. Once off the ridge the route turns to the northwest and passes the junction with Windy Trail. You are now following the haul road used to dig the tunnel that drains Spirit Lake. The route passes through a small brushy area 0.8 mile after passing the Windy Trail. The brush and the flowing water make this spot seem like an oasis in the desert. About a mile past the oasis the route crosses another watercourse. There is usually water here but don't depend on it.

Approximately 5 miles from the Windy Ridge Trailhead, at 3,600 feet elevation, the trail begins to ascend through the hummocks up toward The Spillover. The Spillover is the place where the Debris Avalanche from the 1980 landslide and eruption climbed and crossed over Johnston Ridge. The path winds its way up through the hummocks to the junction with the Boundary Trail near the top of Johnston Ridge. The junction, at 4,150 feet elevation, is 5.9 miles from Windy Ridge Trailhead.

Options: The first 1.7 miles of Truman trail is the access route to the Plains of Abraham Loop. See Hike 36 for the details about the Plains of Abraham Loop. If you want a longer hike, with a long car shuttle, turn left on the Boundary Trail and follow it to the Johnston Ridge Observatory 2.5 miles to the west. See Hike 6 for details. Turning right on the Boundary Trail will take you to the Mount Margaret Backcountry where there are many hiking possibilities.

Camping & services: The closest developed campsites are at Iron Creek Campground, 9.7 miles south of Randle on FR 25. Other services can be obtained in Randle and Morton.

For more information: USDA Forest Service at Woods Creek Information Station or Pine Creek Information Station. See Appendix A.

Truman Trail (Trail 207)

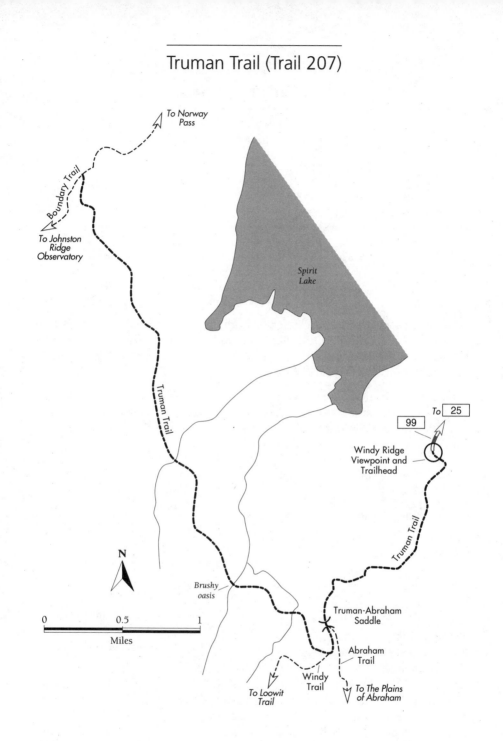

To Norway Pass

Boundary Trail

To Johnston Ridge Observatory

Spirit Lake

Truman Trail

To 25

99

Windy Ridge Viewpoint and Trailhead

Truman Trail

N

Brushy oasis

0   0.5   1
Miles

Truman-Abraham Saddle

Abraham Trail

Windy Trail

To Loowit Trail

To The Plains of Abraham

36 Plains of Abraham Loop (Trails 216D, 216, and 216E)

Type of hike: Day hike, backpack option, loop.
Total distance: 5.3 miles.
Difficulty: Moderate to strenuous.
Best months: July–September.
Elevation gain: 730 feet.
Trailhead elevation: 4,160 feet.
Permits: Mount St. Helens National Volcanic Monument Visitors Pass.
Maps: MSHNVM. USGS Mount St. Helens quad covers the area but this trail is not shown.
Starting point: Junction with Truman Trail, in Truman-Abraham Saddle, 1.7 miles south of Windy Ridge Trailhead.

General description: The Plains of Abraham Loop, an *internal* loop, climbs a flower-covered ridge to the plains then climbs over Windy Pass and returns across the Pumice Plain. This entire loop is within the Blast Zone of the 1980 eruption.

Finding the trailhead: Follow the driving directions in Hike 35 to Windy Ridge Viewpoint and Trailhead. Then hike south along the Truman Trail, also described in Hike 35, for 1.7 miles to the junction with the Abraham Trail.

Key points:
2.2 Junction with Loowit Trail on the Plains of Abraham.
3.3 Windy Pass.
4.3 Junction with Windy Trail.
5.1 Junction with Truman Trail.
5.3 Junction with Abraham Trail in Truman-Abraham Saddle.

The hike: In the Truman-Abraham Saddle, at 4,160 feet elevation, the Abraham Trail bears left (southeast) off the Truman Trail. The path climbs a narrow pumice ridge with Smith Creek Canyon to the left and Mount St. Helens ahead to the right. In late July the flowers along this ridge are

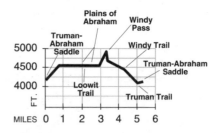

unrivaled. Penstemon and paintbrush nearly cover the slopes. The route climbs its first sand ladder 0.3 mile from the junction. A sand ladder is a series of wooden rungs held together with cables. The purpose of a sand ladder is to allow easier climbing and descending over steep, loose soil. A little farther up you will climb another sand ladder and regain the ridgeline. The route then follows the ridge to the south and climbs to a high point.

Here the path flattens out for a short distance. Leopard lilies and columbines line the trail.

The route climbs a bit more then bears left off the ridgeline, 0.9 mile from Truman Trail. You will cross six draws in the next 0.7 mile. A couple of these draws may have water through midsummer. All of them are flower gardens in late July. The wetter draws grow stands of monkeyflowers. After crossing the sixth draw the Plains of Abraham come into view ahead.

The tread descends, then crosses a wash as it nears the plains. You will make a switchback as you climb out of the wash onto the desert-like plains. Few plants can withstand the rigors of this pumice desert, but a few penstemons seem to prosper and bloom.

The route crosses the plains heading south-southeast for 0.3 mile to the junction with the Loowit Trail. It is about 1.6 miles straight ahead and across the plains to the south to the junction with the Ape Canyon Trail. See Hike 28 for a description of Ape Canyon Trail.

To continue on the loop, turn right at the junction and hike west across the plains on the Loowit Trail. Ape and Nelson Glaciers hang to the mountain slopes ahead and above. As you get closer to the base of the mountain the path bears slightly to the right and crosses a couple of washes. This section of the Loowit Trail is marked with large cairns. In the washes the trail is rough and vague in spots. You will leave the plains and begin to climb toward Windy Pass 0.7 mile from the junction. The route climbs the south-facing, penstemon-covered slope, making a couple of switchbacks before reaching Windy Pass. This is a pumice slope and the path tends to slip away in places if it has not been recently maintained.

Plains of Abraham.

Plains of Abraham Loop (Trails 216D, 216, and 216E)

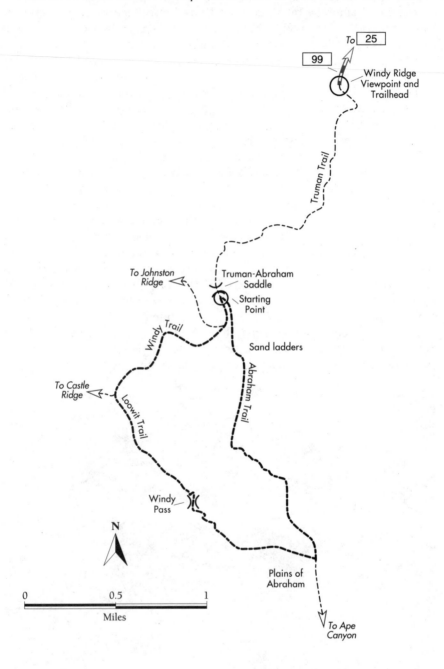

To 25

99

Windy Ridge
Viewpoint and
Trailhead

Truman Trail

To Johnston
Ridge

Truman-Abraham
Saddle

Starting
Point

Sand ladders

Windy Trail

To Castle
Ridge

Loowit Trail

Abraham Trail

Windy
Pass

N

0   0.5   1
Miles

Plains of
Abraham

To Ape
Canyon

The pass at 4,890 feet elevation is the highest spot on this loop. At the pass Spirit Lake comes into view to the north. The trail descends off the pass making four switchbacks as it drops. It then descends a gully that may be snowfilled through July. Leaving the gully the tread traverses northwest, in and out of a couple more washes, and passes a small waterfall to the junction with Windy Trail.

The junction with the Windy Trail is 4.3 miles from the junction with the Truman Trail where this loop started. As of late summer 1998 the Loowit Trail is closed from this junction 4 miles west to Studebaker Ridge. This section of the Loowit Trail may be replaced in 1999, making an around-the-mountain hike again possible. The junction of Windy and Loowit trails is very close to the pre-eruption site of the Timberline Campground. Before the 1980 eruption the most popular climbing routes to the summit of Mount St. Helens started here, at the end of a paved road. Nothing remains of the campground today.

Turn right on the Windy Trail and hike northeast. You will descend gently through the mounds of pumice. The path descends into a large wash 0.6 mile after leaving the Loowit Trail. Another 0.2 mile brings you to the junction with the Truman Trail. Turn right on the Truman Trail and climb gently up the roadbed for 0.2 mile to the junction with the Abraham Trail in the Truman-Abraham Saddle to complete the loop.

Options: Hike south from the junction of the Abraham and Loowit trails, across the Plains of Abraham to the Ape Canyon Trail, then from there along the Ape Canyon Trail to the Ape Canyon Trailhead; this makes a great day hike. The car shuttle to Ape Canyon Trailhead is, however, quite long. A multi-day backpack from Windy Ridge Trailhead to Sheep Canyon Trailhead, two-thirds of the way around Mount St. Helens can be done with a car shuttle to Sheep Canyon Trailhead. See Hikes 29, 27, 20, and 10 for the details.

Camping & services: The closest developed campground to Windy Ridge Trailhead is Iron Creek Campground on FR 25, 9.7 miles south of Randle. Other services can be obtained in Randle or Morton.

For more information: USDA Forest Service at Woods Creek or Pine Creek information stations. See Appendix A.

37 Harmony Trail (Trail 224)

Type of hike: Day hike, out and back.
Total distance: 2.4 miles.
Difficulty: Moderate.
Best months: Mid June–September.
Elevation loss: 640 feet.
Trailhead elevation: 4,050 feet.
Permits: Mount St. Helens National Volcanic Monument Visitors Pass.
Maps: MSHNVM or Spirit Lake East USGS quad.
Starting point: Harmony Viewpoint and Trailhead.

General description: Hike from the Harmony Viewpoint to the shore of Spirit Lake. This trail is the only legal access to Spirit Lake.

Finding the trail: From Portland drive north on Interstate 5 to Exit 21 at Woodland, Washington. Then follow Washington 503 (which becomes WA 503 spur) for 27.5 miles east to Cougar. From Cougar drive east on Washington 503 spur (which becomes Forest Road 90) for 18.6 miles to the junction with FR 25. At the junction, FR 25 goes straight ahead (northeast). Follow FR 25 north for 24.3 miles to the junction with FR 99.

From Seattle take I-5 south to Exit 133 and then follow WA 7 for 55 miles to Morton. From Morton drive east on U.S. Highway 12 for 17 miles to Randle. Turn right and take WA 131 then FR 25 south for 20 miles to the junction with FR 99.

Turn west on FR 99 and drive 13.5 miles to the Harmony Trailhead. GPS coordinates are 46 15.499 N 122 07.027 W.

Parking & trailhead facilities: There is parking for several cars but no other facilities at the trailhead.

Key points:
0.4   Tiny waterfall.
1.2   Spirit Lake.

The hike: The Harmony Trail immediately starts to descend from the trailhead. This north-facing slope is covered with low brush and blown-down logs. In a few yards the trail enters the restricted area as it begins a descending traverse to the west. In the restricted area hikers may not leave the trail or camp.

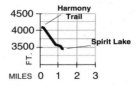

After descending the traverse for 0.2 mile the trail makes a switchback to the right. It then turns left to continue its moderate descent. You will pass a tiny waterfall 300 yards farther along. Cross the tiny stream below the falls then pass beneath an undercut rock face. On the far side of the face are more tiny falls and streams. These streams may dried up by midsummer.

The tread makes a switchback to the right 250 yards after passing the tiny waterfalls. The trail then descends a short distance and leaves the north-facing slope you have been on since leaving the trailhead. The vegetation becomes more sparse as you leave the slope. Making a turn to the left and heading west again toward the lake you follow a line of posts across the pumice flats. The trail descends again 0.3 mile farther along. It soon makes a couple more switchbacks as it comes alongside Harmony Creek. This rushing stream has several small waterfalls. Shortly the trail comes to an end close to the log-strewn shore of Spirit Lake, at 3,410 feet elevation.

The end of the trail offers an excellent view of Mount St. Helens over the lake. Often the mountain reflects in the still water. Harmony Falls Lodge once sat next to the lakeshore, a short distance west of the end of the trail. The site of the old lodge is below the present lake level, which is about 200 feet higher than it was before the May 1980 eruption. Watch for elk all along this trail. Make the return trip via the same route.

Camping & services: The closest developed campsites are at Iron Creek Campground, 9.7 miles south of Randle on FR 25. Other services can be obtained in Randle and Morton.

For more information: USDA Forest Service at Woods Creek Information Station or Pine Creek Information Station. See Appendix A.

Mount St. Helens over Spirit Lake.

Harmony Trail (Trail 224)

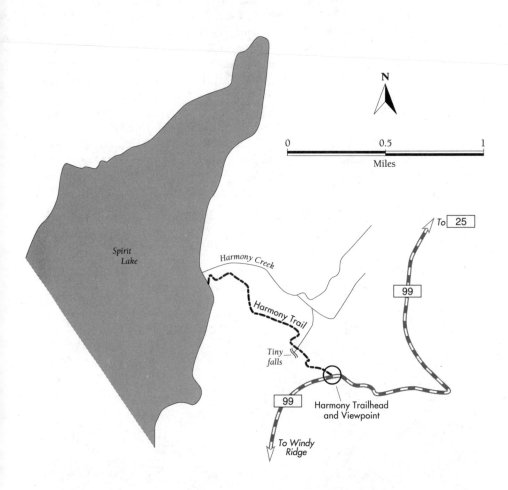

38 Independence Pass (Trail 227, south segment)

Type of hike:	Day hike, out and back, with shuttle option.
Total distance:	2.8 miles.
Difficulty:	Moderate.
Best months:	Mid June–September.
Elevation gain:	520 feet.
Trailhead elevation:	4,010 feet.
Permits:	Mount St. Helens National Volcanic Monument Visitors Pass.
Maps:	MSHNVM. Spirit Lake West and Spirit Lake East USGS quads cover the area but this trail is not shown.
Starting point:	Windy Ridge Viewpoint and Trailhead.

General description: A short hike along Windy Ridge from the Windy Ridge Viewpoint to Donnybrook Viewpoint. Hiking along this volcanically blasted ridge offers the best view of Spirit Lake to be found.

Finding the trailhead: Head north from Portland on Interstate 5 to Exit 21 at Woodland (21 miles north of the Columbia River Bridge). Then drive east for 27.5 miles on Washington 503 (which becomes WA 503 spur) to Cougar. Continue east through Cougar on WA 503 spur (which becomes Forest Road 90 at the Skamania County line) for another 18.6 miles to the junction with FR 25. Bear left (nearly straight ahead) and head northeast on FR 25 for 24.3 miles to the junction with FR 99.

From Seattle take I-5 south to Exit 133 in Tacoma and then follow WA 7 for 55 miles to Morton. Turn left at the south edge of Morton and drive east for 17 miles to Randle on U.S. Highway 12. Turn right and take WA 131 then FR 25 south for 20 miles to the junction with FR 99.

Turn right (west) on FR 99 and drive 15.8 miles to Windy Ridge Viewpoint and Trailhead. This segment of the Independence Pass Trail starts next to the restrooms at the north end of the parking area. GPS coordinates are 46 15.990 N 122 08.200 W.

Parking & trailhead facilities: There are restrooms and adequate parking at the trailhead.

Key points:
- 0.2 Viewpoint.
- 1.4 Donnybrook Viewpoint.

The hike: Originally the first 0.2 mile of the trail was a true sand ladder. A sand ladder is a series of wooden rungs held together with cables. The purpose of a sand ladder is to allow easier climbing and descending over steep, loose soil.

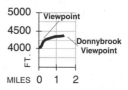

Independence Pass (Trail 227, south segment)

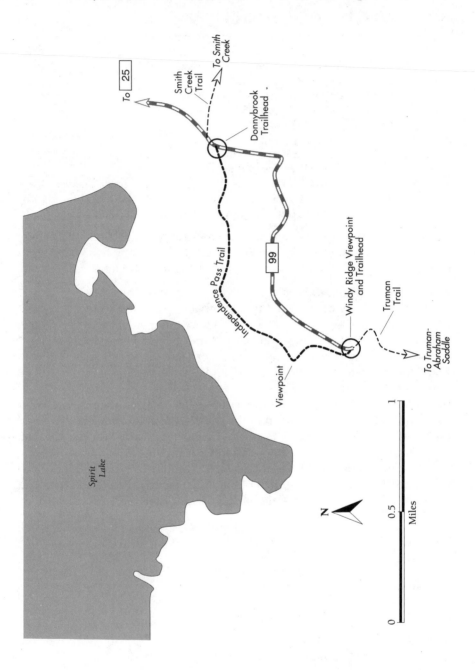

To 25

Smith Creek Trail

To Smith Creek

Donnybrook Trailhead

Independence Pass Trail

99

Windy Ridge Viewpoint and Trailhead

Truman Trail

To Truman-Abraham Saddle

Viewpoint

Spirit Lake

N

0   0.5   1
Miles

Viewpoint overlooking Spirit Lake.

Now eight rock and 428 wooden steps replace the old sand ladder.

Climb the steps and then bear left to the viewpoint at 4,230 feet elevation on a pumice-covered slope. Take some time here to admire nature's violent handiwork. Look into the crater and see what was once the inside of a mountain. Spirit Lake, with its thousands of floating logs, is below. To the west the Johnston Ridge Observatory sits perched atop Johnston Ridge. At this viewpoint, 0.2 mile from the parking area, the majority of tourists turn around.

A sign near the viewpoint "Rd. 99, 1" points to the northeast. Follow the trail past the sign. As you hike to the northeast Mount Margaret and Mount Rainier come into view, while penstemon dots the landscape between the downed logs. These flowers bloom through July. As you get farther along into a slightly more protected area, paintbrush, fireweed, elderberries, and huckleberries join the penstemon.

The path rounds a ridgeline 0.6 mile from the trailhead. Here you begin to traverse east along a north-facing slope. The vegetation becomes much more lush on this hillside. Columbine and lupine bloom here in July. The route passes beneath cliffs 0.3 mile into the traverse. It then rounds another ridge and continues east. The path then descends gently, through the silvered snags, alder brush, and fireweed to Donnybrook Viewpoint and Trailhead on FR 99.

Options: A short (five minutes or less) car shuttle can be made between the two trailheads, or just walk the road back to Windy Ridge Viewpoint.

Camping & services: The nearest campground is located on FR 25 at Iron Creek, 10 miles north of the junction of FR 99 and FR 25, mentioned in the finding the trail section. Other services can be had in Randle or Morton.

For more information: USDA Forest Service at Pine Creek or Woods Creek information stations. See Appendix A.

39 Independence Pass (Trail 227)

See Map on Page 162

Type of hike:	Day hike, out and back, with shuttle and loop options.
Total distance:	7 miles.
Difficulty:	Moderate.
Best months:	Late June–September.
Elevation gain:	490 feet.
Trailhead elevation:	4,090 feet.
Permits:	None.
Maps:	MSHNVM or USGS Spirit Lake East quad.
Starting point:	Independence Pass Trailhead.

General description: A hike along the ridge east of Spirit Lake from Independence Pass to Norway Pass, with great views of Spirit Lake and Mount St. Helens.

Finding the trailhead: Head north from Portland on Interstate 5 to Exit 21 at Woodland (21 miles north of the Columbia River Bridge) . Then drive east for 27.5 miles on Washington 503 (which becomes WA 503 spur) to Cougar. Continue east through Cougar on WA 503 spur (which becomes Forest Road 90 at the Skamania County line) for another 18.6 miles to the junction with FR 25. Bear left (nearly straight ahead) and head northeast on FR 25 for 24.3 miles to the junction with FR 99.

From Seattle take I-5 south to Exit 133 at Tacoma and then follow WA 7 for 55 miles to Morton. From Morton drive east 17 miles to Randle. Turn right and take WA 131 then FR 25 south for 20 miles to the junction with FR 99.

Turn west on FR 99 and follow it 11.9 miles to Independence Pass Trailhead. The trailhead is on the right (west) side of FR 99. GPS coordinates at the trailhead are 46 16.916 N 122 05.798 W.

Parking & trailhead facilities: There is parking for several cars but no other facilities at the trailhead.

Key points:
0.9   Junction with Independence Ridge Trail. GPS 46 17.396 N 122 05.997 W.
3.5   Norway Pass.

The hike: As it leaves the trailhead the route climbs 30 steps, then makes a couple of switchbacks as it heads west to the ridgeline. Once you reach the ridge Spirit Lake comes into view. From the ridge you can see Mount Hood far to the south and slightly to the left of the blasted-out remains

of Mount St. Helens. The ridge is covered with blown-down timber; scattered small firs and huckleberry bushes grow between the logs. The berries are ripe in late August.

The path turns right along the ridge and heads north through stands of fireweed and other flowers. The tread makes a couple more switchbacks 0.5 mile from the trailhead. It then begins to traverse a southwest-facing slope. Along this slope grow columbine and beargrass. Another 0.4 mile brings you to the junction with the Independence Ridge Trail, on the side of a little valley. The Independence Ridge Trail turns to the right (northeast). See Hike 40 for a description of the Independence Ridge Trail. The USGS map shows this junction incorrectly.

Independence Pass Trail bears left at the junction and descends a few feet, crossing the tiny valley. Through midsummer there is usually a spring in the bottom of the valley a few yards below the trail to the south. Leaving the valley the route climbs slightly to the west. Soon it descends and turns north along a steep slope above Spirit Lake.

The route passes beneath some cliffs, 0.9 mile after leaving the junction with the Independence Ridge Trail. Look for pinnacles of rock below the trail as you pass the cliffs. The tread soon begins to climb, making a couple of switchbacks. Then it winds up through a saddle. At 4,580 feet elevation this is the highest point on the Independence Pass Trail.

Past the saddle the path traverses the west-facing slope. Soon Mount Rainier comes into view ahead. In the shaded, damper spots along this slope a few avalanche lilies manage to survive and bloom in early July. A few yards to the right of the trail at 3.4 miles a viewpoint shows Mount Adams to the east. Descend the last 0.1 mile to Norway Pass and the junction with the Boundary Trail, at 4,520 feet elevation.

Options: A loop hike can be made by turning right on the Boundary Trail and following it 1 mile to the junction with Independence Ridge Trail. Then turn right on the Independence Ridge Trail and take it back to its junction with Independence Pass Trail. Once back on the Independence Pass Trail, follow it south for 0.9 mile to the Independence Pass Trailhead.

Camping & services: The closest developed campground to the trailhead is Iron Creek Campground, 9.7 miles south of Randle on FR 25. Other services can be obtained in Randle or Morton.

For more information: USDA Forest Service at Woods Creek Information Station or Pine Creek Information Station. See Appendix A.

Rock pinnacle and Spirit Lake.

40 Independence Ridge (Trail 227A)

Type of hike:	Day hike, out and back, with loop and shuttle options.
Total distance:	2.6 miles.
Difficulty:	Moderate.
Best months:	Late June–September.
Elevation gain:	370 feet.
Trailhead elevation:	4,300 feet at junction with Boundary Trail.
Permits:	None.
Maps:	MSHNVM. Spirit Lake East USGS quad shows the trail incorrectly.
Starting point:	Junction with Boundary Trail 1 mile west of Norway Pass Trailhead.

General description: A short hike on an *internal* trail along the ridge east of Spirit Lake. This trail is generally used as part of a loop from either the Norway Pass Trailhead or the Independence Pass Trailhead.

Finding the trailhead: Head north from Portland on Interstate 5 to Exit 21 at Woodland (21 miles north of the Columbia River Bridge). Then drive east for 27.5 miles on Washington 503 (which becomes WA 503 spur) to Cougar. Continue east through Cougar on WA 503 spur (which becomes Forest Road 90 at the Skamania County line) for another 18.6 miles to the junction with FR 25. Bear left (nearly straight ahead) and head northeast on FR 25 for 24.3 miles to the junction with FR 99.

From Seattle take I-5 south to Exit 133 at Tacoma and then follow WA 7 for 55 miles to Morton. From Morton drive east 17 miles to Randle. Turn right and take WA 131 then FR 25 south for 20 miles to the junction with FR 99.

Turn west on FR 99 and drive 8.8 miles to the junction with FR 26. Turn right and drive northwest on FR 26 to the Norway Pass Trailhead. The trailhead is on the left side of the road. There are restrooms at the trailhead.

Hike west on the Boundary Trail for 1 mile to the signed junction with the Independence Pass Trail. See Hike 44 for a description of this section of the Boundary Trail.

Key points:
- 0.5   Pass.
- 1.3   Junction with Independence Pass Trail.

The hike: Leaving the signed junction with the Boundary Trail, the Independence Ridge Trail climbs gradually to the south. Meta Lake is in view below to the east as you hike. Mount Adams rises above the green hills in the distance. Columbines, lupines, asters, bluebells, and leopard lilies cover the more open slopes

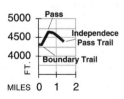

Independence Pass (Trail 227)
Independence Ridge (Trail 227A)

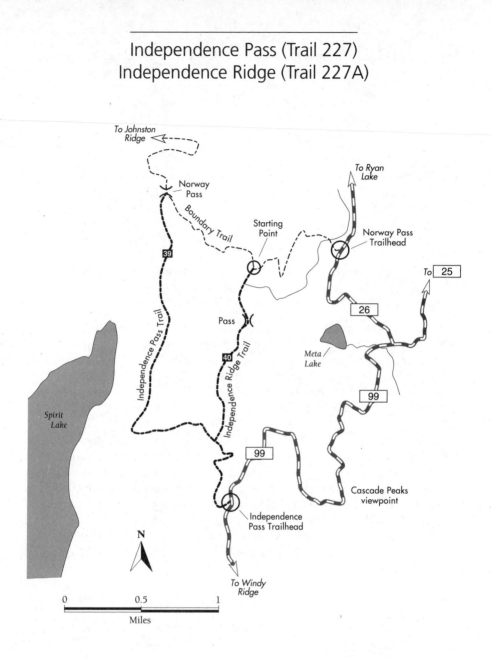

To Johnston Ridge

Norway Pass

Boundary Trail

Starting Point

39

To Ryan Lake

Norway Pass Trailhead

To 25

26

Pass

Independence Pass Trail

Independence Ridge Trail

Meta Lake

40

99

Spirit Lake

99

Cascade Peaks viewpoint

Independence Pass Trailhead

N

To Windy Ridge

0   0.5   1
Miles

as you climb. The vegetation on these slopes is as lush as any within the Blast Zone.

The route reaches a pass 0.5 mile from the junction. At the pass, 4,670 feet above sea level, the slope becomes drier and the vegetation becomes less dense. After crossing the pass the path crosses a large gully then traverses a slope, crossing several small gullies, for 0.5 mile to another ridgeline. Paintbrush and penstemon color this slope. The tread follows the ridge for a short distance then bears slightly to the right. Then you descend through short silvered snags, young firs and fireweed to the junction with the Independence Pass Trail. This junction, which is shown incorrectly on the USGS map, is 1.3 miles from the junction with Boundary Trail. Return via the same route

Options: Make a loop by turning right on the Independence Pass Trail and following it to the Boundary Trail at Norway Pass. Then turn right again and return to the Norway Pass Trailhead via the Boundary Trail. See Hikes 39 and 44 for trail details.

Another option is to turn left on the Independence Pass Trail and follow it to the Independence Pass Trailhead. This option requires a car shuttle to the Independence Pass Trailhead. See Hike 39 for the details.

Camping & services: The closest developed campground is Iron Creek Campground, 9.7 miles south of Randle on FR 25. Other services can be obtained in Randle or Morton.

For more information: USDA Forest Service at Woods Creek Information Station or Pine Creek Information Station. See Appendix A.

Leopard lily.

41 Meta Lake (Trail 210)

Type of hike: Day hike, out and back.
Total distance: 0.6 mile.
Difficulty: Easy.
Best months: Mid June–September.
Elevation gain: Minimal.
Trailhead elevation: 3,630 feet.
Permits: Mount St. Helens National Volcanic Monument Visitors Pass.
Maps: None needed, Spirit Lake East USGS quad.
Starting point: Miners Car Exhibit site.

General description: A short walk from the Miners Car Exhibit through the blown-down forest of the Blast Zone to Meta Lake.

Finding the trailhead: Head north from Portland on Interstate 5 to Exit 21 at Woodland (21 miles north of the Columbia River Bridge). Then drive east for 27.5 miles on Washington 503 (which becomes WA 503 spur) to Cougar. Continue east through Cougar on WA 503 spur (which becomes Forest Road 90 at the Skamania County line) for another 18.6 miles to the junction with FR 25. Bear left (nearly straight ahead) and head northeast on FR 25 for 24.3 miles to the junction with FR 99.

From Seattle take I-5 south to Exit 133 at Tacoma and then follow WA 7 for 55 miles to Morton. From Morton drive east 17 miles to Randle. Turn right and take WA 131 then FR 25 south for 20 miles to the junction with FR 99.

Turn west on FR 99 and drive 8.8 miles to the junction with FR 26 and the Miners Car Exhibit site. GPS coordinates are 46 17.743 N 122 04.507 W.

Parking & trailhead facilities: Water, restrooms, and adequate parking are all found at the trailhead.

Key points:
0.0   Miners Car Exhibit.
0.1   Meta Lake parking area.
0.3   Meta Lake.

The hike: Take a few minutes to check out the Miners Car and imagine what it must have been like to have been here on May 18, 1980 when the volcano blew. From the Miners Car Exhibit, the paved trail parallels FR 99 for a couple hundred yards southwest to the Meta Lake parking area. Fireweed lines this section of trail along a sluggish stream. At the parking area the trail bears right and goes away from the road; after the parking area it is no longer paved. The tread winds its way through the small fir trees and fireweed from

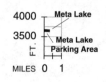

Meta Lake (Trail 210)

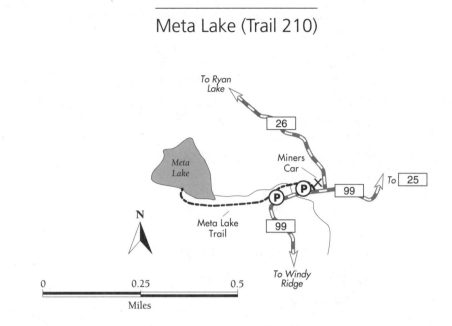

Meta Lake.

the parking area to the lake. Along the way, stop and read the interpretive sign "Survivors."

At the lake, 0.3 mile from where you started, another "Survivors" sign explains how frogs and brook trout survived the blast and ash under a covering of snow and ice. Return is made via the same trail.

Camping & services: The closest developed campground is Iron Creek Campground, 9.7 miles south of Randle on FR 25. Other services can be obtained in Randle or Morton.

For more information: USDA Forest Service at Woods Creek Information Station or Pine Creek Information Station. See Appendix A.

42 Boundary Trail (Trail 1, Bear Meadows to Norway Pass Trailhead)

Type of hike:	Day hike or backpack, shuttle.
Total distance:	5 miles.
Difficulty:	Moderate.
Best months:	Late June–September
Elevation loss:	410 feet.
Trailhead elevation:	4,120 feet.
Permits:	None.
Maps:	MSHNVM or Spirit Lake East USGS quad.
Starting point:	Bear Meadows Viewpoint and Trailhead.

General description: The hike first climbs gently through old-growth forest, passes rushing streams, and then enters the Blast Zone of the 1980 Mount St. Helens eruption. The route passes through a sheltered patch of large timber and along a ridge, and then descends through the blasted forest to FR 26 at the Norway Pass Trailhead.

Finding the trailhead: Head north from Portland on Interstate 5 to Exit 21 at Woodland (21 miles north of the Columbia River Bridge). Then drive east for 27.5 miles on Washington 503 (which becomes WA 503 spur) to Cougar. Continue east through Cougar on WA 503 spur (which becomes Forest Road 90 at the Skamania County line) for another 18.6 miles to the junction with FR 25. Bear left (nearly straight ahead) and head northeast on FR 25 for 24.3 miles to the junction with FR 99.

From Seattle take I-5 south to Exit 133 at Tacoma and then follow WA 7 for 55 miles to Morton. From Morton drive east 17 miles to Randle. Turn right and take WA 131 then FR 25 south for 20 miles to the junction with FR 99.

Turn right (west) on FR 99 and follow it for 4.5 miles to the Bear Meadows Trailhead. The trail leaves from the right side of the road across from the parking area. GPS coordinates at the trailhead are 46 18.799 N 122 02.167 W.

To reach the the Norway Pass Trailhead continue on FR 99 another 4.3 miles and then turn right on FR 26. Follow FR 26 for 1 mile to the trailhead. The parking area and restrooms are on the left (west) side of FR 26. The Boundary Trail crosses FR 26 at the trailhead. GPS coordinates are 46 18.330 N 122 04.948 W.

Parking & trailhead facilities: There are restrooms and adequate parking at either trailhead.

Key points:
    0.6   Junction with Strawberry Mountain Trail.
    3.3   Junction with Ghost Lake Trail.
    5.0   Norway Pass Trailhead. GPS 46 18.330 N 122 04.948 W.

The hike: The pumice-covered trail climbs through small timber intermingled with paintbrush and penstemon as it leaves the Bear Meadows Trailhead. Three hundred yards from the trailhead you will enter old-growth forest of fir and hemlock. The path climbs gently but steadily for 0.6 mile to the junction with the Straw-

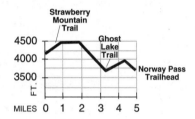

berry Mountain Trail, at 4,360 feet elevation. The Strawberry Mountain Trail turns right (northwest) and ascends Strawberry Mountain. See Hike 57 for a description of the Strawberry Mountain Trail. Bear left at the junction and continue through the large timber. Traverse the slope to the south where avalanche lilies dot the forest floor.

The route rounds the end of a ridge where you can spot FR 99 below. Mount St. Helens looms to the southwest through the trees. The tread crosses a small stream 1 mile from the trailhead. It then crosses a larger stream at the base of a stepped waterfall. Continue the traverse of this steep side hill, crossing a couple more small streams. In an opening on the slope shooting stars, larkspur, and paintbrush grow in profusion. Watch for a view of Mount Adams to your left.

The trail enters the Blast Zone 2 miles from Bear Meadows. The standing dead snags attest to the heat and power of the 1980 eruption. Huckleberries are plentiful here in August. You will make five switchbacks as you descend to a broken wooden bridge over a usually dry stream. A short distance past the bridge is the unmarked junction with the Ghost Lake Trail. At the junction, 3.3 miles from Bear Meadows, Ghost Lake is 0.7 mile to the right (north). See Hike 43 for the details on Ghost Lake.

Author at Bear Meadows Trailhead. SUZI BARSTAD PHOTO

Just past the junction the trail crosses another broken-down wooden bridge, this one over Clearwater Creek. Cross the bridge and pass through a stand of large trees spared by the eruption. The route then climbs gently through the snags and young firs. The path makes a switchback 0.3 mile past the junction then passes through another stand of old trees. The trail continues to climb, winding and switchbacking up and past a meadow.

A very poor and hard-to-find path 0.9 mile past the Ghost Lake junction leads a short distance up a gully to a small, unnamed lake. There are no fish in this lake. The shallow lake warms up quite nicely for swimming late in the summer.

Shortly after passing the path to the unnamed lake, the Boundary Trail crosses a pass at 3,950 feet elevation. Then it begins to descend toward the Norway Pass Trailhead. From the pass Mount Adams can be seen far to the east. As you cross the pass you enter an area where the timber was completely blown down by the 1980 eruption. Fireweed, paintbrush, and a few small trees grow between the downed logs. Late in the summer pearly everlastings cover the ground in spots. The route crosses another wooden bridge over a tiny stream 4.8 miles from Bear Meadows. It then turns to the right and descends between two small knobs to FR 26. Cross the road to the parking area at the Norway Pass Trailhead.

Options: The side trip to Ghost Lake and back will add only 1.2 miles to your hike.

A longer side trip can be made to Strawberry Mountain. The hike to the summit and back adds about 4.2 miles.

Camping & services: The closest developed campground is Iron Creek Campground, 9.7 miles south of Randle on FR 25. Other services can be obtained in Randle or Morton.

For more information: USDA Forest Service at Woods Creek Information Station or Pine Creek Information Station. See Appendix A.

Boundary Trail (Trail 1, Bear Meadows to Norway Pass Trailhead) • Ghost Lake (Trail 1H)

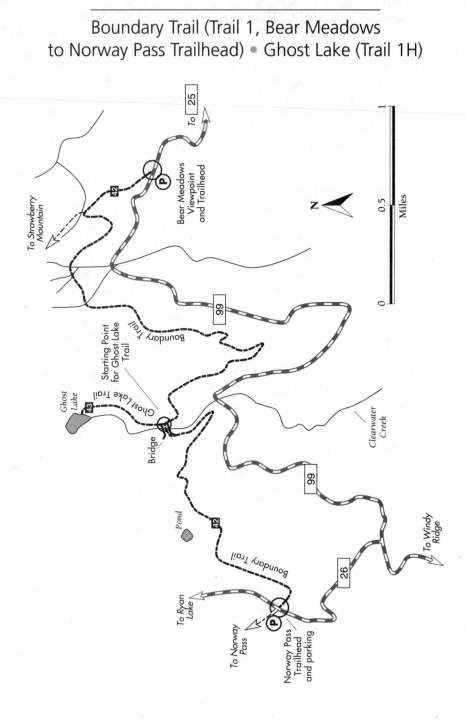

To 25

Bear Meadows Viewpoint and Trailhead

To Strawberry Mountain

N

0.5

Miles

0   1

42

99

Starting Point for Ghost Lake Trail

Boundary Trail

Ghost Lake

43

Ghost Lake Trail

Bridge

Clearwater Creek

99

Pond

42

Boundary Trail

To Windy Ridge

26

To Ryan Lake

To Norway Pass

Norway Pass Trailhead and parking

P

43 Ghost Lake (Trail 1H)

See Map on Page 170

Type of hike: Day hike or backpack, out and back.
Total distance: 1.2 miles.
Difficulty Easy.
Best months: Mid June– September.
Elevation gain: Minimal.
Trailhead elevation: 3,710 at junction with Boundary Trail.
Permits: None.
Maps: MSHNVM or Spirit Lake East USGS quad.
Starting point: Junction with Boundary Trail, 3.3 miles west of Bear Meadows Trailhead.

General description: The trail to Ghost Lake, an *internal* trail, is a short side trip off the Boundary Trail to a small lake with good fishing near the edge of the Blast Zone.

Finding the trailhead: See Hike 42 for driving directions to the Bear Meadows Trailhead and a description of the Boundary Trail which leads to the starting point of Ghost Lake Trail. The unmarked junction is a few feet east of the Clearwater Creek Bridge.

Key points:
0.6   Ghost Lake.

Ghost Lake.

The hike: From the unmarked junction with Boundary Trail, the Ghost Lake Trail leads north. The path is right on the edge between the green forest on your left and the silver snags to your right. The green timber is a pocket of trees that were shielded by a hill and survived the 1980

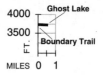

eruption. As the route heads up the east side of Clearwater Creek it passes a small meadow. Soon you leave the large green trees behind and travel through dead snags and fallen timber. The forest is regenerating itself; young trees are growing up between the snags. Huckleberries cover the ground between the trees. The tread enters an area of pumice landslide debris 0.5 mile from the Boundary Trail. Here the path nearly disappears.

Turn left (west) on the pumice to reach the lakeshore. As you approach the lake several flat spots on the pumice make acceptable campsites. Mosquitoes can be bad at Ghost Lake so come prepared. Trout, some of them fairly good sized, are plentiful in the lake.

Options: This is an optional side trip off Boundary Trail. Ghost Lake Trail ends at Ghost Lake.

Camping & services: The closest developed campground is Iron Creek Campground, 9.7 miles south of Randle on FR 25. Other services can be obtained in Randle or Morton.

For more information: USDA Forest Service at Woods Creek Information Station or Pine Creek Information Station. See Appendix A.

44 Boundary Trail (Trail 1, Norway Pass Trailhead to Coldwater Trail)

Type of hike:	Backpack, out and back, with loop and shuttle options.
Total distance:	20.2 miles.
Difficulty:	Moderate to strenuous.
Best months:	July–September.
Elevation gain:	2,000 feet.
Trailhead elevation:	3,670 feet.
Permits:	A backcountry permit is required for camping.
Maps:	MSHNVM. Spirit Lake East and Spirit Lake West USGS quads. The Spirit Lake West quad does not show the trail.
Starting point:	Norway Pass Trailhead.

General description: This section of the Boundary Trail climbs through the Blast Zone from the trailhead to Norway Pass. It then follows the ridgeline west to the junction with the Coldwater Trail, passing Mount Margaret, The Dome, and Coldwater Peak along the way.

Finding the trailhead: Head north from Portland on Interstate 5 to Exit 21 at Woodland (21 miles north of the Columbia River Bridge). Then drive east for 27.5 miles on Washington 503 (which becomes WA 503 spur) to Cougar. Continue east through Cougar on WA 503 spur (which becomes Forest Road 90 at the Skamania County line) for another 18.6 miles to the junction with FR 25. Bear left (nearly straight ahead) and head northeast on FR 25 for 24.3 miles to the junction with FR 99.

From Seattle take I-5 south to Exit 133 at Tacoma and then follow WA 7 for 55 miles to Morton. From Morton drive east 17 miles to Randle. Turn right and take WA 131 then FR 25 south for 20 miles to the junction with FR 99.

Turn west on FR 99 and follow it for 8.8 miles to the junction with FR 26. Turn right on FR 26 and follow it 1 mile to the Norway Pass Trailhead. The trailhead is on the left (west) side of the road. GPS coordinates are 46 18.330 N 122 04.948 W.

Parking & trailhead facilities: There are restrooms and adequate parking at the trailhead.

Key points:
    1.1   Junction with Independence Ridge Trail.
    2.1   Norway Pass.
    2.8   Junction with Lakes Trail.
    4.9   Junction with Whittier Trail.
    5.6   Junction with Mount Margaret Trail.
    9.7   Junction with Coldwater Peak Trail.
    10.1 Junction with Coldwater Trail.

The hike: The Boundary Trail crosses a wooden bridge over the Green River as it leaves the Norway Pass Trailhead. The river is just a small stream here. Climbing through blown-down timber and huckleberry bushes it reaches a small saddle 0.3 mile from the trailhead. In

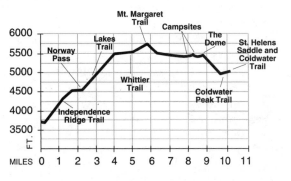

August, fireweed brightens the stark scene of dead, standing snags. In the saddle grows a patch of foxglove. Their bell-shaped flowers add a splash of color in July. Continuing to climb the route makes a couple of switchbacks and reaches the junction with the Independence Ridge Trail 1.1 miles from the trailhead. See Hike 40 for information on the Independence Ridge Trail.

Mount St. Helens from near Mount Margaret.

The Boundary Trail turns right at the junction. Climbing to the northwest the path soon crosses a ridgeline. It then cuts back into a gully and crosses a tiny stream, which may be dry by midsummer. After crossing the gully the tread traverses along the northeast-facing slope to Norway Pass, elevation 4,520 feet, and the junction with the Independence Pass Trail. Mountain ash and huckleberries line the trail as it approaches the pass, 2.1 miles from the trailhead. See Hike 39 for details on the Independence Pass Trail and a possible loop option. At the pass Spirit Lake and Mount St. Helens come into view to the south. From Norway Pass to the junction with the Coldwater Trail at the end of this hike description the Boundary Trail is the boundary of the Restricted Zone. No camping or travel is allowed on the left (south) side of the trail.

As it leaves the pass the path climbs a ridge a short way, then bears right to traverse around the head of a basin. Bleeding hearts grow in a few damp spots on the slopes. The route switches back to the left 0.5 mile from the pass. Another 0.2 mile and you reach the junction with the Lakes Trail, at 4,870 feet elevation. The junction, 2.8 miles from the Norway Pass Trailhead, was not marked when I hiked this trail in August 1998, but it may be in the future. The Lakes Trail turns to the right and climbs to the northeast over Bear Pass. See Hike 46 for a description of the Lakes Trail.

Past the junction with the Lakes Trail you climb another 0.4 mile to a saddle. This saddle, at 5,120 feet elevation, is a good place to stop, rest, and enjoy the view. Grizzly Lake is below to the northeast and Mount Rainier's icy summit rises above the hills in the distance. Far to the northwest, on very clear days, the Olympic Mountains can be seen on the horizon.

Soon after leaving the saddle the route begins a traverse along the south side of the ridge. Far in the distance, to the south-southeast, Mount Jefferson breaks the horizon between Mount St. Helens and Mount Hood. Columbines and cat's ear lilies dot the ground. After crossing several small gullies and ridges the route reaches the ridgeline again in a small saddle, 1.9 miles from the junction with the Lakes Trail. Step a few feet to the right here for a view of Boot and Obscurity Lakes far below to the northeast. Another 0.2 mile will bring you to the junction with the Whittier Trail. This unmarked junction, at 5,560 feet elevation, is in another saddle. The Whittier Trail turns to the right (north) to traverse Mount Whittier. See Hike 45 for the details about this rough trail.

As you leave the junction with the Whittier Trail the Boundary Trail traverses south around a high point on the ridge to another saddle, then traverses an east-facing slope to the junction with the Mount Margaret Trail. This unmarked junction, at 5,700 feet elevation, is 0.7 mile from the Whittier Trail and 5.6 miles from the Norway Pass Trailhead. Take the time to climb the 0.2 mile west to the summit of Mount Margaret and take in the great view.

The Boundary Trail descends southwest then west from the Mount Margaret junction. It crosses a spur ridge and makes a couple of switchbacks before reaching another saddle. When I hiked this trail in early August, there was a large herd of elk below this saddle to the north. In another saddle, 0.4 mile farther along, a vague path marked "1–f" turns left and climbs a small hill to a viewpoint and an abandoned volcano monitoring site.

Another couple hundred yards along the Boundary Trail, on the north side of the hill with the monitoring site, a path turns right (north) to a campsite. There is a restroom and tent platforms at this designated site, and water is available from a small stream just to the east. The route then traverses around the south side of a high point on the ridge to another saddle where there is another campsite with a restroom, tent platforms, and water.

After traversing the slopes above St. Helens Lake, and passing several more small saddles you will come to the junction with the Coldwater Peak Trail. Wild strawberries cover much of the ground between the downed timber beside the trail. At the junction, 1.1 miles from the last camp, the route to Coldwater Peak turns to the right (west). See Hike 9 for the details of the Coldwater Peak hike to the summit. Leave the junction and head south along the Boundary Trail for another 0.4 mile to the junction with the Coldwater Trail. The junction is in the St. Helens Saddle at 5,080 feet elevation. See Hike 6 to continue along the Boundary Trail to Johnston Ridge or to take the Coldwater Trail to the Lakes Trailhead.

Options: Options for loops and side trips along the Boundary Trail abound. The Whittier Trail north from the Boundary Trail to the Lakes Trail makes a spectacular but demanding loop backpack. The Lakes Trail heads east, passes several lakes, and climbs over Bear Pass back to the Boundary Trail. See Hikes 45 and 46 for more information.

Boundary Trail (Trail 1, Norway Pass Trailhead to Coldwater Trail)

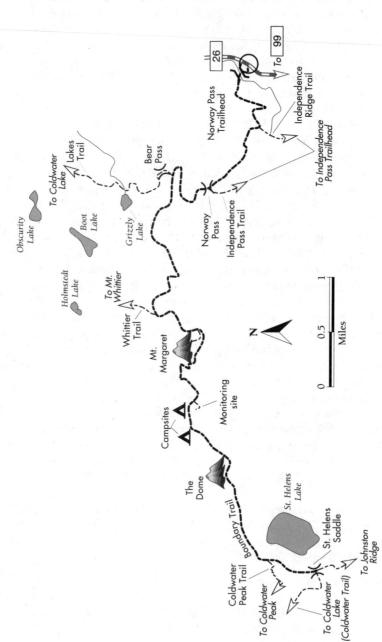

A short side hike to the summit of Mount Margaret is a must do, and the climb to Coldwater Peak is a should do. See Hike 9 for details of the hike to Coldwater Peak.

Hikes requiring a long car shuttle can be made via either continuing on the Boundary Trail to Johnston Ridge or taking the Coldwater Trail and the Lakes Trail to the Lakes Trailhead. See Hike 6 for details.

Camping & services: The closest developed campground is Iron Creek Campground, 9.7 miles south of Randle on FR 25. Other services can be obtained in Randle or Morton.

For more information: USDA Forest Service at Woods Creek Information Station or Pine Creek Information Station. See Appendix A.

45 Mount Whittier (Trail 214)

Type of hike:	Backpack, part of loop.
Total distance:	2.3 miles.
Difficulty:	Very strenuous.
Best months:	July–September.
Elevation gain:	220 feet.
Trailhead elevation:	5,560 feet at the junction with Boundary Trail.
Permits:	A backcountry permit is required for camping.
Maps:	MSHNVM. Spirit Lake West USGS quad covers the area but this trail is not shown.
Starting point:	Junction with Boundary Trail 4.9 miles west of Norway Pass Trailhead.

General description: A very rough and exposed scramble along the crest of Mount Whittier. This *internal* trail connects the Boundary Trail and the Lakes Trail.

Finding the trailhead: Follow the driving directions in Hike 44, then follow the Boundary Trail, also described in Hike 44, for 4.9 miles to the unmarked junction with the Whittier Trail.

Key points:
- 0.5   Ridgeline of Mount Whittier.
- 1.1   Summit of Mount Whittier.
- 2.3   Junction with Lakes Trail.

The hike: Don't use this route unless you are an agile and experienced hiker. Some mountaineering experience would be of great help here. This is also not a trail for children. The Whittier Trail traverses north from the junction with the Boundary Trail, across a slope covered with

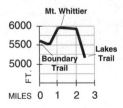

Author on the Whittier Trail. MIKE BARSTAD PHOTO

small firs and hemlocks. Silver snags stick up between the small trees and lupine covers the open spots in between. You will reach a ridgeline 0.5 mile from Boundary Trail. Boot and Obscurity Lakes come into view below to the northeast as you reach the ridgeline.

On the ridge the path quickly deteriorates. In order to follow the route you will need to watch very closely for any and all signs of it. You will descend and climb steps, scramble over steep sections of rock, and traverse very exposed slopes along this narrow path. Holmstedt Lake comes into view 0.4 mile after reaching the ridge. A little more rough scrambling brings you to the summit of Mount Whittier.

On the summit, at 5,883 feet above sea level, the views in all directions are breathtaking. Panhandle Lake sits in a canyon below Holmstedt Lake. Shovel Lake sparkles beneath cliffs to the north. Below and south is Coldwater Canyon. Far down the canyon is the upper end of Coldwater Lake. Coldwater Lake is one of the lakes that were formed by the 1980 eruption and resulting mudflow.

Leaving the summit the rough path continues along the crest for another mile. Then the route bears to the right and descends north to the junction with the Lakes Trail. The junction, at 5,190 feet elevation, is in the saddle between Shovel and Snow lakes.

The hike or scramble along this ridge is well worth the effort, but be very careful. A very serious fall is a real possibility in many spots.

Options: By turning right onto the Lakes Trail and hiking east back to the Boundary Trail you can make a loop. See Hikes 46 and 44 for more information.

Turning left on the Lakes Trail will eventually take you to the Lakes Trailhead. See Hikes 46 and 6 for the details.

Camping & services: The closest developed campground is Iron Creek Campground, 9.7 miles south of Randle on FR 25. Other services can be obtained in Randle or Morton.

For more information: USDA Forest Service at Woods Creek Information Station or Pine Creek Information Station. See Appendix A.

Mount Whittier (Trail 214)

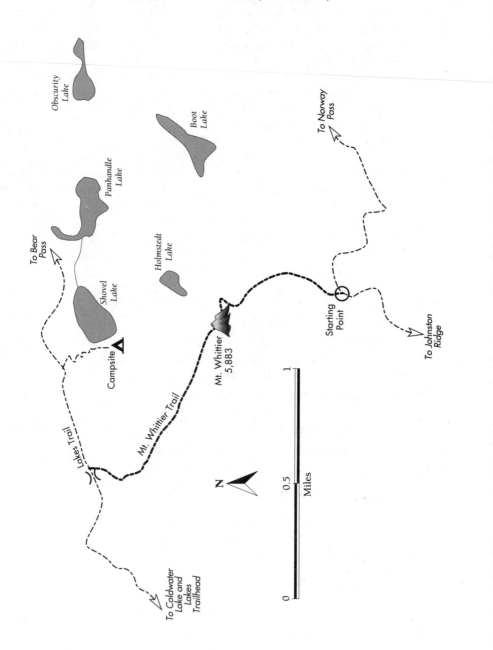

Obscurity Lake

Boot Lake

To Norway Pass

Panhandle Lake

To Bear Pass

Holmstedt Lake

Shovel Lake

Starting Point

To Johnston Ridge

Campsite

Mt. Whittier 5,883

Mt. Whittier Trail

Lakes Trail

N

To Coldwater Lake and Lakes Trailhead

0   0.5   1
Miles

46 Lakes Trail (Trail 211)

Type of hike:	Backpack, out and back, with loop and shuttle options.
Total distance:	19.2 miles.
Difficulty:	Strenuous.
Best months:	July–September.
Elevation gain/loss:	800 feet/3,000+ feet.
Trailhead elevation:	4,870 at junction with Boundary Trail.
Permits:	Backcountry permit is required for camping.
Maps:	MSHNVM. Spirit Lake East and Spirit Lake West USGS quads. The Spirit Lake West quad does not show the trail.
Starting point:	Junction with Boundary Trail 2.8 miles west of Norway Pass Trailhead.

General description: The Lakes Trail, an *internal* trail, first climbs over Bear Pass, then descends to Grizzly Lake. From Grizzly Lake the route passes four more lakes as it undulates through the Blast Zone to the junction with the Coldwater Trail.

Finding the trailhead: Head north from Portland on Interstate 5 to Exit 21 at Woodland (21 miles north of the Columbia River Bridge). Then drive east for 27.5 miles on Washington 503 (which becomes WA 503 spur) to Cougar. Continue east through Cougar on WA 503 spur (which becomes Forest Road 90 at the Skamania County line) for another 18.6 miles to the junction with FR 25. Bear left (nearly straight ahead) and head northeast on FR 25 for 24.3 miles to the junction with FR 99.

From Seattle take I-5 south to Exit 133 at Tacoma and then follow WA 7 for 55 miles to Morton. From Morton drive east 17 miles to Randle. Turn right and take WA 131 then FR 25 south for 20 miles to the junction with FR 99.

Turn west on FR 99 and follow it for 8.8 miles to the junction with FR 26. Turn right on FR 26 and follow it 1 mile to the Norway Pass Trailhead. The trailhead is on the left (west) side of the road. There are restrooms at the trailhead but no other facilities.

From the Norway Pass Trailhead hike west on the Boundary Trail, as described in Hike 44, for 2.8 miles to the junction with the Lakes Trail.

Key points:
- 0.1 Bear Pass.
- 1.2 Grizzly Lake.
- 2.7 Obscurity Lake.
- 3.7 Panhandle Lake.
- 5.3 Junction with Shovel Lake Trail, GPS 46 20.134 N 122 08.245 W.
- 5.9 Junction with Whittier Trail at Pleasant Pass.
- 6.4 Snow Lake.
- 9.6 Junction with Coldwater Trail.

Lakes Trail (Trail 211)

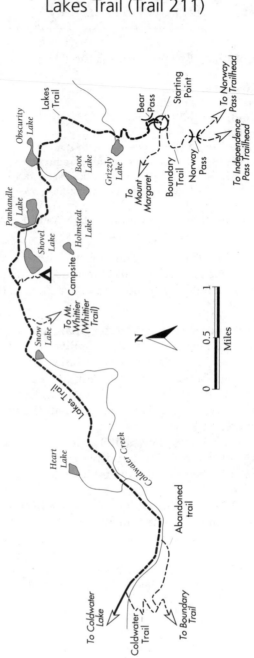

The hike: The Lakes Trail climbs to the northeast from the junction with the Boundary Trail. The sandy route makes its way through mountain ash and huckleberry bushes as it ascends to Bear Pass, elevation 4,940 feet. Near the pass, 0.1 mile from Boundary Trail, asters and everlastings grow from the pumice soil. The route

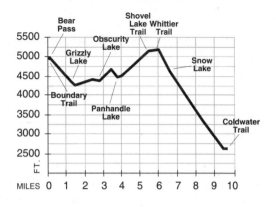

crosses Bear Pass and descends a north slope covered with small fir trees. Grizzly Lake comes into view 0.4 mile after crossing the pass. The path descends on the left side of a small ridge, then crosses a small saddle, before reaching Grizzly Lake at 4,300 feet elevation. Cross the outlet of Grizzly Lake, 1.2 miles from the Boundary Trail, on stepping stones. After the lake, the path crosses slopes covered with fireweed and everlastings that bloom in August. The route crosses a small stream as it rounds the head of a basin 0.4 mile farther along. Monkeyflowers grow next to the stream. A little farther along the path follows a ledge for a short distance, then passes beneath a cliff. The tread crosses a small stream as it goes by Obscurity Lake. At the northeast end of the lake a path leads a few yards to the left to a campsite and restroom. You are now 2.7 miles from the Boundary Trail.

After leaving Obscurity Lake, the trail heads southwest along the inlet stream for a short distance, then crosses the stream on a single log bridge. This stream is also the outlet from Boot Lake, which is about 0.5 mile to the southwest. The route now climbs, sometimes steeply, passing a waterfall to the saddle between Obscurity Lake and Panhandle Lake. At the saddle Panhandle Lake comes into view. The path descends to a creek crossing, then traverses well above Panhandle Lake. As you traverse above the lake there will be a trail to the right. This trail leads to a campsite with a restroom down on the lakeshore. The Lakes Trail now descends gently and crosses the inlet stream at the west end of Panhandle Lake, 3.8 miles from the Boundary Trail, at 4,490 feet elevation. This stream is also the outlet stream from Shovel Lake. Monkeyflowers and cow parsnips cluster along the stream and among the groves of mountain ash.

Now the route really begins to climb. The path climbs to a ridgeline then turns west to ascend the ridge. You climb along the right side of the ridge for a short distance. Then the path makes a switchback and climbs to the crest. As you look ahead along the nearly vertical left side of the ridge, Shovel Lake comes into view. You continue up the ridge making a couple more switchbacks. One mile above the stream crossing at the west end of Panhandle Lake the trail bears right off the ridgeline and the grade moderates. The tread now traverses the north slope of the ridge through standing dead snags and small fir trees. Lupine blooms along this slope in August. You reach the junction with the trail to Shovel Lake 0.5 mile after leaving the ridgeline.

The junction with Shovel Lake Trail is in a saddle, at 5,160 feet elevation, on the same ridge you have been climbing since leaving Panhandle Lake. Shovel Lake is in view far below to the left. The poor path to Shovel Lake turns to the left (southeast) at the junction sign. See Hike 47 for a description of the Shovel Lake Trail. Leaving the junction the trail traverses a south-facing slope for 0.6 mile to Pleasant Pass and the junction with the Mount Whittier Trail. Whittier Trail turns off to the south and follows a rough ridge to the Boundary Trail. See Hike 45 for the details of the Mount Whittier Trail.

From Pleasant Pass at 5,190 feet elevation, the Lakes Trail begins its long descent into Coldwater Canyon. The route descends through blown-down timber and crosses green slopes for 0.5 mile to Snow Lake. Below Snow Lake the descent continues at a fairly even grade. Here small firs grow between the downed logs and snags. The route skirts the base of a cliff then crosses several slide areas. As you near the bottom of the canyon alders appear next to the trail. The path crosses the outlet stream from Heart Lake 1.8 miles after passing Snow Lake. At another 0.8 mile is the junction with the old Coldwater Trail. This section of the Coldwater Trail has recently been abandoned in favor of a new route farther west. Hike another 0.6 mile to the junction with the Coldwater Trail.

From the junction the Lakes Trail continues on to the Lakes Trailhead. The Coldwater Trail turns left and climbs out of the canyon to the south. To continue on the Lakes Trail see Hikes 6 and 4.

Options: There are several options for side trips and loop hikes off the Lakes Trail. The shortest loop involves turning south at Pleasant Pass on the Whittier Trail and following this difficult route over Mount Whittier to the Boundary Trail. Turn left (east) on the Boundary Trail and take it back to the junction with the Lakes Trail to complete the loop. See Hikes 45 and 44 for a description of these trails.

To make a longer loop, turn left (south) on the Coldwater Trail and follow it to the Boundary Trail. Then turn left on the Boundary Trail and hike north and east back to the junction with the Lakes Trail to complete the loop. See Hikes 6 and 44 for details.

Camping & services: The closest developed campground is Iron Creek Campground, 9.7 miles south of Randle on FR 25. Other services can be obtained in Randle or Morton.

For more information: USDA Forest Service at Woods Creek Information Station or Pine Creek Information Station. See Appendix A.

Grizzly Lake.

47 Shovel Lake (Trail 211C)

Type of hike:	Backpack, out and back.
Total distance:	1.6 miles.
Difficulty:	Strenuous.
Best months:	July–September.
Elevation loss:	510 feet.
Trailhead elevation:	5,160 feet at the junction with the Lakes Trail.
Permits:	Backcountry camping permit is required to camp.
Maps:	MSHNVM. Spirit Lake East USGS quad covers the area but does not show this trail.
Starting point:	Junction with the Lakes Trail 8.1 miles from Norway Pass Trailhead.

General description: A short but demanding side trip on an *internal* trail from a junction with the Lakes Trail to Shovel Lake.

Finding the trailhead: Follow the driving directions in Hike 44 to the Norway Pass Trailhead. Then hike, as described in Hike 44, 2.8 miles west on the Boundary Trail to the junction with the Lakes Trail. Follow the Lakes Trail, described in Hike 46, for 5.3 miles to the junction with the Shovel Lake Trail. There is a sign marking the junction. GPS coordinates at the junction are 46 20.134 N 122 08.245 W.

Key points:
0.8 Shovel Lake.

The hike: The sign at the junction says "Shovel Lake, 0.5 mile." This is a conservative estimate. The Shovel Lake Trail descends south from the junction with the Lakes Trail. Its pumice-covered path soon becomes very vague. Shovel Lake is in view to the southeast and far below as you descend through the snags and blown-down timber. Mountain ash, everlasting, and

beargrass grow between the logs, adding some color to the gray landscape. The rounded form of Mount Adams highlights the eastern horizon.

The route switchbacks down the slope, but it is hard to follow it exactly. Watch ahead for logs that have been cut to make way for the trail. Even if you lose the trail you can see your destination ahead. Shortly before reaching the campsite the path flattens. Head south across the pumice flats to the campsite at Shovel Lake.

Options: The options are camping and fishing at the lake, as this is an out and back side trip from the Lakes Trail.

Camping & services: The closest developed campground is Iron Creek Campground 9.7 miles south of Randle on FR 25. Other services can be obtained in Randle or Morton.

Shovel Lake and Mount Whittier.

Shovel Lake (Trail 211C)

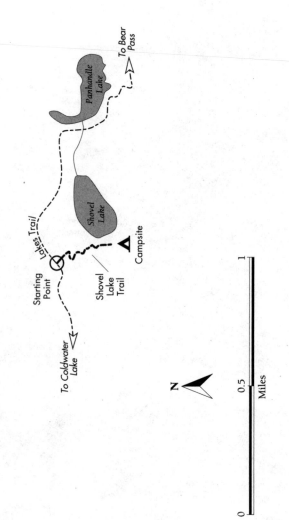

To Bear Pass

Panhandle Lake

Shovel Lake

Lakes Trail

Starting Point

Shovel Lake Trail

Campsite

To Coldwater Lake

N

0   0.5   1
Miles

Northern Region
Access from US 12 and Forest Roads 25, 26

The Northern Region is the outback country of Mount St. Helens National Volcanic Monument. Road access to the trailheads in this region is generally over gravel roads that may or may not be marked. The exceptions to this are **Hike 59 Woods Creek Watchable Wildlife Loop** and **Hike 60 Iron Creek Falls,** which are along Forest Road 25 south of Randle.

From the Goat Mountain Trailhead, on FR 2612 near Ryan Lake, **Hike 48 Goat Mountain,** follows the ridge along the northern edge of the Blast Zone then descends slightly in to the virgin forest to the north, allowing the hiker to experience both environments on the same hike. The short hike to the summit of Strawberry Mountain described in **Hike 57** provides a view of most of the Blast Zone as well as the Mount Margaret Backcountry. **Hike 58** to Strawberry Lake follows abandoned roads to a campsite next to a lake surrounded by standing silver snags. The trails in the Vanson Peak area in **Hikes 53, 54, 55, and 56** are mostly in virgin woods and make a great place for a few days of easy backpacking and fishing.

The Northern Region receives only light to moderate use, so it's the best place to hike in the monument if you want to stay away from crowds.

Mount Rainier from Goat Mountain.

Northern Region
Overview Map

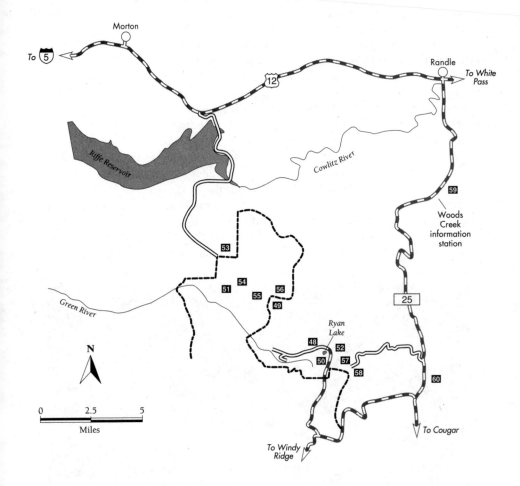

48 Goat Mountain (Trail 217, To Vanson Peak Trail)

Type of hike:	Day hike or backpack, out and back, with loop option.
Total distance:	16.6 miles
Difficulty:	Moderate to strenuous.
Best months:	July–September
Elevation gain:	1800 feet.
Trailhead elevation:	3,280 feet.
Permits:	None
Maps:	MSHNVM or Spirit Lake East, Cowlitz Falls and Vanson Peak USGS quads.
Starting point:	Goat Mountain Trailhead, near Ryan Lake.

General description: The Goat Mountain Trail climbs the east ridge of Goat Mountain. It then follows the ridge with its beautiful alpine scenery for some distance before descending to Deadman Lake. The route continues through the forest from the lake to a junction with the Goat Creek Trail near Vanson Peak.

Finding the trailhead: Head north from Portland on Interstate 5 to Exit 21 at Woodland (21 miles north of the Columbia River Bridge). Then drive east for 27.5 miles on Washington 503 (which becomes WA 503 spur) to Cougar. Continue east through Cougar on WA 503 spur (which becomes Forest Road 90 at the Skamania County line) for another 18.6 miles to the junction with FR 25. Bear left (nearly straight ahead) and head northeast on FR 25 for 24.3 miles to the junction with FR 99.

From Seattle take I-5 south to Exit 133 at Tacoma and then follow WA 7 for 55 miles to Morton. From Morton drive east 17 miles to Randle on U.S. Highway 12. Turn right and take WA 131 then FR 25 south for 20 miles to the junction with FR 99.

Turn right (west) on FR 99 and follow it for 8.8 miles to the junction with FR 26. Turn right on FR 26 and drive 5 miles north. Turn left (west) on FR 2612, just past Ryan Lake. Follow FR 2612 for 0.5 mile to the trailhead where Goat Mountain Trail crosses the road. There is a parking area on the right side of FR 2612 at the trailhead. GPS coordinates are 46 21.368 N 122 04.212 W.

Parking & trailhead facilities: There is parking for several cars but no other facilities at the trailhead.

Key points:
- 3.7   Goat Mountain Saddle.
- 5.4   Junction with Deadman Lake and Deep Lake Trails.
- 5.5   Junction with Tumwater Mountain Trail. GPS 46 22.852 N 122 07.754 W.
- 8.3   4-way junction with Goat Creek and Vanson Peak trails. GPS 46 24.238 N 122 09.167 W.

The hike: Where Goat Mountain Trail begins you are still inside but very near the edge of the Blast Zone. The route starts out as a roadbed through the young forest of douglas and noble fir. You soon leave the roadbed and wind your way up to a rounded ridgeline. The route climbs the ridge and crosses another roadbed 0.7 mile from

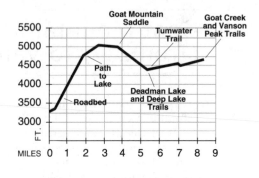

the trailhead. Above the road you climb steeply and enter larger timber. The route then traverses north-northeast for 0.6 mile to the main ridge of Goat Mountain. On the ridge the path switches back to the southwest. You now traverse a slope through the timber for 0.6 mile to the top edge of a clearcut. Here the route starts a series of four switchbacks taking you up to the ridgeline. At the edge of the clearcut, penstemon and paintbrush dot the slope. As you climb, huckleberries line the trail. Watch for the beautiful leopard lilies that grow here.

As you reach the ridge Mount Rainier comes into view to the north. The route heads west along the semi-open ridge, through groves of subalpine fir and hemlock. A poor, hard-to-see path turns to the right 0.3 mile after reaching the ridge. This path leads northwest through a meadow for a couple hundred yards to an unnamed lake and campsite. The lake has no fish.

Unnamed lake on Goat Mountain.

The Goat Mountain Trail soon leaves the ridgeline to traverse the south slope. The route continues to climb, regaining the ridgeline 0.4 mile farther along. This is the highest point on Goat Mountain Trail at 5,080 feet elevation. You then follow the semi-open ridge for 0.6 mile. Penstemon and paintbrush grow from the rocky soil and bloom in July. The tread bears left off the ridge again 2.7 miles from the trailhead. You will stay on this south-facing slope for 1 mile to the Goat Mountain Saddle, closely approaching the ridgeline only once. The slope becomes more open as you head west. Wonderful flower gardens grace this slope. Larkspur, lupine, and leopard lilies are common, as is beargrass.

At Goat Mountain Saddle you cross the ridgeline and begin to descend. North of the ridgeline the vegetation becomes much more dense. Below to the right are a couple of ponds and Mount Rainier is again in view. The route descends this brushy slope, then traverses beneath cliffs. Shortly you will enter larger timber. The path winds and switchbacks its way down through the timber. The junction with the trail to Deadman Lake is reached 5.4 miles from the trailhead, at 4,370 feet elevation. At the junction, Deadman Lake is 0.2 mile to the left (southwest). There are several good campsites and a restroom at Deadman Lake. Fishing can be good at Deadman Lake and swimming is quite good too. Another path turns to the right at the same junction. This path leads 0.7 mile to Deep Lake. See Hike 49 for the details on the hike to Deep Lake.

After passing the junction with the trails to Deadman Lake and Deep Lake it is only 0.1 mile to the junction with Tumwater Mountain Trail. Tumwater Mountain Trail turns to the right (northeast). See Hike 56 for a description of the Tumwater Mountain Trail.

Leaving the junction with the Tumwater Mountain Trail, the Goat Mountain Trail climbs very gently to the northwest. As you hike through the forest, leopard lilies and lupine greet you with their bright blooms. The route climbs to a ridgeline. It then follows the ridge to the junction with Goat Creek and Vanson Peak Trails. As you near the junction Mount Rainier and Goat Rocks are in view to the north and northeast. In July spiraea blooms next to the trail in scattered spots. At the four-way junction in a timbered saddle, Goat Creek Trail turns hard to the right (southeast). The Vanson Peak Trail is straight ahead (north). The Goat Mountain Trail descends heading northwest. For a trail description of the rest of the Goat Mountain Trail and the Vanson Peak Trail, see Hike 53. Goat Creek Trail is Hike 55.

Options: Make a loop by continuing another 0.8 mile on the Goat Mountain Trail to the junction with the Vanson Ridge Trail. Then turn left and descend the Vanson Ridge Trail to the Green River Trail. Hike east back to the junction with the Goat Mountain Trail, then turn left and follow the Goat Mountain Trail a short distance to FR 2612. Cross the road to the parking area at the Goat Mountain Trailhead, completing the 20.8 mile loop.

The side trip to Deep Lake is easy from a camp at Deadman Lake. See Hike 49 for more information.

Goat Mountain (Trail 217)

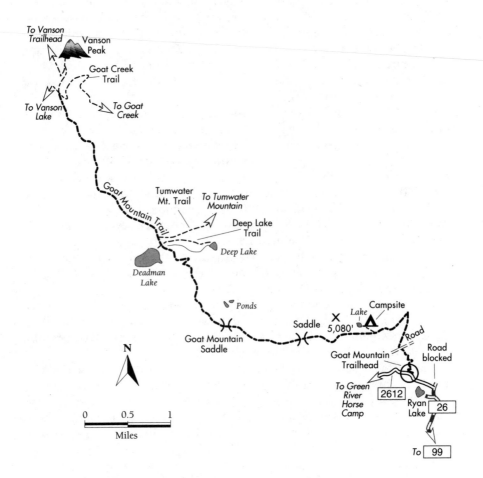

Camping & services: Dispersed camping is allowed in the Gifford Pinchot National Forest outside the monument. Green River Horse Camp is a bit over a mile west of the trailhead on FR 2612. The camp is supposed to be reserved for horse camping, but when there are few or no horse parties it is often used by other campers. Except for the horse camp the closest developed campground is Iron Creek Campground, 9.7 miles south of Randle on FR 25. Other services can be obtained in Randle or Morton.

For more information: USDA Forest Service at Woods Creek Information Station or Pine Creek Information Station. See Appendix A.

49 Deep Lake (Trail 217E)

Type of hike: Day hike or backpack, out and back.
Total distance: 1.4 miles.
Difficulty: Strenuous.
Best months: July–September
Elevation loss: 380 feet.
Trailhead elevation: 4,370 at the junction with Goat Mountain Trail.
Permits: None.
Maps: MSHNVM. Cowlitz Falls and Vanson Peak USGS quads.
Starting point: Junction with the Goat Mountain Trail near Deadman Lake.

General description: Deep Lake Trail is a short but demanding hike on an *internal* trail from the junction with Goat Mountain Trail near Deadman Lake down to Deep Lake.

Finding the trailhead: Follow the driving directions in Hike 48. Then hike the Goat Mountain Trail, also described in Hike 48, to the junction with the Deep Lake Trail. The unmarked trail is directly across the Goat Mountain Trail from the path to Deadman Lake.

Key points:
  0.7   Deep Lake

The hike: Turn northeast off the Goat Mountain Trail and follow the path through the open woods. This path was at one time a section of the Goat Mountain Trail. This section is now abandoned in favor of the present route. After hiking 0.2 mile turn left on a much poorer path. The spot where you turn off is 100 yards before you reach a stream

Deep Lake (Trail 217E)

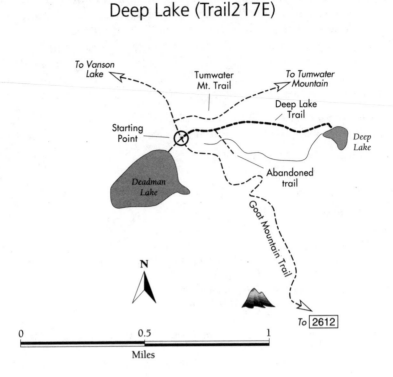

crossing with the remains of a wooden bridge. If you reach the stream, turn around and backtrack 100 yards then turn east on the poor path. Soon after leaving the old trail the route becomes steep and braided. The path descends a steep hillside to the shore of Deep Lake.

There are lots of trout in Deep Lake, but the brush-lined shore can make fishing a little difficult.

Options: A good option would be to camp at Deadman Lake, then take a day hike to Deep Lake and back.

Camping & services: Dispersed camping is allowed in the Gifford Pinchot National Forest outside the monument. The Green River Horse Camp is slightly over a mile west of the Goat Mountain Trailhead on Forest Road 2612. The camp is supposed to be reserved for horse camping, but when there are few or no horse parties it is often used by other campers. Except for the horse camp the closest developed campground is Iron Creek Campground, 9.7 miles south of Randle on FR 25. Other services can be obtained in Randle or Morton.

For more information: USDA Forest Service at Woods Creek Information Station or Pine Creek Information Station. See Appendix A.

Deep Lake.

50 Green River (Trail 213)

Type of hike:	Day hike or backpack, long shuttle or out and back with loop option.
Total distance:	11.3 miles, shuttle, 22.6 miles out and back.
Difficulty:	Easy to moderate.
Best months:	June–mid-October.
Elevation loss:	1,580 feet.
Trailhead elevation:	3,460 feet.
Permits:	None.
Maps:	MSHNVM or Spirit Lake East, Spirit Lake West and Vanson Peak USGS quads. The Weyerhaeuser Mount St. Helens Tree Farm map locates the west end of the trail.
Starting point:	Junction of the Green River Trail and Forest Road 26.

General description: A long but gentle hike down the Green River Valley, starting in the Blast Zone, then passing through old growth forest.

Finding the trailhead: Head north from Portland on Interstate 5 to Exit 21 at Woodland (21 miles north of the Columbia River Bridge). Then drive east for 27.5 miles on Washington 503 (which becomes WA 503 spur) to Cougar. Continue east through Cougar on WA 503 spur (which becomes Forest Road 90 at the Skamania County line) for another 18.6 miles to the junction with FR 25. Bear left (nearly straight ahead) and head northeast on FR 25 for 24.3 miles to the junction with FR 99.

From Seattle take I-5 south to Exit 133 at Tacoma and then follow WA 7 for 55 miles to Morton. From Morton drive east 17 miles to Randle on U.S. Highway 12. Turn right and take WA 131 then FR 25 south for 20 miles to the junction with FR 99.

Turn right (west) on FR 99 and follow it for 8.8 miles to the junction with FR 26. Turn right on FR 26 and drive 4.5 miles to the point where Green River Trail crosses the road. There are small trail signs on both sides of FR 26.

To reach Green River Horse Camp, where many hikers will want to start this hike, drive another 0.5 mile north to the junction with FR 2612, just after passing the Ryan Lake parking area. Turn left on FR 2612 and follow it 1.6 miles to the entrance road for Green River Horse Camp. There is a sign pointing to the camp, which is some distance off FR 2612.

To reach Green River Trail where it crosses FR 2612 continue west past the horse camp entrance on FR 2612 for 0.9 mile. There is a small trail sign where the trail crosses the road. Be sure to bear left at the junction 0.1 mile before reaching the trail crossing.

To reach the west end of the Green River Trail where this hike ends, take Exit 49 off Interstate 5. Drive east on Washington 504 for 23.9 miles to the junction with Weyerhaeuser Road 2500. There is a small sign at the junction. Follow Road 2500 for 14.1 miles to the junction with Road 2800. Turn right and follow Road 2800 for 7 miles. Be careful not to take Road 3900 which bears right 2.9 miles after leaving Road 2500. Road 2800 becomes Road 2500 after going the 7 miles. Continue on Road 2500 for 4.2 more miles to a bridge over the Green River. The trailhead is just across the bridge on the north side of the river. There is no sign pointing out this trailhead. Road 2800 is rough and steep; a high-clearance vehicle is required.

If you wish to reach the west end of the Green River Trail without driving the rough Road 2800, go straight ahead at the junction with Road 2800, 14.1 miles after leaving WA 504. You will be able to drive 1.6 more miles to where the road is blocked. From here it is 1.8 more miles along the closed and washed-out road to the trailhead.

A good map is a big help in finding this out-of-the-way trailhead. I would suggest you get a Weyerhaeuser Mount St. Helens Tree Farm map.

Parking & trailhead facilities: Green River Horse Camp has ample parking, restrooms, and water for horses. This water can be boiled, filtered, or treated for human use.

The other places where there is road access to Green River Trail have parking for a couple of cars but no other facilities.

Key points:
0.7	Junction with Goat Mountain Trail.
1.3	Green River Horse Camp. GPS 46 20.978 N 122 05.079 W.
2.9	Trail crosses FR 2612. GPS 46 20.998 N 122 06.576 W.
4.9	Mount St. Helens National Volcanic Monument boundary.
8.3	Junction with Vanson Ridge Trail. GPS 46 23.114 N 122 10.817 W.
11.3	Road 2500. GPS 46 23.357 N 122 13.608 W.

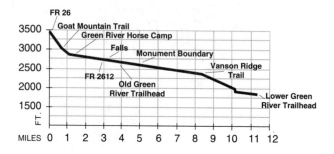

The hike: The Green River Trail was built in the late nineteenth century to provide access to the mines along the Green River Valley. Very few hikers will hike the entire length of this trail at one time. Mountain bikers and horsemen and women do ride the full length occasionally. The main reason hikers use parts of Green River Trail is to make connections with other trails. This description takes you from east to west down the river.

Where the Green River Trail crosses FR 26 you are within the devastated Blast Zone of the 1980 eruption of Mount St. Helens. The route starts as a roadbed, heading west. After descending gently along this road for a couple hundred yards, through a young Douglas-fir forest, the trail turns to the right. There is a sign marking the place where the path leaves the roadbed. The wide tread heads northwest to the junction with the Goat Mountain Trail 0.7 mile from FR 26. The Goat Mountain Trail turns north and climbs to the Goat Mountain Trailhead 0.5 mile away. The Green River Trail bears left at the junction and continues west. You will cross a wooden bridge as you hike through the young forest to the Green River Horse Camp.

The Green River Horse Camp, 1.3 miles from FR 26 at 2,850 feet elevation, is where most hikers and bikers begin their trip down the Green River Valley. There are several campsites, a restroom, and horse facilities at the camp. The trail cuts through a corner of the parking area then heads on down the river. The route goes through a finger of large green timber 0.8 mile from the horse camp. The trail crosses FR 2612, 1.6 miles below the horse camp; this is the last place you can reach the trail by car until you get to Road 2500. Just past FR 2612 the path crosses a wooden bridge then comes close to the river on the edge of a little canyon. The river drops over falls as it enters the canyon.

Three quarters of a mile farther along you will reach the site of the old Green River Trailhead. This was the main upper Green River trailhead before mudslides closed the road used to reach it. Above the trail to the north on top of the mudslide debris seems to be a favorite bedding area for elk. The route soon crosses another slide. On the slide the route is marked with three large rock cairns. The path enters Mount St. Helens National Volcanic Monument 0.3 mile farther along. At the monument boundary you are 4.9 miles from FR 26.

Just past the monument boundary the tread enters old-growth forest. You will hike through large old growth most of the way to the junction with the Vanson Ridge Trail. Just before reaching the junction the trail crosses a

Green River (Trail 213)

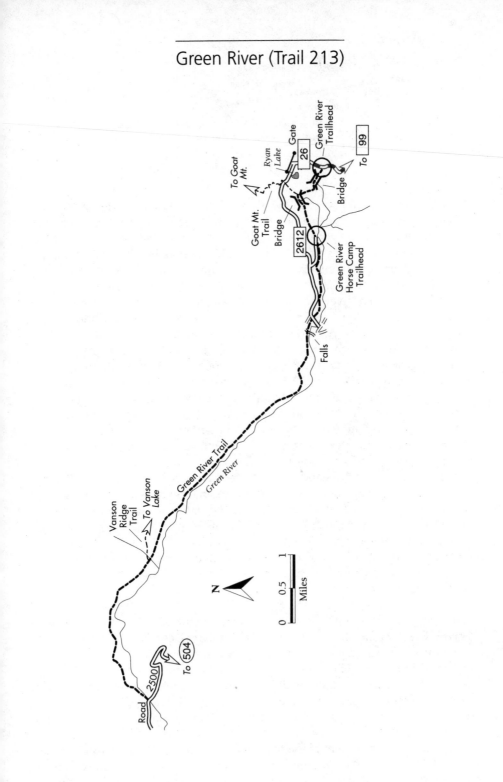

Green River Trailhead

To 99

Gate

Ryan Lake

26

To Goat Mt.

Goat Mt. Trail

Bridge

Bridge

2612

Green River Horse Camp Trailhead

Falls

Green River Trail

Green River

Vanson Ridge Trail

To Vanson Lake

N

0   0.5   1

Miles

Road 2500

To 504

wooden bridge over a clear little stream. At the junction 8.3 miles from FR 26, the Vanson Ridge Trail heads north and climbs to meet the Goat Mountain Trail near Vanson Lake. See Hike 51 for a description of the Vanson Ridge Trail.

The Green River Trail continues west from the junction. Besides the huge Douglas-fir trees the forest here also contains some very large red cedar. The route crosses several streams in the next mile. Just after crossing a wide, log-strewn streambed you may notice a path to your right. This path is the now abandoned Old Vanson Ridge Trail. Soon after passing the path the trail climbs a little. Then it descends again, making a couple of switchbacks. Half a mile past the last switchback the route leaves the old-growth forest.

You will cross several more small streams as the path winds through the alder brush and small trees. Foxglove and fireweed brighten the sides of the trail as it approaches its end at Road 2500. The route descends fairly steeply for a short distance before reaching the road.

Options: A good option is to use the Green River Trail as a return route for a hike along the Goat Mountain Trail. See Hikes 48 and 51 for details.

Camping & services: Dispersed camping is allowed in the Gifford Pinchot National Forest outside the monument. The Green River Horse Camp is supposed to be reserved for horse camping, but when there are few or no horse parties it is often used by other campers. Except for the horse camp the closest developed campground is Iron Creek Campground, 9.7 miles south of Randle on FR 25. Other services can be obtained in Randle or Morton.

For more information: USDA Forest Service at Woods Creek Information Station or Pine Creek Information Station. See Appendix A.

Green River.

51 Vanson Ridge (Trail 213A)

General description:	A descent of the mostly wooded Vanson Ridge from Goat Mountain Trail to Green River Trail.
Type of hike:	Day hike or backpack.
Total distance:	3.5 miles.
Difficulty:	Moderate.
Best months:	Late June–September.
Elevation loss:	1,780 feet.
Trailhead elevation:	4,120 feet at the junction with Goat Mountain Trail.
Permits:	None.
Maps:	MSHNVM. Vanson Ridge USGS quad covers the area but doesn't show this trail correctly.
Starting point:	Four-way junction with Goat Mountain Trail 0.9 mile from Vanson Lake Trailhead.

General Description: A descent of the mostly wooded Vanson Ridge on an *internal* trail from Goat Mountain Trail to Green River Trail.

Finding the trailhead: Follow the driving directions in Hike 53 to reach Vanson Trailhead. Then hike Goat Mountain Trail (sign at the trailhead says Lander Trail) for 0.9 mile to the 4-way junction near Vanson Meadows. There is no trail sign at this junction. GPS coordinates are 46 24.471 N 122 09.739 W.

If you want to reach the Vanson Ridge Trail at its lower end, use the driving directions to the Green River Trail in Hike 50. Hike up the Green River Trail for 3 miles to the junction with the Vanson Ridge Trail.

Key points:
- 0.1 Creek Crossing
- 2.0 Falls
- 2.8 Viewpoint
- 3.5 Junction with Green River Trail. GPS 46 23.114 N 122 10.871 W.

The hike: The Vanson Ridge Trail is seldomly hiked as a primary route. Usually hikers use this trail as a connector trail between the Goat Mountain Trail and the Green River Trail when making a loop hike.

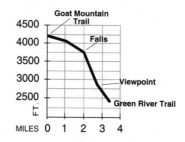

From the four-way junction with the Goat Mountain and the Vanson Meadow Trails, at 4,120 feet elevation, the Vanson Ridge Trail heads west. You will cross a creek, which is the outlet stream from Vanson Lake, 0.1 mile from the junction. The route is nearly level at first as it passes through forest and open areas. After about 0.6 mile the path starts to descend. The grade is gentle at first

Vanson Ridge (Trail 213A)

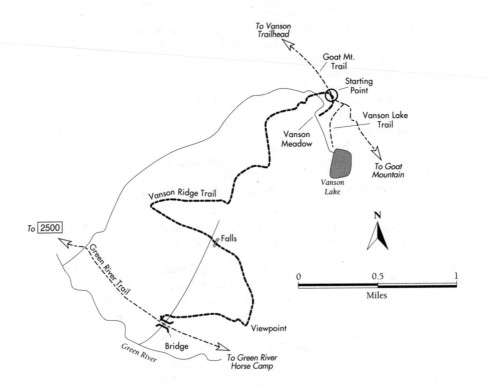

but soon steepens. Farther along, about 1.3 miles from the junction, the trail bears left to begin a descending traverse along a steep hillside. Half a mile into the traverse the route passes a waterfall.

Soon after passing the falls the path steepens as you descend to a viewpoint overlooking the Green River Valley. From the viewpoint the tread works its way down to the west. You will cross a stream shortly before reaching the junction with the Green River Trail. At the junction Weyerhaeuser Road 2500 is 3 miles to the right (west). The Green River Horse Camp and Trailhead is 7 miles to the left (east).

Options: Just before you start your hike down the Vanson Ridge Trail it is worthwhile to make a side trip to Vanson Meadow. From the unsigned, four-way junction, head southwest for 0.2 mile to the meadow. Through the small meadow runs the outlet stream from Vanson Lake. Hellebore, leopard lilies, and many other flowers cover the meadow in July. A campsite can be found next to the east edge of the meadow. The out-of-the-way meadow is a great place to relax and enjoy the sun.

Camping & services: Taidnapam Park, run by Tacoma Public Utilities, is a very nice place to camp. The park is located near the north end of the bridge over the Riffe Reservoir you crossed on the way to the trailhead. There is no camping allowed at the trailhead. Other services are available in Morton.

For more information: USDA Forest Service at Woods Creek Information Station or Cowlitz Valley Ranger Station in Randle. See Appendix A.

Vanson Meadow.

52 Ryan Lake Loop (Trail 222)

Type of hike:	Day hike, loop.
Total distance:	0.6 mile.
Difficulty:	Easy.
Best months:	June–mid-October.
Elevation gain:	Minimal.
Trailhead elevation:	3,300 feet.
Permits:	None.
Maps:	MSHNVM or Spirit Lake East USGS quad. No map is really needed to follow this short, well-maintained loop.
Starting point:	Ryan Lake parking area.

General description: A short loop hike through young forest and blown-down timber, just south of Ryan Lake. The loop offers excellent views of Ryan Lake and the Green River Valley.

Finding the trailhead: Head north from Portland on Interstate 5 to Exit 21 at Woodland (21 miles north of the Columbia River Bridge). Then drive east for 27.5 miles on Washington 503 (which becomes WA 503 spur) to Cougar. Continue east through Cougar on WA 503 spur (which becomes Forest Road 90 at the Skamania County line) for another 18.6 miles to the junction with FR 25. Bear left (nearly straight ahead) and head northeast on FR 25 for 24.3 miles to the junction with FR 99.

From Seattle take I-5 south to Exit 133 at Tacoma and then follow WA 7 for 55 miles to Morton. From Morton drive east 17 miles to Randle on U.S. Highway 12. Turn right and take WA 131 then FR 25 south for 20 miles to the junction with FR 99.

Turn right and head west on FR 99 for 8.8 miles to the junction with FR 26. Turn right on FR 26 and drive 5 miles to the Ryan Lake parking area. The parking area is on the left (west) side of the road.

Parking & trailhead facilities: There are restrooms and adequate parking at the trailhead.

Key points:
0.3 Bench
0.6 Return to parking area.

The hike: The Red Zone was a circle 10 miles wide drawn around Mount St. Helens in the months preceding the 1980 eruption that was supposed to be the danger area. It did not extend as far as Ryan Lake, so there were three campers here when the mountain blew. All three died in the hot gases and ash cloud that reached the lake shortly after 8:30 A.M. on May 18, 1980.

The Ryan Lake Loop Trail leaves from the south side of the parking area. You wind and switchback up through the young forest for 150 yards. The path then turns west leaving the young trees for a slope covered with silver snags and blown-down timber. Paintbrush line the trail as you pass beneath some fallen logs. Hike through a few more small trees and reach the rounded ridgeline. Between the snags, Ryan Lake sparkles below.

Some hikers will welcome a resting bench 0.3 mile from the parking area. Stop and read the interpretive sign next to the bench. The bench is at the high point of the trail, so from here the tread begins to descend. As you drop gently through the young Douglas-fir woods you will pass more interpretive signs. Take the time to stop and read them, and learn more about the regenerating forest. The route returns to the parking area 0.6 mile after leaving it.

Options: You may want to walk down to the shore of Ryan Lake from the parking area. At present there are no fish in Ryan Lake.

Camping & services: Dispersed camping is allowed in the Gifford Pinchot National Forest outside the monument. The Green River Horse Camp, a couple of miles to the west, on FR 2612, is supposed to be reserved for horse camping, but when there are few or no horse parties it is often used by other campers. Except for the horse camp the closest developed campground is at Iron Creek 9.7 miles south of Randle on FR 25. Other services can be obtained in Randle or Morton.

For more information: USDA Forest Service at Woods Creek Information Station or Pine Creek Information Station. See Appendix A.

Ryan Lake.

Ryan Lake Loop (Trail 222)

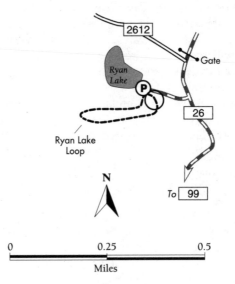

53 Vanson Peak Loop (Trails 217 and 217A)

See Map on Page 212

Type of hike: Day hike, loop.
Total distance: 3.9 miles.
Difficulty: Moderate
Best months: July–September.
Elevation gain/loss: 1,040 feet.
Trailhead elevation: 3,910 feet.
Permits: None.
Maps: MSHNVM or Vanson Peak USGS quad. The quad map shows the trail somewhat incorrectly.
Starting point: Vanson Trailhead.

General description: A loop hike through mostly old-growth forest to the top of Vanson Peak and back.

Finding the trailhead: From Portland drive north on Interstate 5 to Exit 68. Take Exit 68 and drive 36 miles east on U.S. Highway 12. Turn south off US 12, 5 miles east of Morton, onto Kosmos Road.

From Seattle take I-5 south to Exit 133 at Tacoma and then follow Washington 7 for 55 miles to Morton. From Morton drive east for 5 miles to Kosmos Road.

Drive south on Kosmos Road for 0.1 mile and then turn left on Champion Haul Road 100. Follow the haul road 4.2 miles to the bridge over Riffe Reservoir. Cross the bridge, then turn right on Road 400. Follow Road 400 for 7 miles to the junction with Road 430. Turn left on Road 430 and drive 3.3 miles to the junction with Road 436. (Don't take Road 433.) Turn left on Road 436. Then pass the junction with Road 2689. (Road 436 becomes very rough just before reaching the junction with Road 2689.) Shortly after passing the junction with Road 2689, turn right at an unmarked junction. This junction is 1.3 miles from Road 430. You will pass an inverted Y intersection 0.5 mile farther along. There are some watertanks on the left side of the road next to the inverted Y junction. Just past the tanks bear left on Road 2600 (as of summer 1998 Road 2600 had a sign that appeared to mark it as Forest Road 2750). Follow Road 2600 for 0.9 mile to the trailhead. The trailhead is on the right side of the road. The sign at the trailhead says Landers Trail 217c. This is an old sign and may be changed in the future to say Goat Mountain Trail. GPS coordinates are 46 24.991 N 122 10.440 W.

Parking & trailhead facilities: There is parking for several cars and horse hitching rail at the trailhead.

Key points:
    0.7   Junction with Vanson Peak Trail.
    0.9   4-way junction with Vanson Ridge and Vanson Meadow Trails.
    1.0   Junction with Vanson Lake Trail. GPS 46 24.428 N 122 09.579 W.
    1.7   4-way junction with Vanson Peak and Goat Creek Trails.
    2.2   Vanson Peak.
    3.2   Junction with Goat Mountain Trail.
    3.9   Vanson Trailhead.

The hike: Ignore the sign that says this is Landers Trail 217c; it will quickly become the Goat Mountain Trail 217. Leaving the trailhead you hike east through a clearcut. About 0.3 mile from the trailhead the path bears right and enters old-growth forest. As you enter the woods you also enter Mount St. Helens National Volcanic Monument. You will pass a path to the left as you enter the

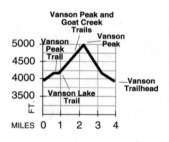

woods. This path connects with the road a short distance east of the trailhead. A little farther along another path to the left also connects with the road. Leopard lilies and bunchberries bloom along the trail in July.

You may notice a path blocked with sticks to the right 0.6 mile from the trailhead. This path is the old and now abandoned Vanson Ridge Trail. One hundred yards farther along is the junction with the Vanson Peak Trail. As you will probably note by looking at the trail sign, you are now on the Goat Mountain Trail. Vanson Peak Trail turns to the left. Hike straight ahead to the southeast for 0.2 mile to another junction. At this four-way junction

Riffe Reservoir from Vanson Peak.

Vanson Ridge Trail turns hard to the right. See Hike 51 for a description of Vanson Ridge Trail. The trail to Vanson Meadow also turns to the right but not as hard as Vanson Ridge Trail does. Vanson Meadow is 0.2 mile away to the southwest.

Continue southeast on the Goat Mountain Trail. The junction with the Vanson Lake Trail is reached 0.1 mile past the four-way junction. Vanson Lake is to the right. See Hike 54 for the details on the Vanson Lake Trail. The Goat Mountain Trail begins to climb at a steeper grade, just before reaching the junction with the Vanson Lake Trail. After passing the junction the route climbs to the southeast. You may see a path to the right 0.3 mile past the junction. This path was once the trail to Vanson Lake. It was short but very steep.

In a saddle 0.4 mile farther up the trail is another four-way junction. Here the Goat Creek Trail bears left to descend Goat Creek Canyon. See Hike 55 for a description of the Goat Creek Trail. The Vanson Peak Trail turns hard to the left (north) and the Goat Mountain Trail bears slightly to the right. See Hike 48 for the details on the rest of the Goat Mountain Trail. Turn hard to the left and take the Vanson Peak Trail to continue on the loop.

The route climbs steadily from the junction. As you climb the ridge Mount Adams comes into view to the east. A small rock outcropping on the right side of the trail, 0.4 mile from the junction, is a good viewpoint. Just past the viewpoint the trail forks. Bear right and climb the last few yards to the summit of Vanson Peak, at 4,948 feet elevation.

Take time to sit and enjoy a 360-degree view from the summit. The spectacular view includes Mount Rainier to the northeast and Mount Adams to the east. Below to the northwest are the reservoirs along the Cowlitz River. The open areas near the summit are nearly covered with flowers in July.

When you are ready to leave the summit, retrace your steps to the last fork in the trail and turn right. The route makes five switchbacks as it descends west for 1 mile to the junction with the Goat Mountain Trail. When you reach the junction the loop is completed. Turn right and hike the 0.7 mile back to Vanson Trailhead.

Options: The best option is to make a side trip to Vanson Lake. See Hike 54 for the details.

Camping & services: Taidnapam Park, run by Tacoma Public Utilities, is a very nice place to camp. The park is located near the north end of the bridge over Riffe Reservoir you crossed on the way to the trailhead. There is no camping allowed at the trailhead. Other services are available in Morton.

For more information: USDA Forest Service at Cowlitz Valley Ranger Station in Randle or Woods Creek Information Station. See Appendix A.

Vanson Peak Loop (Trails 217 and 217A)
Vanson Lake (Trail 217B)

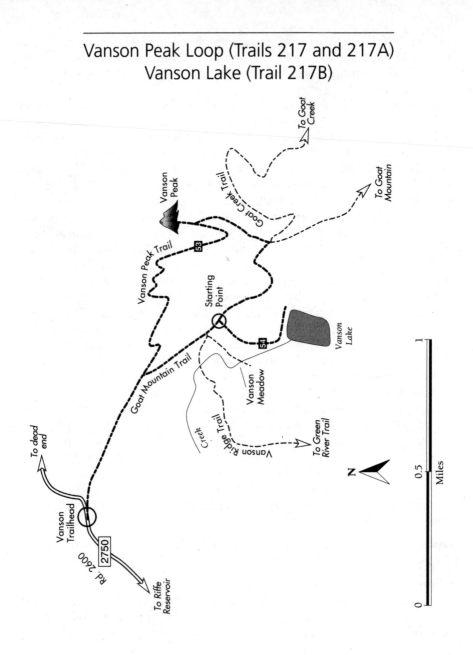

54 Vanson Lake (Trail 217B)

See Map on Page 212

Type of hike: Day hike or backpack, out and back.
Total distance: 0.6 mile.
Difficulty: Easy.
Best months: July–September.
Elevation gain: Minimal.
Trailhead elevation: 4,140 at the junction with Vanson Lake Trail.
Permits: None.
Maps: MSAHNVM or Vanson Peak USGS quad; the quad map shows the old and now abandoned route from Goat Mountain Trail to Vanson Lake.
Starting point: Junction with Vanson Lake Trail, 1.1 mile from the Vanson Trailhead.

General description: A short side trip off Goat Mountain Trail, on an *internal* trail, to Vanson Lake.

Finding the trailhead: Follow the driving directions in Hike 53. Then hike 0.7 mile on the Goat Mountain Trail to the junction with the Vanson Peak Trail. There is a sign at the junction. Continue southeast on Goat Mountain Trail 0.3 mile to the junction with the Vanson Lake Trail. This section of the Goat Mountain Trail is part of the Vanson Peak Loop described in Hike 53. The GPS coordinates at the junction of the Goat Mountain Trail and the Vanson Lake Trail are 46 24.428 N 122 09.579 W.

Key points
0.3   Vanson Lake

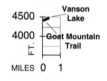

The hike: The route to Vanson Lake heads south from the Goat Mountain Trail. As you hike through the medium-aged forest watch the ground for avalanche lilies. Avalanche lilies bloom shortly after the snow melts. You will cross a small stream which flows beneath the trail through a culvert 150 yards from the junction. Trilliums sprout from the forest floor close to the stream. The path reaches Vanson Lake 0.3 mile from the junction with Goat Mountain Trail.

At the lake a path turns to the left. This rough path follows the shore around to the northeast corner of the lake where there is a good campsite. There are trout in Vanson Lake. Flies work well but fishing with them from shore can be a challenge because of the alder brush.

Options: The Vanson Peak Loop described in Hike 53 makes a rewarding trip when done from Vanson Lake. Since camping is not allowed at the Vanson Trailhead, pack your camp the 1.3 miles to the lake and make the loop from there.

Vanson Lake.

Camping & services: Taidnapam Park, run by Tacoma Public Utilities, is a very nice place to camp. The park is located near the north end of the bridge over Riffe Reservoir you crossed on the way to the trailhead. There is no camping allowed at the trailhead. Other services are available in Morton.

For more information: USDA Forest Service at Woods Creek Information Station or Cowlitz Valley Ranger Station in Randle. See Appendix A.

55 Goat Creek (Trail 205)

Type of hike:	Long day hike or backpack, shuttle, with out and back options.
Total distance:	9 miles.
Difficulty:	Moderate
Best months:	July–September
Elevation loss:	3,640 feet.
Trailhead elevation:	4,700 feet at the junction with Goat Mountain Trail.
Permits:	None.
Maps:	MSHNVM does not show this trail. Vanson Peak USGS quad covers the area but this trail is not shown.
Starting point:	Junction with Goat Mountain Trail, 1.7 miles from Vanson Trailhead.

General description: The Goat Creek Trail is a fairly long downhill hike on a trail with an *internal* start from a junction with the Goat Mountain Trail near Vanson Peak to the point where Forest Road 2750 is blocked nearly all the way to Riffe Reservoir.

Finding the trailhead: Follow the driving directions and trail description in Hike 53 to the junction where Goat Creek Trail begins. GPS coordinates are 46 24.238 N 122 09.167 W.

To reach the lower end of the Goat Creek Trail follow the driving directions in Hike 53 as far as the bridge over Riffe Reservoir. Then turn right on Road 400 and drive 0.8 mile to the junction with Forest Road 2750. Turn left on FR 2750 and follow it 0.2 mile to where it is blocked. Park there and hike up the road for 3.3 miles to the old trailhead. FR 2750 may not be marked.

Key points:

1.9   Lake.
4.0   Junction with Tumwater Mountain Trail. GPS 46 25.142 N 122 07.900 W.
5.7   Old trailhead.
9.0   FR 2750 (blocked). GPS 46 27.630 N 122 10.701 W.

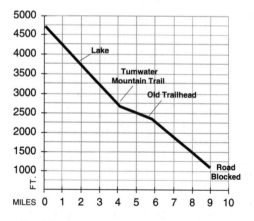

The hike: Leaving the four-way junction with the Goat Mountain and Vanson Peak Trails, the Goat Creek Trail begins its descent to the southeast. You descend along a forested hillside for a couple hundred yards then switchback to the left. The route continues down at a moderate grade to the north then northeast. Through openings in the timber Mount Adams is in view to the east. Lupine blooms in the open spots and Mount Rainier is sometimes in view to the north.

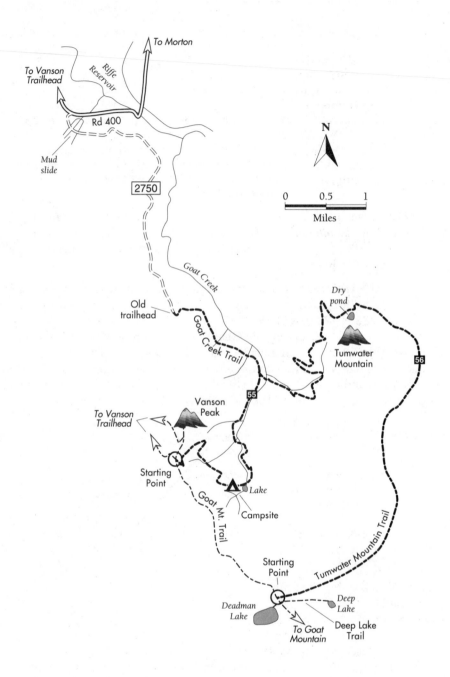

To Morton

To Vanson
Trailhead

Riffe
Reservoir

Rd 400

Mud
slide

2750

N

0   0.5   1
Miles

Goat Creek

Old
trailhead

Goat Creek Trail

Dry
pond

Tumwater
Mountain

56

55

To Vanson
Trailhead

Vanson
Peak

Starting
Point

Lake

Goat Mt. Trail

Campsite

Tumwater Mountain Trail

Starting
Point

Deadman
Lake

Deep
Lake

To Goat
Mountain

Deep Lake
Trail

The route bears right to head down a small ridge 0.6 mile from the junction with the Goat Mountain Trail. It soon switchbacks off the ridge to descend to a small swampy meadow. The path crosses a wooden bridge over one of the forks of Goat Creek as it leaves the meadow. A steep path turns right off the trail 0.8 mile after crossing the bridge. This path descends to an unnamed lake. Continue on the main trail a bit farther to another path to the right. This nearly level path also leads to the lake.

The lake, at 3,745 feet elevation and 1.9 miles from the Goat Mountain Trail, makes an ideal spot to end your hike if you are planning an out and back trip. There is a small pumice beach at the south end of the lake and a good campsite south on the other side of the meadow. Ducks nest at the lake and flowers cover the meadow in July. Yellow alpine monkeyflowers line the lake's inlet stream. If your timing is right (July), you can find wild strawberries in the meadow. There are also trout in the lake.

If you are going to hike on down Goat Creek Canyon, go back to the main trail. Then cross the outlet stream at the north end of the lake. A few yards below the crossing the stream splashes over falls. There is an excellent view of these falls a few more yards down the trail. The route descends along the east side of the creek for 0.9 mile, making five switchbacks along the way. It then re-crosses the creek to the west side. One mile below the crossing, after you have crossed a couple of side streams, there are more falls in the main creek. You will cross another small stream and duck beneath two huge logs that hang over the trail before you reach the junction with the Tumwater Mountain Trail.

The junction with the Tumwater Mountain Trail, at 2,560 feet elevation, is 4 miles from the junction with the Goat Mountain Trail. A quarter of a mile to the right (southeast) on the Tumwater Mountain Trail, Goat Creek flows over a ledge to form a picturesque waterfall. See Hike 56 for a description of the Tumwater Mountain Trail. As you leave the junction with the Tumwater Mountain Trail, the Goat Creek Trail climbs a few feet then traverses northwest along the steep slope. As you hike through the large Douglas-firs, deer fern and sword fern dot the slope. Small patches of foxglove bloom to add color to the green landscape. Seven-tenths of a mile from the junction, after crossing a creek, the path crosses a small steep stream. This little creek drops over many tiny steps above the trail. You will then pass beneath an overhanging cliff. The route follows a ledge for a few yards then goes under more cliffs. This spot is almost a cave. The path goes behind some tiny falls then leaves the undercut area.

After crossing a couple more tiny streams the route reaches the end of an abandoned roadbed. Walk the roadbed through the alders and round a point. Then hike southwest along the roadbed to the old Goat Creek Trailhead. The road (FR 2750) leading to this trailhead has slid away in several spots. A mudslide blocks the road 3 miles below the old trailhead. To continue on to what is now the end of the driveable section of the road, you have to hike the 3 miles.

Options: The best option here is to camp at the lake 1.9 miles from the Goat Mountain Trail, then explore the lower section of Goat Creek Trail as a day hike from there. Alternately, you may want to park at the point where FR 2750 is blocked and hike up the closed road and trail to the junction with the Tumwater Mountain Trail. Then follow the Tumwater Mountain Trail as far as the falls.

Camping & services: Taidnapam Park, run by Tacoma Public Utilities, is a very nice place to camp. The park is located near the north end of the bridge over Riffe Reservoir you crossed on the way to the trailhead. There is no camping allowed at the trailhead. Other services are available in Morton.

For more information: USDA Forest Service at Woods Creek Information Station or Cowlitz Valley Ranger Station in Randle. See Appendix A.

Cave on Goat Creek Trail.

56 Tumwater Mountain (Trail 218)

See Map on Page 216

Type of hike: Long day hike or backpack.
Total distance: 9.7 miles.
Difficulty: Moderate to strenuous.
Best months: July–September.
Elevation loss: 2,600 feet.
Trailhead elevation: 4,410 feet at junction with Goat Mountain Trail.
Permits: None.
Maps: Cowlitz Falls and Vanson Peak USGS quads.
Starting point: Junction with Goat Mountain Trail near Deadman Lake.

General description: The Tumwater Mountain Trail, an *internal* trail, follows the ridgeline of Tumwater Mountain for 6 miles from a junction with the Goat Mountain Trail near Deadman Lake. Then it descends into the Goat Creek Canyon and passes a beautiful waterfall before joining the Goat Creek Trail.

Finding the trailhead: The closest road access to the junction of the Tumwater Mountain and Goat Mountain trails is the Vanson Trailhead. To reach the Vanson Trailhead follow the driving directions in Hike 53. From the trailhead hike the Goat Mountain Trail (sign says Landers Trail at the trailhead) for 4.5 miles southeast to the junction with the Tumwater Mountain Trail. GPS coordinates at the junction of the Goat Mountain Trail and the Tumwater Mountain Trail are 46 22.851 N 122 07.754 W.

The junction can also be reached from the east via Goat Mountain Trail. See Hike 48 for driving directions and trail details.

The north end of the Tumwater Mountain Trail is at a junction with Goat Creek Trail. For driving directions and a trail description see Hike 55.

Key points:
6.0 Dry pond below Tumwater Mountain summit.
9.2 Cross Goat Creek.
9.5 Falls.
9.7 Junction with Goat Creek Trail.

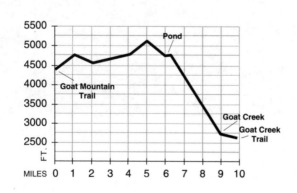

Falls in Goat Creek.

The hike: The Tumwater Mountain Trail is lightly used mostly because views from it are sparse for 9 of its 9.7-mile length; nearly the full length of this trail is in the timber. Also there are no really good campsites along this trail.

Leaving the marked junction with the Goat Mountain Trail, near Deadman Lake, the Tumwater Mountain Trail heads northwest, climbing gently. The view opens up a little as you cross a rocky outcrop 0.9 mile from the junction. Cat's ear lilies and lupine grow in the open spots along this section. Mount Adams is in view to the east. Slightly farther after the view, the route reaches the ridgeline.

For the next 5 miles the path generally follows the ridge through the timber. At times you will be below the ridge on the west and at others on the east, but the route is never far from the ridgeline. At 4.2 miles from the junction with Goat Mountain Trail, the timber opens up enough to catch a glimpse of Mount Rainier to the north. A couple miles farther along you pass a dry, or nearly dry, pond on the left side of the trail. The summit of Tumwater Mountain rises above the south side of the dry pond. This area offers about the only reasonable camping along the Tumwater Mountain Trail.

The route starts to descend into Goat Creek Canyon 0.3 mile past the dry pond. After a few yards you will make a switchback to the left next to a rock outcropping. Look for delphinium growing along the path after making the switchback. After making three more switchbacks there is a viewpoint overlooking Goat Creek Canyon on the right side of the trail. You will cross a creek 0.4 mile below the viewpoint. The route passes a waterfall 0.3 mile farther down. Another 0.5 mile and a couple more switchbacks down is Goat Creek. Cross Goat Creek and turn right to descend along the steep side hill above the creek. Where the trail crosses Goat Creek you are 9.2 miles from the junction with Goat Mountain Trail.

One of the prettiest waterfalls in the Northwest is in Goat Creek, 0.3 mile below the crossing. After passing the falls another 0.2 mile of walking brings you to the crossing of the west fork of Goat Creek. There are actually two streams to cross here as a side stream enters the west fork just below the crossing. This crossing and the one 0.2 mile back can be difficult during times of high water. Be careful. Just past the last crossing you will reach the junction with the Goat Creek Trail. To the right it is 5 miles on the Goat Creek Trail and closed FR 2750 to the point where the road is blocked by a mudslide near the Riffe Reservoir. The Goat Mountain Trail is 4 miles to the left.

Options: A good option is to hike the lower 0.5 mile of the Tumwater Mountain Trail as a side trip off the Goat Creek Trail. See Hike 55 for a description of the Goat Creek Trail.

Camping & services: Taidnapam Park, run by Tacoma Public Utilities, is a very nice place to camp. The park is located near the north end of the bridge over Riffe Reservoir you crossed on the way to the trailhead. There is no camping allowed at the trailhead. Other services are available in Morton.

For more information: USDA Forest Service at Woods Creek Information Station or Cowlitz Valley Ranger Station in Randle. See Appendix A.

Strawberry Mountain.

57 Strawberry Mountain (Trail 220)

Type of hike: Day hike, out and back, with shuttle options.
Total distance: 1.6 miles to summit, 4.4 miles to Boundary Trail.
Difficulty: Moderate.
Best months: Mid-July–September.
Elevation gain: 600 feet.
Trailhead elevation: 4,870 feet.
Permits: None.
Maps: MSHNVM or Spirit Lake East USGS quad.
Starting point: Junction of Forest Road 2516, FR 069 and Strawberry Mountain Trail.

General description: A short climb to the summit of Strawberry Mountain with a magnificent 360-degree view, or a hike along an open ridge and a descent through deep forest to a junction with the Boundary Trail.

Finding the trailhead: Head north from Portland on Interstate 5 to Exit 21 at Woodland (21 miles north of the Columbia River Bridge). Then drive east for 27.5 miles on Washington 503 (which becomes WA 503 spur) to Cougar. Continue east through Cougar on WA 503 spur (which becomes FR 90 at the Skamania County line) for another 18.6 miles to the junction with FR 25. Bear left (nearly straight ahead) and head northeast on FR 25 for 26 miles to the junction with FR 2516. The junction with 2516 is 1.7 miles north of the junction with FR 99.

From Seattle take I-5 south to Exit 133 at Tacoma and then follow WA 7 for 55 miles to Morton. From Morton drive east 17 miles to Randle on U.S. Highway 12. Turn right and take WA 131 then FR 25 south for 18.3 miles to the junction with FR 2516.

Turn west on FR 2516. Follow FR 2516 for 5.6 miles to a saddle and the junction with the Strawberry Mountain Trail and FR 069. At this junction FR 2516 is blocked. GPS coordinates at the junction and trailhead are 46 20.654 N 122 02.281 W.

This section of the Strawberry Mountain Trail starts 200 yards south of the junction. Hike 200 yards south up FR 069 to the point where the trail turns to the right off the road. GPS coordinates 46 20.573 N 122 02.350 W.

Strawberry Mountain Trail ends at a junction with Boundary Trail, 0.6 mile northwest of Bear Meadows Trailhead. For a description of this section of the Boundary Trail and directions to the Bear Meadows Trailhead see Hike 42.

Strawberry Mountain (Trail 220)
Strawberry Lake

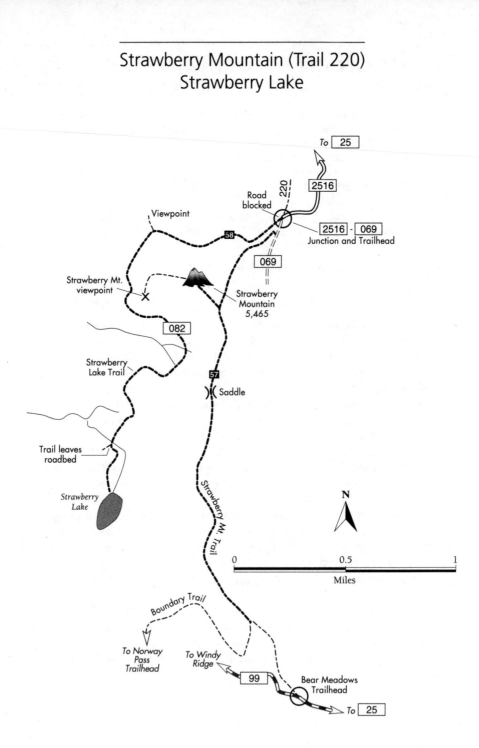

Parking & trailhead facilities: There is parking for a couple of cars at the junction of FR 2516, FR 069, and the Strawberry Mountain Trail but no other facilities. There is no parking where the Strawberry Mountain Trail leaves FR 069.

There is parking for several cars and restrooms at Bear Meadows Trailhead.

Key points:
- 0.6   Junction with path to summit.
- 1.1   Cross saddle and leave ridgeline.
- 2.2   Junction with Boundary Trail.

The hike: There is no sign where the trail leaves the road but there is a trail sign a few yards up the trail. As it leaves FR 069, the trail climbs northwest for about 100 yards. It then switches back to the southwest to follow the ridgeline through the forest. After climbing along the ridge for 0.3 mile the

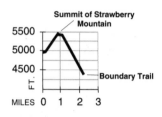

tread bears slightly left and traverses the wooded slope along the east side of Strawberry Mountain. The route reaches the southeast ridge of Strawberry Mountain, at 5,300 feet elevation, 0.6 mile after leaving FR 069.

As the trail reaches the ridgeline a path turns off to the right (northwest). This rough path goes to the summit of Strawberry Mountain, where a lookout once stood. If your destination is the summit, turn right and climb steeply along the open ridgeline. Shortly the path crosses an old log landing with a couple of propane tanks on it. The route then climbs very steeply for a few feet as it leaves the landing. The grade soon moderates somewhat as you continue to climb through scattered small firs and hemlocks. Between the trees mountain ash grows in abundance. The summit, elevation 5,465 feet, is reached 0.2 mile after leaving the Strawberry Mountain Trail.

From the top the view is marvelous in all directions. To the west are Ryan Lake and the Green River Valley, flanked by Goat Mountain and the Mount Margaret Backcountry. To the north Mount Rainier looms above the green hills. Looking east Mount Adams is in full view and to the south is the gaping crater of Mount St. Helens. Elk seem to like this summit for a bedding spot. You may see them or at least their tracks in the dust on the summit.

To continue on the main trail after passing the path to the summit, head south along the ridge. Soon the route bears slightly off the west side of the ridgeline on the mostly open slope. As you traverse the slope look for a few stunted Alaska cedars growing between the huckleberries and rocks. The abundant berries may cause you some delays if you hike here in late August. Half a mile past the junction with the path to the summit, the trail crosses another saddle and begins its descent through the forest. The descent continues for 1.1 miles to the junction with the Boundary Trail at 4,360 feet elevation.

If you have made a car shuttle to the Bear Meadows Trailhead turn left and follow the Boundary Trail 0.6 mile to the trailhead. For a description of this section of the Boundary Trail see Hike 42.

Options: Just going to the summit and back is a great short hike. If you want a longer hike turn right at the junction with the Boundary Trail and follow it to the Norway Pass Trailhead. This option would necessitate a longer car shuttle. For directions to the Norway Pass Trailhead see Hike 44.

Camping & services: The closest developed campsites are at Iron Creek Campground, 9.7 miles south of Randle on FR 25. Other services can be obtained in Randle or Morton.

For more information: USDA Forest Service at Woods Creek or Pine Creek Information Stations. See Appendix A.

---

58 Strawberry Lake

See Map on Page 224

Type of hike:	Day hike or backpack, out and back.
Total distance:	4.8 miles.
Difficulty:	Moderate
Best months:	Mid-July–September.
Elevation loss:	130 feet.
Trailhead elevation:	4,860 feet.
Permits:	None.
Maps:	MSHNVM or Spirit Lake East USGS quad.
Starting point:	Junction of Forest Road 2516, Strawberry Mountain Trail and FR 069.

General description: A hike through salvaged, blown-down forest around Strawberry Mountain to Strawberry Lake. The route follows closed and abandoned roads most of the way.

Finding the trailhead: The route to Strawberry Lake starts at the same junction as the trail to Strawberry Mountain. For driving directions to the starting point see Hike 57. GPS coordinates at the junction and trailhead are 46 20.654 N 122 02.281 W.

Parking & trailhead facilities: There is parking for a couple of cars at the junction of FR 2516, FR 069, and Strawberry Mountain Trail but no other facilities.

Key points:
0.9   Change roadbeds near Strawberry Mountain Viewpoint.

Strawberry Lake.

2.1   Leave roadbed.
2.4   Strawberry Lake. GPS 46 19.641 N 122 03.200 W.

The hike: The route to Strawberry Lake follows the now closed FR 2516 west-southwest
from the junction and trailhead. The route
goes around a pile of rock that was dumped
here to prevent vehicle access. Within a few
yards the roadbed enters a salvage-logged
area, and the view opens up. At 0.1 mile a

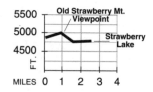

section of road has slid away. A path skirts the slide then the route continues
west along the roadbed. Mount Rainier is in view to the north.

A spur road goes a short distance to the right to a viewpoint overlooking
the head of Quartz Creek, 0.5 mile from the trailhead. The route then heads
southwest, traversing along the slopes of Strawberry Mountain. Looking
west you can see the Mount Margaret Backcountry and Goat Mountain,
with the Green River Valley in between. Mount St. Helens is now in view to
the southwest.

The route leaves the roadbed 0.9 mile from the trailhead. The place where
you leave the roadbed can be a little hard to spot. It is about 150 yards
before reaching the now closed parking area for the Strawberry Mountain
Viewpoint. Turn right off the road and drop steeply for a short distance to
the long-abandoned roadbed of FR 082. Then turn left and follow that abandoned road, heading southeast. If you miss the spot where the path leaves

the road it is possible to bushwhack down from the viewpoint parking area and reach FR 082. Strawberry Lake can be seen to the south from here.

Hike along abandoned FR 082, through the huckleberries and lupine and everlasting, for 1.2 miles. You will cross a couple of washouts and pass several spur roads along the way. Then 2.1 miles from the trailhead the route leaves the roadbed. A small stream has washed out a gully across the roadbed here. The path drops into the gully then climbs steeply for a few feet out the other side. Then the route flattens and heads south through the standing dead snags. The route is very vague after leaving the roadbed, but finding the lake is fairly easy. It can be more difficult to find the roadbed when you are heading back so take careful note of the route as you approach the lake. Reach Strawberry Lake 0.3 mile after leaving the roadbed of FR 082.

There are possible campsites available near the lake and some decent fishing. The open country all along the route to Strawberry Lake abounds with both blacktail deer and Roosevelt elk. In September, you may hear the bull elk bugling.

Options: If you are an agile hiker it is possible to follow game trails up the open ridge from the Strawberry Mountain Viewpoint to the summit of Strawberry Mountain, and then return to the trailhead on the trails from there. See Hike 57 for a description of Strawberry Mountain Trail.

Camping & services: Disbursed camping is permitted along FR 2516 as you approach the trailhead. The closest developed campsites are at Iron Creek Campground, 9.7 miles south of Randle on FR 25. Other services can be obtained in Randle or Morton.

For more information: USDA Forest Service at Woods Creek Information Station. See Appendix A.

59 Woods Creek Watchable Wildlife Loop (Trails 247 and 247A)

Type of hike: Day hike, loop.
Total distance: 2.4 miles.
Difficulty: Easy.
Best months: March–October.
Elevation gain: Minimal.
Trailhead elevation: 1,140 feet.
Permits: None.
Maps: The one in this book or in pamphlet at trailhead.
Starting point: Woods Creek Trailhead and Picnic Area.

General description: Woods Creek and Old Growth loops make a figure eight hike through this diverse lowland forest. This is an excellent hike to take with small children.

Finding the trailhead: Head north from Portland on Interstate 5 to Exit 21 at Woodland (21 miles north of the Columbia River Bridge). Then drive east for 27.5 miles on Washington 503 (which becomes WA 503 spur) to Cougar. Continue east through Cougar on WA 503 spur (which becomes Forest Road 90 at the Skamania County line) for another 18.6 miles to the junction with FR 25. Bear left (nearly straight ahead) and head northeast on FR 25 for 36.6 miles to Woods Creek Information Station.

From Seattle take I-5 south to Exit 133 at Tacoma and then follow WA 7 for 55 miles to Morton. From Morton drive east 17 miles to Randle on U.S. Highway 12. Turn right at Randle and take WA 131 then FR 25 south for 5.7 miles to the Woods Creek Information Station.

The trailhead is on the east side of FR 25 across from the information station. GPS coordinates are 46 27.668 N 121 57.574 W.

Parking & trailhead facilities: There are restrooms, a picnic area, adequate parking, and an information sign at the trailhead.

Key points:
0.3 Junction with Woods Creek Loop.
0.8 Junction with Old Growth Loop.
2.1 Junction with start of Woods Creek Loop.
2.4 Picnic area.

The hike: As you leave the parking area pick up one of the pamphlets covering the Woods Creek Watchable Wildlife Interpretive Trail. A dispenser for the pamphlets (and a donation box) are located on the signboard next to the trailhead.

The 4-foot-wide gravel tread heads east from the parking area through dense second-growth forest. Fir, big leaf maple, and red cedar trees furnish the canopy. Beneath the big, moss-hung trees grows vine maple. Ferns and

Woods Creek Watchable Wildlife Loop
(Trails 247 and 247A)

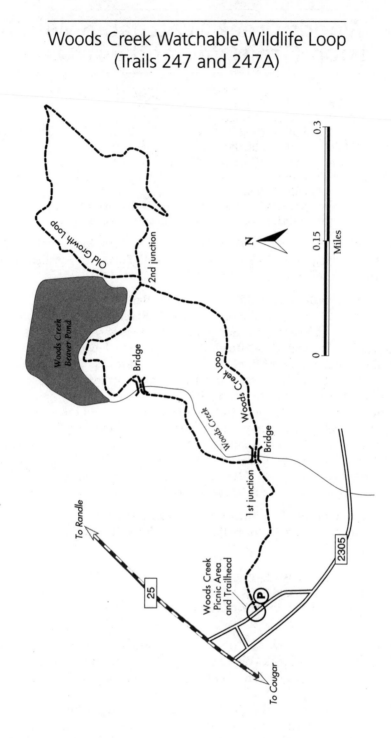

moss cover the ground. Soon after leaving the trailhead you will want to stop and read the first interpretive sign about deer tracks, which you may have already seen along the trail. After hiking 0.3 mile you will reach a trail junction. At the junction there is a clearing and a marsh next to the trail, as well as a bench and sign about elk tracks.

Turn left at the junction and hike northwest along the sluggish Woods Creek. Foxglove and blackberries line the creek, as do nettles. After passing another bench and sign about hare tracks you cross a wooden bridge over Woods Creek. One-tenth of a mile farther along is a lookout porch to the left of the trail. The porch, which was constructed in memory of Joe Frinche, is a viewpoint for Woods Creek Beaver Pond. Just past the porch are another bench and a sign describing raccoon tracks.

Soon you will reach the junction with the Old Growth Loop Trail. Turn left then quickly turn right at another junction a few yards away. The Old Growth Loop climbs gently and makes a couple of switchbacks as it enters the larger trees of the old-growth forest. The largest of these trees are Douglas-fir. Four-tenths of a mile into the Old Growth Loop you will find another bench and a sign about martin tracks. This bench is at the highest point of the hike. From here the trail descends, making another switchback, and returns to the junction with the Woods Creek Loop. At this junction first turn right then left.

Once back on the Woods Creek Loop the path heads east, then south, passing yet another bench and a sign about coyote tracks. Before long, after crossing a wooden bridge, you will reach another junction. This junction is the first one you came to when you began this hike. Turn left at the junction and hike the remaining 0.3 mile back to the trailhead.

Options: For a shorter hike do not take the Old Growth Loop.

Camping & services: The closest developed campground is at Iron Creek Campground, 4 miles south on FR 25. Other services can be obtained in Randle or Morton.

For more information: USDA Forest Service at Woods Creek Information Station. See Appendix A.

60 Iron Creek Falls (Trail 91)

Type of hike:	Day hike, out and back.
Total distance:	0.2 mile.
Difficulty:	Easy.
Best months:	May–October.
Elevation loss:	Minimal.
Trailhead elevation:	2,800 feet.
Permits:	None.
Maps:	None needed.
Starting point:	Iron Creek Falls Trailhead.

General description: A short walk to beautiful Iron Creek Falls. This is not a barrier-free trail.

Finding the trailhead: Head north from Portland on Interstate 5 to Exit 21 at Woodland (21 miles north of the Columbia River Bridge). Then drive east for 27.5 miles on Washington 503 (which becomes WA 503 spur) to Cougar. Continue east through Cougar on WA 503 spur (which becomes Forest Road 90 at the Skamania County line) for another 18.6 miles to the junction with FR 25. Bear left (nearly straight ahead) and head northeast on FR 25 for 24.8 miles to the trailhead.

From Seattle take I-5 south to Exit 133 at Tacoma and then follow WA 7 for 55 miles to Morton. From Morton drive east 17 miles to Randle on U.S. Highway 12. Turn right and take WA 131 then FR 25 south for 19.5 miles to the trailhead. The parking area is on east side of Forest Road 25.

Parking & trailhead facilities: There is parking for several cars but no other facilities at the trailhead.

Key points:
0.1   Iron Creek Falls Viewpoint.

The hike: A few yards from the trailhead you will start to descend the first of 58 wooden steps that take you to a switchback. Hemlock and fir line the path along the moss-covered slope as you walk to the switchback. At the switchback turn right and walk 30 yards to a viewpoint looking at Iron Creek Falls. Past the switchback there are 16 more wooden steps then a long step down to the creek bed. Walk up the creek bed 40 yards to get close to the falls. Iron Creek Falls drops over an undercut cliff and splashes with a roar into a beautiful pool at its base. As you climb the steps back to the parking area watch for the tiny white flowers that hug the side of the trail.

Options: None.

Camping & services: Camping is close by at Iron Creek Campground 10 miles north on FR 25. Other services are in Randle or Morton.

For more information: USDA Forest Service at Woods Creek Information Station. See Appendix A.

Iron Creek Falls (Trail 91)

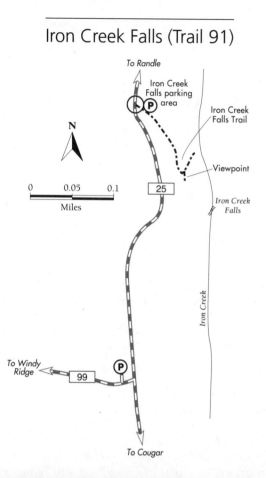

To Randle

Iron Creek Falls parking area

Iron Creek Falls Trail

Viewpoint

Iron Creek Falls

N

0   0.05   0.1
Miles

25

Iron Creek

99

To Windy Ridge

P

To Cougar

Iron Creek Falls. SUZI BARSTAD PHOTO

Summit Climb

61 Monitor Ridge Summit Climb (Trails 216A and 216H to the summit of Mount St. Helens)

Type of hike: Day climb, out and back.
Total distance: 9.2 miles.
Difficulty: Strenuous.
Best months: June–September.
Elevation gain: 4,615 feet.
Trailhead elevation: 3,750 feet.
Permits: Climbing permit.
Maps: Mount St. Helens USGS quad, or Green Trails Mount St. Helens NW, Wash–No 364s. Neither of these maps has the route marked above 4,800 feet elevation.
Starting point: Climbers Bivouac Trailhead.

General description: A non-technical but strenuous climb up the south side of Mount St. Helens to the summit on the crater rim.

Finding the trailhead: Head north from Portland or south from Seattle on Interstate 5 to Exit 21 at Woodland (21 miles from the Columbia River Bridge or about 150 miles from Seattle). Then drive east on Washington 503 (which becomes WA 503 spur then Forest Road 90) for 34.3 miles, passing Cougar, to the junction with FR 83. Turn left on FR 83 and follow it for 3.1 miles north to the junction with FR 81. Turn left on FR 81 and drive northwest 1.6 miles to the junction with FR 830. Turn right and head northeast on FR 308 for 2.6 miles to Climbers Bivouac Trailhead. GPS coordinates are 46 08.799 N 122 10.991 W.

Parking & trailhead facilities: There are restrooms and adequate parking at the trailhead. Camping is allowed at Climbers Bivouac Trailhead.

Key points:
2.1 Junction with Loowit Trail.
2.3 Trail ends and climbing route begins.
4.4 Crater Rim.
4.6 Summit of Mount St. Helens.

The hike: While climbing Monitor Ridge to the summit of Mount St. Helens is not a technical climb, it is a rough scramble much of the way. The weather above timberline is very changeable. It may be warm, clear, and sunny when you leave the trailhead; by the time you reach the summit you could

Monitor Ridge Summit Climb
(Trails 216A and 216H to the summit of Mount St. Helens)

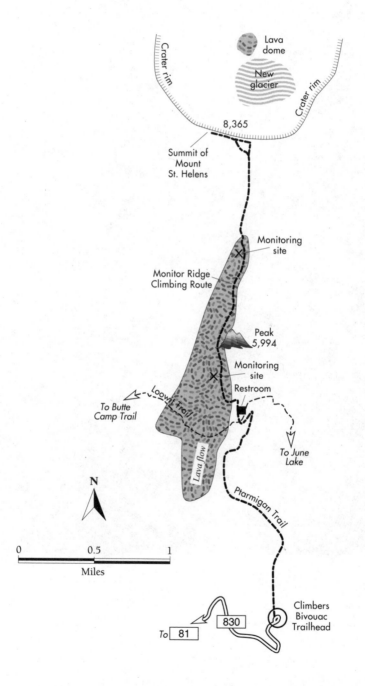

Lava dome

New glacier

Crater rim

Crater rim

8,365

Summit of Mount St. Helens

Monitoring site

Monitor Ridge Climbing Route

Peak 5,994

Monitoring site

Restroom

Loowit Trail

To Butte Camp Trail

To June Lake

Lava flow

N

0   0.5   1

Miles

Ptarmigan Trail

To 81

830

Climbers Bivouac Trailhead

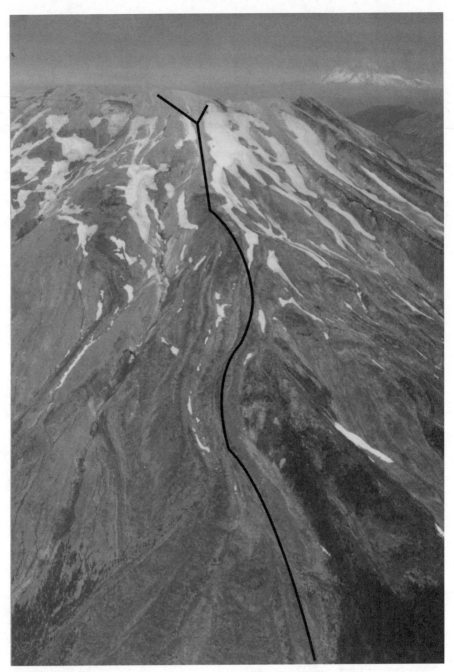

Summit Climb.

experience a dust storm or even a blizzard. Rain and snow are normal before late June and possible all summer. During sunny weather these south-facing slopes can be very warm and dry. There is no water along this route after the snow melts. Under these conditions take plenty of water with you; 3 quarts is not too much. When the route is snow covered long slides are possible so take your ice axe and know how to use it.

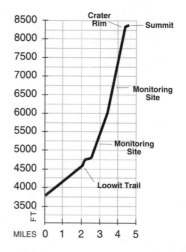

The first 2.1 miles of this hike follow the Ptarmigan Trail described in Hike 23. From Climbers Bivouac Trailhead hike north up the Ptarmigan Trail for 2.1 miles to the junction with the Loowit Trail at 4,600 feet elevation. Cross the Loowit Trail and hike on up through the timber. Just after passing the junction with the Loowit Trail a short path to the right goes to a restroom. The trail bears left and leaves the larger timber 0.2 mile from the Loowit Trail at about 4,750 feet elevation. The trail heads west for a short distance through small alpine firs. This is where the trail ends and the climbing route begins.

After heading west for a few yards the route climbs onto a lava flow. From here up to the pumice slopes near the summit the route is marked with wood posts. Once you are on the lava flow turn right and continue to climb to the north along a small ridge. At 5,200 feet elevation you may notice a now unused monitoring site a short distance west of the route. As you scramble up through the boulders watch for pikas and golden mantle ground squirrels. The view improves steadily as you gain elevation. Mount Adams is to the east and Mount Hood to the southeast. If the atmosphere is really clear you can also see Mount Jefferson slightly to the right of Mount Hood. Swift and Yale reservoirs are far below to the south and southwest.

The line of posts follows the tiny ridgeline up to 5,400 feet elevation. There are paths on both sides of the small ridge so you can take your choice of which one to use. Then the line of posts bears slightly left of the ridgeline, and the main path closely follows them. At 6,000 feet elevation the route regains the ridgeline well above the peak marked 5,994 on both the USGS and Green Trails maps. This is a good spot for a rest break.

The steepest part of the climb is between 6,000 feet and 7,000 feet elevation. You will scramble up and over several humps on the ridgeline. The route passes another monitoring site at 6,700 feet elevation and reaches the top of the dark lava rocks at 7,000 feet elevation. Above the dark rock the route becomes better defined. The path continues up a light colored ridge to the base of the pumice slopes at about 7,800 feet elevation. As you climb the pumice slope you may want to bear to the left where the path forks. The left fork is a shorter way to the summit. The route reaches the crater rim at 8,280 feet elevation. On the rim turn left and climb gently for 0.2 mile to the summit.

Summit of Mount St. Helens. ERIC VALENTINE PHOTO

Try to allow yourself plenty of time to enjoy the view from the summit, 8,365 feet above sea level. Stay back from the edge of the crater since the loose rock snow cornice may give away. To the north Mount Rainier rises above the smaller peaks. In the crater below notice the new glacier that is forming behind the Lava Dome. It is often windy on the summit. The wind picks up the fine particles of pumice dust and at times creates a minor dust storm.

Options: From the summit you can take an alternate descent route to the southwest. Descend to the junction of the Loowit and Butte Camp trails. Then follow the Butte Camp and Toutle trails to the Redrock Pass Trailhead. See Hikes 19 and 14 for trail descriptions. This route should only be used when it is completely or nearly completely snow covered to avoid damage to the fragile alpine environment. Descending via this route requires a car shuttle to Redrock Pass Trailhead.

Camping & services: Beaver Bay and Cougar campgrounds located along WA 503 spur, just east of Cougar are the closest developed campsites. Gas ,groceries, restaurant, and motel are available in Cougar. The closest medical services are in Woodland.

For more information: USDA Forest Service at Mount St. Helens National Volcanic Monument Headquarters in Chelatchie, Ape's Headquarters at the Ape Cave parking area, or at Jack's Restaurant 5 miles west of Cougar at the junction of WA 503 and WA 503 spur. See Appendix A.

Appendix A: Additional Resources

USDA Forest Service
Mount St. Helens National Volcanic Monument Headquarters
42218 NE Yale Bridge Road
Amboy (Chelatchie), WA 98601
(360) 247-3900
(360) 247-3961 (climbing hotline)
FAX (360) 247-3901

Mount St. Helens Visitor Center
3029 Spirit Lake Highway (MP 5)
Castle Rock, WA 98611
(360) 274-2100

Coldwater Ridge Visitor Center
3029 Spirit Lake Highway (MP 43)
Castle Rock, WA 98611
(360) 274-2131

Johnston Ridge Observatory
3029 Spirit Lake Highway (MP 51)
Castle Rock, WA 98611
(360) 274-2140

Cowlitz Valley Ranger Station
Randle Ranger District
P.O. Box 670
Randle, WA 98377

Other Information Sources
Jack's Restaurant
Junction of WA 503 and WA 503 spur, 5 miles west of Cougar, WA.
(360) 231-4276

Weyerhaeuser Company
P.O. Box 1645
Tacoma, WA 98401-9970
(800) 458-0274

Emergency Phone Numbers
Cowlitz County Sheriffs Department
(360) 577-3092

Lewis County Sheriffs Department
(360) 748-8887

Skamania County Sheriffs Department
(509) 427-9490

Appendix B: Glossary

aa: Lava that flowed when the outer layer of lava was in a nearly solid state causing a very rough surface.

Blast Zone: The area of eradicated downed or dead vegetation caused by the volcanic eruption.

borrow pit: A place where native rock or soil has been removed for road building purposes.

cirque: A bowl-shaped area where a glacier has eaten its way into a mountain slope, then melted. A cirque is formed at the head of a glacier.

cornice: A wind-caused snowdrift that overhangs a cliff or steep slope.

Debris Avalanche: A fast-moving flow of unsorted rock debris. In this book it refers to the debris from a huge slide that preceded the 1980 eruption by a few seconds.

dome: A pile of rock extruded from a volcanic vent. Same as lava dome.

Eruption Impact Zone: A zone that includes the Blast Zone and the Singe Zone but does not include areas that were only affected by lahars and ashfall in the 1980 eruption.

hummocks: Low mounds or ridges of earth. In this book, it refers to the parts of the pre-1980 Mount St. Helens that were left by the Debris Avalanche: see **Debris Avalanche.**

internal trail: A trail that begins and/or ends at a junction with another trail. Internal trails do not reach any trailhead.

lahar: A volcanic mudflow. Lahars are a mixture of rock, sand, and soil that flows swiftly off a mountain as a result of volcanic activity or that are the solidified remains of such a flow.

lateral blast: A volcanic blast that is directed horizontally rather than vertically.

lava flow: A stream of molten rock flowing from a volcano or a stream of rock after it has cooled and hardened.

lava tube: An opening beneath or in a lava flow where a stream of molten rock continuesto flow after the outer crust of the lava flow has cooled and hardened. The lava flow leaves a tube as it flows out.

lava tube cave: A lava tube large enough for a person to enter. Ape Cave on Mount St. Helens is the longest lava tube cave in North America.

MSHNVM (map): USDA Mount St. Helens National Volcanic Monument map (the one with the waterfall on the cover). AKA the Brown Map.

pumice: The solidified froth of volcanic rock. Pumice is a light-colored rock that weighs so little it can float.

pyroclastic flow: A mass of hot volcanic debris and gases that move swiftly along the surface of the ground.

Red Zone: A 10-mile wide circle (5-mile radius from the old summit) around Mount St. Helens in 1980 prior to the eruption.

Restricted Zone: The area in which the public is not allowed to travel off established roads or trails. The Restricted Zone was created for both environmental and safety reasons.

sand ladder: A device that makes it easier to climb and descend loose slopes. A sand ladder is a series of wooden steps (round or square) that are tied together with cables and laid on the slope to give the hiker better footing when climbing or descending.

second-growth forest: Forest that has been logged many years ago and has regrown to medium-sized timber.

Singe Zone: The area where the timber is still standing but dead as a result of the volcanic eruption. The Singe Zone is at the outside edge of the Blast Zone.

spur highway: A highway that is a side route off another highway and is designated with the word "spur" or "s" after the highway number.

spur ridge: A smaller ridge on the side of a main ridge. Spur ridges may be very steep.

spur trail: A short side trail.

USDA: United States Department of Agriculture.

USGS: United States Geological Survey.

wash: A creek bed that is dry most of the time, usually with steep, unstable banks.

whistle pig: A common name for a hoary marmot.

winter range: The area where migrating animals spend the winter.

Appendix C: Hiker's Checklist

Use the following lists to help you prepare for your Mount St. Helens National Volcanic Monument hikes. Your equipment need not be new or expensive, but it should be well tested.

EQUIPMENT

☐ Day pack or fanny pack
☐ Water bottles
☐ First-aid kit
☐ Survival kit
☐ Compass
☐ Maps
☐ Toilet paper
☐ Sunscreen
☐ Flashlight with extra batteries
☐ 2 light sources per person if you are going into the caves
☐ Pocketknife
☐ Sunglasses
☐ Anti-fog solution *(If you wear glasses, especially if you are going in the caves in the spring)*

Optional

☐ Binoculars
☐ Camera and extra film
(with flash for the caves)

Added Equipment for Overnight Trips

☐ Tent and waterproof fly
☐ Sleeping bag and stuffsack
(Synthetic bags are best for this damp climate)
☐ Sleeping pad
☐ Water filter or purification tablets
☐ More water bottles
☐ Cooking pots and holder
☐ Cup, bowl, and eating utensils
☐ Lightweight stove and plenty of fuel *(a must in the Blast Zone where campfires are prohibited.)*
☐ Plastic zip-locked bags

- [ ] Nylon cord (*50 feet*)
- [ ] Small towel
- [ ] Personal toilet kit

Optional

- [ ] Paper towels
- [ ] Stuffsacks
- [ ] Notebook and pencil

CLOTHING

Day hikes

- [ ] Large-brimmed hat or cap
- [ ] Sturdy hiking boots *(well broken in)*
- [ ] Hiking shorts or long pants
- [ ] Long-sleeved shirt
- [ ] Light, windproof parka
- [ ] Raingear
- [ ] Mittens or gloves

Additional Clothing for Overnight Trips

- [ ] Warm hat *(stocking cap)*
- [ ] Long underwear
      (during fall winter and spring)
- [ ] Sweater or insulated vest
- [ ] Waterproof wilderness parka
- [ ] Long pants
- [ ] One pair of socks for each day plus one extra pair
- [ ] Extra underwear
- [ ] Extra shirts
- [ ] Sandals *(for use around camp and wading streams)*

FOOD

For day hiking, take high-energy snacks for munching along the way. For overnight trips, bring enough food, but do not overburden yourself with too much. Include plenty of snacks. Plan meals carefully; bring just enough food plus some emergency rations. Packaged freeze-dried foods are the lightest to carry, but they are expensive and not completely necessary. Bring plenty of cold and hot drinks.

244

Appendix D: Further Reading

Roadside Geology of Mount St. Helens National Volcanic Monument and Vicinity, Patrick T. Pringle, Washington Department of Natural Resources.

Ape Cave, William R. Halliday M.D., ABC Printing and Publishing.

Index

Page numbers in italic type refer to maps.
*Page numbers in **bold** type refer to photos.*

About the Author

Fred Barstad grew up in Oregon's Willamette Valley and developed an interest in the Cascade Mountains at an early age. With his parents he hiked and fished extensively in the range, mostly between Mount Hood and Mount Jefferson in Oregon. The high volcanic peaks of the Cascades were a special interest of his as a child.

By the time he was a teenager in the 1960s this interest had become an addiction for the high and remote country. Fred has climbed most of the Cascades Volcanoes in Washington and Oregon, some of them many times. He climbed Mount St. Helens 11 times before the 1980 eruption and a couple of times since. He has also climbed Mount McKinley in Alaska; Aconcagua in Argentina; and Popocatepetl, Citlaltepetl, and Iztaccihuatl in Mexico.

Fred now lives in Enterprise, Oregon at the base of the Wallowa Mountains. This is his third guidebook for Falcon Publishing, and he intends to write several more. He devotes his time to hiking, climbing, skiing, and snow-shoeing when not working on a book.